DIVERSE TEAMS AT WORK

Capitalizing on the
Power of Diversity

DIVERSE TEAMS AT WORK

Capitalizing on the Power of Diversity

Lee Gardenswartz, PhD

Anita Rowe, PhD

McGraw-Hill

New York   San Francisco   Washington, D.C.   Auckland   Bogotá
Caracas   Lisbon   London   Madrid   Mexico City   Milan
Montreal   New Delhi   San Juan   Singapore
Sydney   Tokyo   Toronto

McGraw-Hill

A Division of The McGraw·Hill Companies

Library of Congress Cataloging-in-Publication Data

Gardenswartz, Lee.
    Diverse teams at work : capitalizing on the power of diversity
/ Lee Gardenswartz and Anita Rowe.
        p.   cm.
    Includes bibliographical references and index.
    ISBN 0–7863–0425–1
    1. Work groups.   2. Multiculturalism.   I. Rowe, Anita
    II. Title.
    HD66.G375 1996
    658.4'036—dc20   95–4181

Printed in the United States of America
2 3 4 5 6 7 8 9 0 QK 2 1 0 9 8

Preface

In today's highly competitive world, organizations with downsized staffs and tighter resources are increasingly turning to teams to achieve performance objectives and maximize productivity by solving problems, creating new products, and improving customer service. Often, organizational survival depends on how well those teams work. Yet in today's complex and pluralistic world, where teams are seldom homogeneous, workers often come with different values, norms, languages, and points of view. In such an environment, traditional team building methods, tools, and techniques are not enough.

The concept for *Diverse Teams at Work* began to emerge as we worked in client organizations on two separate yet parallel tracks. First, with the growing focus on teams and employee empowerment, clients were continuing to search for ways to remove obstacles to teamwork and increase the output of work groups. On the other track, changing workforce demographics had radically altered the composition of the employee base, creating work groups made up of people from different generations, genders, races, ethnicities, and life situations.

It became clear to us that instead of remaining separate, the two tracks needed to be integrated. The very work teams that were struggling to become more harmonious, to solve problems, and to implement change were also diverse groups with the whole spectrum of human differences that organizations were training people to deal with in diversity seminars. The potential for creativity, energy, and commitment was waiting to be tapped in these teams.

Diverse Teams at Work brings these two issues together, giving team leaders and members an understanding of what it takes to build an effective team in a diverse environment and providing the methods to do so. It offers both conceptual information about team functioning—the elements of diversity and how they impact one another—as well as practical techniques and tools for intervening in and facilitating team processes to increase group effectiveness.

WHAT THIS BOOK IS AND ISN'T

This book is not about the statistical process measures or analytical problem-solving approaches found in the many excellent quality-improvement books already available. It is rather about the human side of teamwork, especially when those humans are different from one another. The techniques and methods featured here focus on helping teams build common ground, appreciate and capitalize on differences, and overcome the obstacles that diversity sometimes presents.

Perhaps the most important service this book can provide is to help team leaders and members become more flexible and adaptive in the face of an ever-changing economic and social world.

WHAT'S IN THIS BOOK: A CHAPTER-BY-CHAPTER GUIDE

Chapter 1 explains how diverse teams are different from homogeneous ones and dispels some of the myths about diverse teams.

Chapter 2 answers the frequent question, "What is diversity, anyway?" It goes beyond race and gender to include the wide spectrum of differences that make up diversity. The chapter focuses on the four layers of differences—from personality and internal dimensions to external and organizational categories—that impact behavior, assumptions, and opportunities on the job.

Chapter 3 presents a model of team functioning and shows how the diversity of team members can influence each of the four aspects of how teams work.

Chapter 4 gives the reader information about one aspect of teamwork, task focus, and offers processes for defining the team's mission, goals, objectives, and measurement criteria that build common ground.

Chapter 5 looks at another aspect of team functioning, relationships, and provides activities and tools for building strong interpersonal connections and support among diverse co-workers.

Chapter 6 focuses on ways to build teams through structuring interdependence among employees, which requires diverse staff to work together on common goals, projects, and tasks.

Chapter 7 provides a series of group-process interventions that help teams through difficult spots and keep them on track and moving forward.

Chapter 8 gives suggestions for processes to use for teams at different stages and with different needs. From starting new teams and integrating new members to ending group experiences and diagnosing problem spots, the chapter provides answers to the "What do I do now?" question.

Chapter 9 deals not with teams themselves but with their leadership, offering a new model of leadership for today's diverse work groups and organizations.

Chapter 10 concludes the book with a discussion of considerations, challenges, and caveats in building diverse teams.

A compilation of resources for diverse team building is included at the end of the book. It provides an annotated list of books, training activities, and videos about diversity and team building that can be helpful in developing group members and training team leaders.

Lee Gardenswartz
Anita Rowe

Acknowledgments

O ur most formidable and important learning experiences involving the building of diverse teams began years ago when we helped the Los Angeles Unified School District work through the stresses, strains, and pains of mandatory integration in 1977. That seminal experience became life changing and set us on a path of helping people in organizations come to understand and find value in the phenomenon of differentness. Through all those years, we have had the benefit of working with many excellent teachers and supporters who helped us gain our experience and hone our skills. One person from those early days stands out: We'd like to thank John E. Jones, Ph.D., our first and best teacher in the field of team building and human dynamics.

We'd also like to thank the following people who have been helpful to us on this particular project:

Judy Rosener, Ph.D., an energetic colleague, friend, and cheerleader who gives us endless support.

Virginia Fleming, Melinda Harris, and Maria Pitts, our typical end users but very atypical, exceptional team leaders, facilitators, and clients who gave us helpful feedback.

Red Badgett and Mihran Sarkesian, whose in-the-trenches reality was our guide.

UCLA Extension Diverse Team Building Class, spring 1993, for bringing their real work issues inside our classroom and laying them at our feet—what a laboratory!

Cindy Zigmund, our editor, and Judy Semler, our agent, who removed the roadblocks so we could write.

Ron Matheson, our right-hand man who not only presents us well on paper but is a constant and dependable source of tangible support.

Our dear friends Francey Gray, Ann Petty, and Sharon Dewees, who generously provided wonderful writing retreats so we could work without interruption or distraction.

Anita's husband Darrell, who continues to show her the richness diversity brings and who reminds her daily that that's why we have chocolate and vanilla.

Beth Ojena, Mark Gardenswartz, Ian Gardenswartz, Jill Ebstein, and Wesley Gardenswartz, siblings who always have (and continue to) teach Lee the beauty and wonder of diversity. You were her first teachers regarding tolerance for and appreciation of differences.

To the executive staff at 1339 Stuart Street, the team builders non-pareil, Rosyne and Nathan Gardenswartz (AKA Lee's parents), Lee wishes she knew their magic or understood how they harnessed such different personalities, talents, skills, and interests to forge the loving and devoted unit they did. They have always been Lee's best team building teachers and role models.

Contents

Chapter One

E Pluribus Unum

"The glory of creation is in its infinite diversity."

Gene Roddenberry

In the best of organizational worlds, to paraphrase Voltaire's *Candide*, the vision, creativity, and commitment of the many unify to yield results greater than any single person can achieve. In many organizations, work teams are the functional unit charged with task accomplishment that enables companies to distance themselves from the pack and ensure survival in an extraordinarily competitive environment, both global and domestic. But traditional team-building models, while historically relevant, need to be adapted to suit the richly pluralistic employee base most organizations draw from today.

Team building has become a dominant response as companies try to maximize the output and commitment of their human resources. It traditionally focuses on task accomplishment while also paying attention to relationship building as a means to a productive and lucrative end. The central issue this book addresses is how task and relationship issues need to be adapted to ensure goal accomplishment when team composition is diverse. Whether the numerous diversities your team reflects center on distinctions such as work experience and position in the organization, cultural dissimilarities involving language and ethnicity, or some of the less changeable diversities such as age and race, one thing is clear. The way these differences are managed within the group will have enormous consequences on how the team functions and, ultimately, on how faithful it is to the accomplishment of its performance objectives.

In truth, work teams have always been diverse, even when we believed they were homogeneous. The idea that work teams composed of all white males, for example, were bastions of harmony among individuals who supposedly shared the same world view, solved problems in a similar fashion, and wanted to allocate resources using the same priorities is fallacious. Individual differences and uniqueness have always made every team diverse, yet it is also true that the variety of differentness experienced on teams today far outdistances and challenges those we've seen in the past. Beyond race, gender, ethnicity, variations in age, education levels, parental status, geographic location, sexual orientation, or work experience are a few of the many ways in which people can be different. These same variables that challenge us also provide us with the potential for discovering and building on common ground. Either way, the previously assumed rules regarding team membership and performance require a new and different set of assumptions and expectations in order for teams to remain effective and fully functional within our pluralistic organizations.

Check out some of your own assumptions about diverse teams by comparing the following myths and realities to your own team experiences. Place a checkmark next to any of these myths you subscribe to.

MYTHS AND REALITIES OF DIVERSE TEAMS

Myth 1: The potential for conflict is greater with diverse teams, while achieving cohesion and productivity are more difficult.   Diverse teams have no corner on the market when it comes to conflict. We have been conducting team-building sessions for 18 years with groups in which people have been both similar and different in areas such as race, socioeconomic level, education, and lifestyle. These more obvious diversities have rarely been the source of conflict. Sometimes more subtle differences, such as those due to work experience on cross-functional teams, have produced friction. At other times, differences in values presented serious obstacles to cohesion. Any time human beings come together, the soil is fertile for conflict.

Having acknowledged this universal human tendency for conflict, it is also true that when teams experience dissimilarity based on culture, language, or a host of other factors, education that increases awareness and understanding can go a long way toward mitigating conflict and misunderstanding.

Myth 2: People of like backgrounds (e.g., the same gender or age group) stick together and don't want to mingle.   This is another diversity assumption that in truth more clearly indicates a human behavior reality than it does a reflection of diversity. The human species finds comfort in likeness. It is predictable that people who look like, sound like, or think like you engender greater trust and comfort than those who are different. You will be drawn to likeness. The challenge and opportunity for a good team leader comes in defining new common ground so that team members may come together around issues and for reasons that appear less obvious than age, race, or gender, for example. A common goal has the ability to bring a diverse group together more solidly than any one shared diversity factor.

Myth 3: It is almost impossible to be harmonious and collaborative with team members when fundamentally different values exist on a team. Differences where our most sacred values are concerned make for very difficult bridge building. Nevertheless, we have seen agreement reached painfully but successfully. One of the most striking examples occurred when two team members had differences the size of the Grand Canyon. One was a gay African-American; the other was an admittedly homophobic woman who couldn't reconcile homosexuality with her Christian fundamentalism. Differences in values of this magnitude make peaceful coexistence a challenge, to say the least. The woman assumed that a person's sexual orientation is a preference; therefore, his was an immoral choice. With her upbringing, she found the concept of homosexuality a difficult one for her to grasp; it was sinful in her eyes because she felt people had responsibility and control over their sexual orientation. The two colleagues had some painful one-on-one conversations in which they aired their viewpoints. These conversations, gut wrenching though they were, finally cleared away the anger and animosity. The real healing, however, came in the process of doing their respective jobs. They developed a healthy regard for each other as professionals who shared common organizational objectives. Eventually that respect extended to one another as human beings. While there is much in the world they will never agree on, they can appreciate each other for the jobs they do, and even have some warmth toward one another as colleagues. Getting beyond fundamental differences is not easy, but it is possible by finding a scintilla of overlapping values in the task at hand and slowly building on it. A little courage and honesty don't hurt either.

Myth 4: Just bringing people together who share a common goal will result in effective teamwork and yield results. The assumption is frequently made that people who are functionally interdependent and share common outcomes can be thrown together in the same room and work jointly to solve problems with a high degree of effectiveness. This certainly can and does happen, but team leaders shouldn't assume that merely bringing competent people together who share common responsibilities will produce the desired results. All human beings have egos. Couple Freud's triplets—id, ego, and superego—with organizational politics and you may see a first-stage team alert. Then add to that mix the universal need to belong and the desire to influence others in a group, and you may find that just showing up can sometimes trigger disaster. When methodologies such as many of the techniques suggested throughout this book are strategically applied, team leaders can end up with lemonade, not just smashed lemons.

Myth 5: The quality of work from teams is superior to that from individuals.   There are interesting training exercises that almost always validate the quality of group output and creativity over that of an individual. On a team that is healthy and functional, the significance of multiple viewpoints and the synergy from creativity will be borne out. But the operative word here is *healthy.* On teams in which there are power struggles and interpersonal conflicts or vendettas, the focus often changes from the good of the team to the victory of one individual at the expense of another or to out-and-out sabotage of group goals. Good teams absolutely produce better work than individuals, but don't assume that all teams have members with no hidden agendas and no desire to sabotage.

Myth 6: There is a template for effective team development.   The idea that there is a best way, a formula, or a series of foolproof ways to engineer team development plays into our Walter Mitty fantasies that aren't part of the real world. There are many techniques that foster team development and many factors that influence the consideration of which strategies to use. Consider just a few pertinent questions: How long is the group planning to work together? What is the team's performance objective? Is this a functional work team? If not, how well do people already know each other? Is participation voluntary? What kind of resources are available to support the team's work? These and many other questions need answering before a team-building methodology is defined. Furthermore, how much facilitator skill, knowledge, and experience the team leader has also impacts the team-building design. One-size-fits-all team building is an antithesis to the very processes we are advocating throughout this book. Cookie-cutter formulas don't work any better for teams than they do for individuals.

Myth 7: The ultimate measure of an effective team is whether or not a group gets the job done in a successful and timely fashion.   Effective teams can be measured in several ways, and certainly timely results is at the top of the list. But in addition to such concrete outcomes as delivering a product, there is also the question about the worth of the process itself. What do employees gain from the experience of being on the team? As individuals change from this experience, does their growth have a long-term impact on productivity in other parts of the organization? How does their individual growth add value on subsequent projects? Are loyalty and commitment to the organization and the team rekindled through the team experience? The answers to these questions may be difficult to quantify. Nevertheless, we have seen the end result of a team experience become an epiphany. Dedication to a company and to job performance has been reborn in employees who were about to leave due to apathy or disenchantment. Unarticulated outcomes such as group cohesion, increased meaning, individual growth, and job satisfaction can be stunning personal and organizational rewards that aren't always calculated to the last dollar.

As you think about these myths, consider your own assumptions regarding team building with a diverse group. Once you're open to re-thinking some of them, you're ready to look at the implications of team building, diversity style.

TEAM BUILDING WITH A DIVERSE STAFF: HOW IS IT DIFFERENT?

If you agree that team building can be a worthwhile commitment of human and financial resources, then the legitimate question becomes, "Isn't team building simply team building, regardless of who is on the team?" The two-word answer to that question is not really. Team building is more complex and challenging as more diversities are factored in. Team building may have certain philosophical underpinnings and core relevancies such as mission, goals, and roles, regardless of who is on the team. But the more diversity and complexity you have, the more challenging it becomes to reach agreement on team direction and priorities.

We often face resistance from those who feel that too much time is spent on differences rather than similarities. The prevailing view goes something like this: Our common ground is company XYZ. What does it matter that we're different? We just need to respect each other and get the job done. While there is truth to the statement that task interdependence gives diverse employees common ground, it is also true that there is a different set of assumptions operating when a team is perceived to be homogeneous than when it is perceived to be diverse. Table 1–1 illustrates these differences.

Once you acknowledge or realize that these differences exist, then the questions become: (1) What do I do with this information? (2) What does it mean to me as a team leader or manager? (3) How can I orchestrate an effective experience that pays dividends for both the organization and the individuals involved? The answers to these questions are central to your building a high-performance team that gives you an edge in the marketplace. The content of this book is designed to answer precisely these questions. But before we describe and explain the "hows," we need to define the concept of the team and identify the different kinds of teams that exist.

Teams, diverse or otherwise, are groups of people, preferably between 7 and 12 in number, who come together to achieve certain results or performance goals. The members are functionally interdependent and bring their individual knowledge and complementary skills to the task so that, individually and collectively, they yield the results for which they are held accountable. The following kinds of teams are frequently seen in organizations:

Work teams. Members of this unit work as a team day in and day out because they are functionally dependent on one another's individual contributions in order to create the collective result. Not all work units are teams. Many times people form a group of associates with tangential or similar tasks, but they function independently and come together only occasionally for support, problem solving, or brainstorming; their affiliation is loose. Real work teams are in the trenches together, accepting joint responsibility for producing better-built widgets at less cost and higher quality. Accomplishing that ongoing task forms the heart and soul of their being a team.

Task-force teams. These units come together for a short period of time (say, three months to a year) as they investigate and make recommendations about specific issues or problems that arise. Who the participants are and where they come from in the organization depends on the task they're trying to accomplish. At one organization where we are currently involved in working with four task forces, each is charged with investigating a different piece of the diversity puzzle. After 10

TABLE 1–1

Differences between Homogeneous and Diverse Work Teams in the United States

Aspects	Homogeneous Model (Teams Perceived to Be Homogeneous)	Diversity Model (Teams Perceived to Be Diverse)
Management philosophy	Golden Rule management: I treat everyone the way I want to be treated.	Expanded Golden Rule management: I find out how people want to be treated and I respond accordingly.
Expectations of team members	Assimilation model: I will show you the ropes and you'll adapt; you'll fit in just fine.	Valuing differences: There are many ways to think, behave, and act; none is inherently better than any other.
Problem solving	Pattern of "either–or" options and logical, linear thinking	A wide array of creative options; open to less traditional ways of problem solving
Perception of differentness	"Differentness" equals "less than"	"Differentness" equals "value added"
Team member's role	Press for conformity in norms, thinking, behavior	Greater accommodation and response to individual needs
Leader's role	More of a mentor and coach; emphasis on helping people fit into existing culture	More of a facilitator and catalyst; leadership shapes evolving culture; flexible; knowledgeable about other cultural norms
Team-building paradigm	Combining clear mission with concrete strategies at formal team-building sessions to get the task accomplished; strong task focus	A heavy investment in relationship building, much of it in informal surroundings; still relies on traditional team-building concepts of mission, goals, and roles
Conflict resolution	Use of analytical methods; straightforward thrust in solving problems; highly values assertiveness and "I" statements as tools	Use of one-on-one, informal methods for solving a variety of interpersonal conflicts; sees cultural interpreters as an invaluable resource
Communication mode	Prefers communication to be straight-forward, direct, and to the point; expects members to "put their cards on table"	Prefers communication to be less explicit; attention to individual preferences rather than assuming the mainstream American preference for directness and assertiveness
Caveats in the face of challenges	Avoiding "group think"; developing a wide variety of options in how to do things and to function on a team	Managing the many cultural and other differences that surface; honoring the differences while still creating a common team culture and value base

months, these committees, focusing on themes of how to improve communication, increase tolerance, expand professional development, and demonstrate leadership at all levels of the organization, are making recommendations to the executive committee so that concrete changes will result from their investigative work.

Problem-solving teams. While task forces mostly investigate issues and make recommendations, problem-solving teams are brought together for the purpose of solving specific work problems such as production defects or customer complaints. The total quality management (TQM) movement has had a strong emphasis on using teams to overcome obstacles to quality. How to reduce internal theft or decrease litigation over grievances through the increased use of mediation services might be the focus of such groups.

Cross-functional teams. In the attempt to bring increased productivity and higher quality to products, we see many of our clients using cross-functional teams as a way to minimize myopia and improve creativity, quality, and customer service. One aerospace client, a maker of parts for both the defense industry and commercial airlines, comes to mind. In an attempt to speed up delivery time, improve product excellence, and keep the customer happy, the company formed teams made up of engineers, marketers, machinists, customer service personnel, a quality assurance representative, and an administrator. With all the perspectives represented, they definitely had a diversity of viewpoints; although those differences were a source of conflict, they ultimately led to improved results.

There may be overlaps among these four kinds of teams. They aren't necessarily discreet in function. Nevertheless, you can see that all teams, whether charged with making products or delivering services, have to show results. And on some teams, investigating issues, making recommendations, or solving problems is the primary outcome.

Regardless of the task at hand, the team's results and satisfaction will undoubtedly come from achieving performance objectives and doing so in a way that leaves everyone better off. The reality, however, is that not all team experiences are created equal, and not all leave everyone better off. To get you started on the right path so that your team experience is a constructive and productive one, we offer 10 characteristics of an effective pluralistic team as a tool for analysis. It can become your barometer of a high-performance team. It can also be your road map in building one.

TEN CHARACTERISTICS OF AN
EFFECTIVE PLURALISTIC TEAM

1. *A meaningful mission.* The overarching reason for your work together engenders much more support and commitment when it's in
   the service of something that matters to the people involved. Regarding the four task forces we just finished working with on diversity-related issues, there were certainly conflicts about direction, goals,
   and priorities. The one ace we always had up our sleeve was that
   people showed up with energy because creating a more tolerant,
   humane, and productive organization mattered significantly to everyone, and all participants believed they had a part to play in making this happen. Lagging participation and spotty attendance may
   be signs that the team's mission lacks meaning for some in the group.
2. *A clearly defined performance outcome.* Above all, being on any team
   is about furthering the organization in some way. If you're on a
   professional sports team, the desired performance outcome is clear:
   win the most games and take home the championship. The performance outcomes may be less clear in your organization, but the real
   guts and essence of a team, the steam behind the engine, is having
   some work that needs to be done, some measurable outcome for
   which you are held accountable. It's hard to rally any troops around
   or dig up any passion or commitment for nothing. The spine of the
   team experience is a well-defined performance outcome.
3. *An understanding of different cultural norms and their impact on communication, problem solving and conflict.* Mainstream American
   norms are pretty clear in these areas. They favor the analytical over
   the intuitive in problem solving and, in conflict, directness over
   avoidance. Communication in our "tell it like it is" culture is straightforward, both in and out of conflict. Not so in other cultural or
   ethnic groups, where harmony is more highly prized than dealing
   with differences, and where communication is much more vague
   and inexplicit than direct. Understanding these norms is critical to
   team functioning because, as subsequent chapters will show, you
   have both personal and cultural differences to deal with and meld.
4. *A set of shared values that clearly articulate demonstrations of dignity
   and respect.* What is universally true about us human types is that
   we all need, want, and value being treated with dignity and respect.
   What is less clear among different groups is how dignity and respect
   are measured or shown. We know the high cost of not showing

respect. In gang culture, perceptions of disrespect can get you killed. In organizations, team members who don't feel respected can suffer a slow, withering death at work every day. Setting out very clear examples of respectful behavior as determined by all team members is essential. How you do this will be one of the subjects of Chapter 7, on group dynamics.

5. *A cultivation of different viewpoints.* Pluralistic teams deal with their diversity much more easily and flexibly when they embrace differences by following the principle of "no fewer than three viewpoints." What that precept does is inculcate the belief that there is no best way and that the more options you have, the better your potential solutions are. Just sanctioning the belief that things aren't "either–or" and that one way is not intrinsically better than another sets up a norm that values differentness and opens everyone to exploration.

6. *A willingness to do what it takes to get the job done.* One critical determinant of excellent, high-performing teams is a strong commitment from each individual to meet his or her own assignments. Further, there is a willingness to help others when they need it so the group meets its goals. Individually and collectively, there is a determination that, as the group meets obstacles on the way toward completion of its marathon tasks, it will keep running the race until all participants get to the finish line together. This requires that each person does his or her own job and helps others as needed. On high-performing teams with a cohesive environment, no one weighs contributions with a postal scale. What we see is that team members would never let their fellow teammates down; nor would they let the job go unfinished.

7. *Loyalty and devotion to the team experience.* Loyalty, and particularly devotion, are strong words rarely mentioned as a necessity when talking about team performance. Nevertheless, they are important because they imply passion and energy, not just run-of-the-mill work. It is possible to accomplish outcomes without a true devotion to the whole experience, but it leaves one wanting. If you take a trip to Niagara and don't see Niagara Falls, you may very well have had a nice vacation and managed to accomplish a relaxing getaway. But you will have missed much of the magnificence and beauty that could have shaped your adventure. A team experience without loyalty and devotion as an integral part of the landscape is like taking a trip to Niagara without seeing the falls.

8. *A desire for individual and collective growth.* Part of the intrigue and

frustration of the team phenomenon is that you have to merge your skills, competencies, ideas, values, and priorities with others. Figuring out how to do that well is a complex undertaking. Although team members' skills and knowledge may be complementary and not necessarily conflicting, aligning priorities, making decisions, and solving problems frequently exposes areas of friction. One of the biggest perks of team building can be found in the growth you realize from working with others—those you agree with and those you don't. We have seen teams nearly erupt until team members acquired skills to deal with present and future conflicts. But once they do, they gain an ongoing competency that will help them anywhere.

9. *An openness to new experiences and processes, both interpersonal and problem solving.*   Being a learner, being open to new experiences, is any employee's best continuous employment strategy in the downsizing, "rightsizing" '90s. An attitude that says, "I am open to new ways of seeing and doing things" may give people skills and tools that they can use over and over in a variety of circumstances. Learning is a potential benefit in all team experiences, the good and the bad. As Alan Teller, a colleague of ours, quips, "Everything in life is for my entertainment or my education. If I'm not having fun, I must be learning."

10. *Shared laughter and humor as an integral part of the team experience.*   While having fun together as teammates in the process of accomplishing a task is not absolutely necessary, it adds immeasurably to the experience of working together; in fact, it is an important determinant in creating more tenacity and follow-through in meeting performance objectives. To some, humor and enjoyment are luxuries, just perks when they occur. We disagree.

In fact, we were recently facilitating a meeting of a task-force team that met once or twice a month, with assignments to complete between meetings. They had been meeting for eight months and were getting ready for a big presentation the next day. Because team members flew in from locations scattered throughout the western United States, we met at the end of the work day and worked until late that night. We were having such a good time doing our work that many people passing by our room at day's end commented on our laughter. Some, tongue in cheek, cautioned us that we were having too much fun, while others just looked at us longingly. What struck the team members was how much our quality and productivity were enhanced, not sacrificed, through our laughter, and the sheer number of people who commented on the enjoyment we were having in the process of doing our job.

Reading about the benefits to be gained from cultivating the 10 dimensions of an effective pluralistic team is a starting point. But this is a lifeless list until you engage your own team in discussing these ideas. Worksheet 1–1 at the end of this chapter, "Characteristics of an Effective Pluralistic Team" will help your team evaluate itself and assess its strengths and weaknesses. This assessment can serve as the precursor to a vital discussion. Once each member has scored his or her own worksheet, tally the scores from all participants and get a team average for each question. Question 1, for example, may have an 8.5 average, while question 4's average may be 6, and question 9's might be 7. In addition to the average score, also note the range for each question because that is useful information for the team as well. If the range of perceptions about shared laughter and humor is from 7 to 9, there is some agreement that you have fun together. However, if the range extends from 2 to 9, it is clear that some people are not sharing in the laughter, nor is humor being perceived in the same way. That would warrant a discussion. The following questions are worth considering as your team evaluates itself:

1. What are our strengths?
2. Where can we improve?
3. On what items are our ranges the broadest? What is the meaning and implication of these disparities of perception? How can this wide range of perception hurt us? Help us?
4. Where is the best place to begin improving our team?

WORKSHEET 1–1

Characteristics of an Effective Pluralistic Team

Directions: Circle the number that best reflects how you see or experience your team.

1. *A meaningful mission.* (What we're doing has merit; it matters to me.)

   1 2 3 4 5 6 7 8 9 10
   Low_____High

2. *A clearly defined performance outcome.* (We all know where we're headed and what we're striving for.)

   1 2 3 4 5 6 7 8 9 10
   Low_____High

3. *An understanding of different cultural norms and their impact on communication, problem solving, and conflict.* (We understand differences in the ways of engaging in interpersonal relationships due to our cultural backgrounds.)

   1 2 3 4 5 6 7 8 9 10
   Low_____High

4. *A set of shared values that clearly articulate demonstrations of dignity and respect.* (We all feel respected and valued on the team.)

   1 2 3 4 5 6 7 8 9 10
   Low_____High

5. *A cultivation of different viewpoints.* (Two ideas or views are never enough; we challenge ourselves to create many options and configurations.)

   1 2 3 4 5 6 7 8 9 10
   Low_____High

6. *A willingness to do what it takes to get the job done.* (Both I as an individual and the team as a whole are accountable for meeting performance outcomes.)

   1 2 3 4 5 6 7 8 9 10
   Low_____High

7. *Loyalty and devotion to the team experience.* (We are committed to the work itself, to the mission, and to other team members.)

   1   2   3   4   5   6   7   8   9   10

   Low_____High

8. *A desire for individual and collective growth.* (I enjoy learning new job skills as well as learning about myself and about being a part of a whole.)

   1   2   3   4   5   6   7   8   9   10

   Low_____High

9. *An openness to new experiences and processes, both interpersonal and problem solving.* (The mantra, "We've always done it that way" is not heard on this team.)

   1   2   3   4   5   6   7   8   9   10

   Low_____High

10. *Shared laughter and humor as an integral part of the team experience.* (Fun is not a dirty word. We believe that the team that plays together stays together and accomplishes!)

   1   2   3   4   5   6   7   8   9   10

   Low_____High

This assessment tool can function as your team-building blueprint. You can use it as a pre- and posttest, and also as a focal point for discussing what constitutes effective team building and where your team can concentrate its development efforts. The rest of the book will show you how to build an effective, high-performing, diverse team. To start you on this process, Chapter 2 will help you define the various diversities that exist on your team.

Chapter Two

Similar Differences
The Power of Infinite Variety

"We all like diversity as long as everyone acts like us."

Howard Phillips

Team members often have much in common, from shared goals, tasks, and experiences in the organization to the basic needs and life problems that all human beings encounter. However, they also bring differences, some as intangible as values and point of view, some as specific as language and personal preference. These variations influence how team members see their tasks and one another, how they relate, and how they perform. These differences also form the "filter" through which each individual team member sees and interacts with the group. Team leaders and members of diverse groups need to understand the elements of diversity that make up each person's filter, as well as how to keep their own filters clear and clean. This chapter will help you understand the four layers of diversity and how they impact teamwork. Succeeding chapters will give you tools and techniques for capitalizing on these differences.

THE FOUR LAYERS OF DIVERSITY

An often-asked question is, "Why do we have to focus so much on the differences?" Indeed, aren't we more similar than different? It's true that we share many similarities but, as seminar participant Tabiri Chukunta, coordinator of diversity at St. Peters Medical Center in New Brunswick, New Jersey, put it, "It's not our similarities that have caused us all our problems, but rather our differences." While people do share the same basic human needs, encounter many like work issues, and experience similar life events, our differences *do* matter. They influence both our assumptions about others and our opportunities in life. Without examining and understanding the layers of diversity that form our filters, we are apt to be victims of our differences, making unconscious assumptions and encountering unexplained and frustrating barriers. On the other hand, when we understand the many influences that have formed our unique filters, we have choices about our behavior and our reactions to others.

As Figure 2–1 shows graphically, each person's filter is made up of four layers of factors. At the center is personality, the innately unique aspect that gives us our own particular style. This core aspect permeates all other layers. Then we are influenced by a group of internal dimensions which Judy Rosener and Marilyn Loden label the primary dimensions of diversity. These are aspects over which we have little or no control, such as gender, age, and race. The next layer of factors, most of which Rosener and Loden refer to as secondary dimensions, is made up of external influences, those brought to bear by society and one's experiences in the world. Examples of external dimensions are where you grew up or live now, whether you have children, and how your religious affiliation guides you. Finally, there are organizational dimensions such as seniority, your level within the company, and your work location. These four layers together form your own diversity filter. Let's take a look at each of them to see their impact on you and the team.

PERSONALITY: THE UNIQUE CORE

Why is it that you feel an immediate closeness with some individuals and an equally quick negative response with others? Why are there some people you'd go miles out of your way for, while others you'd go even more miles to avoid? The answer may have to do with the most basic factor about human beings—personality. Each of us has a unique way of interacting with others. Whether we are seen as charming, irritating, fascinating, nondescript, approachable, or intimidating depends in part on our personality, or what others might describe as our style.

Worksheets 2–1 and 2–2 will give you a chance to analyze your personality to see how it impacts your relationships on the team.

FIGURE 2–1

The Four Layers of Diversity

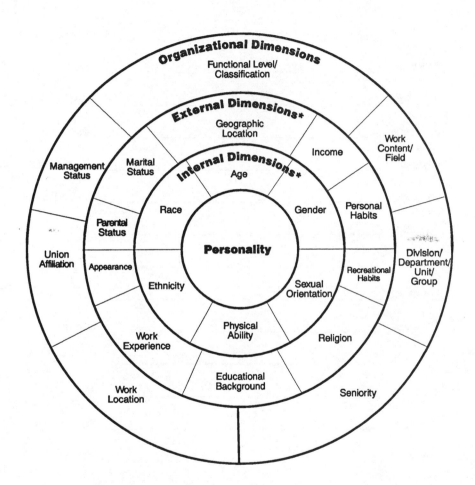

*Internal Dimensions and External Dimensions are adapted from
Marilyn Loden and Judy Rosener, *Workforce America!*
(Business One Irwin, 1991)

WORKSHEET 2–1

Drawing Your Personality Profile

Directions: Mark and *X* along each continuum to represent where you fit.
Then connect your *X's* vertically to form your personality profile.

Patient	Impatient
Introvert	Extrovert
Doer	Thinker
Assertive	Nonassertive
Change maker	Change adapter
Competitive	Collaborative
Supporting	Directing
Leader	Follower
Listener	Talker
Fast-paced	Slow-paced
Serious	Humorous
Spontaneous	Scheduled
Flexible	Rigid
Relaxed	Intense
Gregarious	Loner
Optimist	Pessimist
Realist	Idealist
Rational	Emotional
Conformist	Nonconformist

First, take a look at your profile. Which of these characteristics make you a good team player on your current team? Which may cause problems with others in your group? What personality characteristics of others are hard for you to deal with? To take this assessment one step further, mark each continuum to form the profile of a teammate you have a difficult time getting along with. When you compare the two profiles, what differences or similarities seem to be at the heart of your difficulty? Next, compare your profile with those of the rest of your teammates. Spend time discussing how you see each other. What feedback do they give you about how they view your style? Where are there similarities? Where are there differences? How do these differences enhance the relationships on this team? Do they ever cause conflicts? How can you lessen the negative effects when they occur?

As a whole team you might want to share profiles by drawing them with different colored markers on a large piece of chart paper. What patterns emerge? How does your joint profile help you as a team? How does it hinder you? How do you currently deal with differences among team members? How can you make these variations an asset for the team? How can team members expand their individual ranges so that all members are more adaptable?

All of these personality traits cut two ways at some time during the life of the team. The challenge for each team member is to expand his or her own range of responses and to be appropriately humorous or serious, in a particular context.

Worksheet 2–2 offers another way for you to analyze your personality and your impact on others.

How similar or different are your perceptions about yourselves compared with the way you see each other? Discuss with each other how these personality traits are demonstrated, being as specific as possible. What surprises or insights are there in the feedback you get from your partner? How compatible are your two personalities? Where do your traits help you in your relationships with others on the team? Where do they hinder interactions?

Then as a following step, each member can share with the whole team insights about his or her personal style by responding to one of the following open-ended statements:

- The personality trait that makes me an effective team member is . . .
- One aspect of my personality that sometimes hinders my effectiveness on the team is . . .

WORKSHEET 2–2

Personality: What's Your Style?

Directions: This is a multiple-part personality assessment. Before you begin, pair up with one of your teammates as your partner. Sit together but do not speak to one another as you both complete steps 1 and 2. In step 1, choose the *10* words from the following list that you believe best describe *your* personality style.

____ Friendly	____ Confident	____ Talkative	____ Shy
____ Serious	____ Approachable	____ Easygoing	____ Warm
____ Analytical	____ Unemotional	____ Creative	____ Loyal
____ Nurturing	____ Unconventional	____ Emotional	____ Free
____ Sensitive	____ Cautious	____ Private	____ Brusque
____ Authoritarian	____ Traditional	____ Empathetic	____ Assertive
____ Visionary	____ Aggressive	____ Upbeat	____ Energetic
____ Fun-loving	____ Nonassertive	____ Humble	____ Serene
____ Trustworthy	____ Open	____ Humorous	____ Critical
____ Outgoing	____ Dynamic	____ In charge	____ Bold
____ Organized	____ Flamboyant	____ Intense	
____ Calm	____ Quiet	____ Formal	____ ____

In step 2 choose the *10* words that you believe best describe *your partner's* personality.

____ Friendly	____ Confident	____ Talkative	____ Shy
____ Serious	____ Approachable	____ Easygoing	____ Warm
____ Analytical	____ Unemotional	____ Creative	____ Loyal
____ Nurturing	____ Unconventional	____ Emotional	____ Free
____ Sensitive	____ Cautious	____ Private	____ Brusque
____ Authoritarian	____ Traditional	____ Empathetic	____ Assertive
____ Visionary	____ Aggressive	____ Upbeat	____ Energetic
____ Fun-loving	____ Nonassertive	____ Humble	____ Serene
____ Trustworthy	____ Open	____ Humorous	____ Critical
____ Outgoing	____ Dynamic	____ In charge	____ Bold
____ Organized	____ Flamboyant	____ Intense	
____ Calm	____ Quiet	____ Formal	____ ____

In step 3 compare lists with your partner, sharing your choices and your descriptions of each other.

- The aspect of my personality I like best is . . .
- The aspect of my style I'd most like to change is . . .
- The personality aspect I find most difficult to work with is . . .

The self-disclosure required in sharing responses to these open-ended statements might be difficult for team members who are from cultures or upbringings that discourage such public openness. In those cases the sharing might take place in pairs or small groups, where the comfort is greater.

Team leaders and managers may also find these activities useful as feedback tools to gain insight into the staff's perceptions about the leader's personality. Employees could be asked to complete either personality checklist anonymously. The leader would then have a composite profile or style description of him or herself made up of the collective views of team members. This information could prove extremely valuable to the leader, especially if staff members were also asked to indicate which personality aspect was most helpful to the leader in maintaining productive relationships with employees and which aspect caused the most difficulties.

HOW INTERNAL DIMENSIONS OF DIVERSITY SHAPE THE TEAM

Beyond the central core of personality, the six internal dimensions of diversity have a powerful effect on behavior and attitudes about others. They are, for the most part, not within our control, but they shape expectations, assumptions, and opportunities on the team. Let's take a look at how each might influence the team.

Age

The generation to which each individual belongs leaves an indelible mark in terms of values, norms, and expectations. Loyalty, security, work ethic, and flexibility are factors that people in their twenties see very differently than co-workers in their forties and fifties do. Younger employees tend to place a greater value on individual needs such as time with family and don't necessarily assume that their tenure in the organization is permanent. As long as employment works for both the organization and the employee, the relationship will remain in effect. Older employees, on the other hand, tend to have signed on for life, with an expectation that the organization will repay their loyalty with job security. Team members from these different points of view may find it difficult to understand one another and may make negative judgments about each other, such as disparaging remarks about a declining work ethic or resistance to change. Younger employees complain that their older co-workers don't take them seriously, while older staff members often feel displaced, discarded, and discounted. In addition, both sides may feel it awkward when the boss is a generation or so younger than some of the employees on the team.

> Questions for the team:
> - What is the age range on our team and what difference does it make?
> - How well do people of different ages relate to one another?
> - What do we need to do to overcome any age-related obstacles?

Gender

Men and women grow up in and live in different worlds. They are taught to see themselves and to behave differently. "Big boys don't cry" is the message preached to young lads, while "Sugar and spice and everything nice" is the socialization given to little girls. In addition to setting up fundamentally different expectations, even similar behavior is interpreted differently, as described in the following poem.

> The family picture is on HIS desk.
> *Ah, a solid, responsible family man.*
>
> > The family picture is on HER desk.
> > *Umm, her family will come before her career.*
>
> HIS desk is cluttered.
> *He's obviously a hard worker and a busy man.*
>
> > HER desk is cluttered.
> > *She's obviously a disorganized scatterbrain.*
>
> HE is talking with his co-workers.
> *He must be discussing the latest deal.*
>
> > SHE is talking with her co-workers.
> > *She must be gossiping.*
>
> HE's not at his desk.
> *He must be at a meeting.*

SHE's not at her desk.
She must be in the ladies' room.

HE's not in the office.
He's meeting customers.

SHE's not in the office.
She must be out shopping.

HE's having lunch with the boss.
He's on his way up.

SHE's having lunch with the boss.
They must be having an affair.

The boss criticized HIM.
He'll improve his performance.

The boss criticized HER.
She'll be very upset.

HE got an unfair deal.
Did he get angry?

SHE got an unfair deal.
Did she cry?

HE's getting married.
He'll get more settled.

SHE's getting married.
She'll get pregnant and leave.

HE's having a baby.
He'll need a raise.

SHE's having a baby.
She'll cost the company money in maternity benefits.

HE's going on a business trip.
It's good for his career.

SHE's going on a business trip.
What does her husband say?

HE's leaving for a better job.
He knows how to recognize a good opportunity.

SHE's leaving for a better job.
Women are not dependable.

Natasha Josefowitz, "Impressions from an Office"

In addition, men and women communicate differently. According to Deborah Tannen, in her book, *You Just Don't Understand,* men communicate "vertically" while women do so "horizontally." Men use communication as a means of establishing a hierarchy of order and power and to solve problems. Women, on the other hand, interact to form relationships and share feelings and reactions. This difference can lead to subtle barriers in transmitting information and even subtler unconscious assumptions. She may be seen as wasting time; he may be seen as cold and insensitive. Her comments may be taken as nagging or an attempt to control, while the solutions he offers may be rejected as proof that "he didn't hear what I was saying."

To make matters even more complicated, there is another factor present that may garble the interchange between men and women. Our colleague and friend Judy Rosener, professor of business and management at the University of California, Irvine, and coauthor of *Workforce America!*, has coined the term *sexual static* to describe the invisible yet real interference that exists when men and women communicate. Much like the crackling and hissing of an old radio, sexual static can result in misread signals and mistaken interpretations that lead to frustration and misunderstanding on both sides of the gender gap.

Finally, because of these differences in socialization, all groups and cultures have assigned appropriate and inappropriate roles and behaviors to each sex. Even with all the progress made in gender equity at work, Title IX gender equity legislation in the schools, and consciousness-raising in society, many people are often still surprised when the nurse is a man or when the mechanic is a woman. Women are still asked more often to take notes at meetings or to oversee the refreshments. Eyebrows still raise in many organizations when men take parental leave to stay home with a newborn. What happens when the tables are turned and women supervise men or when men work in support-staff roles?

> Questions for the team:
> - How do men and women interact on our team?
> - Are opportunities equally available to both men and women?
> - What do we need to do to ensure equal access for both genders?

Ethnicity

An individual's nationality or ethnic background is another difference on the team. Some proudly identify themselves as hyphenated Americans such as Mexican-American, Arab-American or Polish-American. Some even sport buttons or bumper stickers heralding their heritage, such as Viva la Raza or I'm Proud I'm Irish. Others are just as proud to be plain American. And some bristle at the mention of hyphenated ethnicities; "We're all American and that's all that matters" might be their motto.

These ethnic differences can bring variations in cultural norms, holiday observances, language proficiency, and group affiliation. What happens when a team begins to separate because one group speaks its own language in front of others? How can you build a cohesive group if the team begins to ghettoize into isolated groups? What can you do when contrasting cultural norms have taught people to respond differently to conflict? These are difficulties that can arise on a team when ethnicity becomes a divisive rather than a unifying force.

An even more subtle demonstration of ethnicity can be seen in culture, the "software" that forms the rules, norms, and assumptions that guide each person's behavior. For some on your team, not making eye contact may be seen as deceitful or unassertive, while others may see it as a sign of respect shown to elders and authority figures. Some team members may beam when complimented publicly at a staff meeting, while others would be embarrassed at being singled out from the group. You may view team members who find brainstorming fun and energizing as go-getters with a lot of good ideas. On the other hand, you may perceive other employees as slow and lacking initiative because their carefully thought-out responses aren't forthcoming in a shoot-from-the-hip, raucous session.

Both behaviors and assumptions about individuals are the products of each teammate's cultural software program. What's more, team members are generally unaware of this factor as an influence on both actions and interpretations. Like a fish that has no concept of water until pulled out of it, we rarely become conscious of culture as an influence until we encounter a different one, a set of rules that is at variance with our own. And when we do, our knee-jerk, ethnocentric response is generally a judgment that the other's behavior is wrong. We may consider the person who stands too close as pushy or rude, the one who talks loudly as ill-mannered or aggressive, the one who nods and says yes when he means no as unassertive or deceitful. On today's multiethnic teams, these differences are becoming more and more apparent. Effective teams recognize, talk about, and spend time learning about these differences. The information and exercises in Chapter 3 will help the team understand and share this vital information.

Another impact of ethnicity is language differences. If some team members are immigrants whose native language is not English, communication can be impaired. When team members literally don't speak the same language, bilingual instruction and interpreters may be needed. However, even when the employees are fluent in English as a second language, blocks can occur if jargon or complicated language is used or if employees pretend to understand each other when they don't. In addition, immigrants' native language often serves as a divider, breaking up the staff into separate groups. Finally, accents are frequently cited as communication inhibitors on both sides. Non-native English speakers often report being discounted and assumed to be stupid because of their accents. On the other hand, native speakers sometimes complain about the difficulty in understanding heavily accented speech, especially over the phone.

Beyond these tangible language issues is the less concrete but volatile impact of the power struggle and turf battles symbolized by language differences. Outrage at concessions to bilingualism or to the fact that in some ethnic communities individuals can live a lifetime without speaking English can bring frustration and anger to your team. Speakers of languages other than English, on the other hand, may feel that they are handicapped when they are prevented from speaking their native languages on the job.

> Questions for the team:
> * What different ethnic backgrounds are on our team?
> * What do we know about our own and each other's cultures and how can we learn more?
> * How can we deal more effectively with language differences and accents?

Race

Another fundamental diversity dimension is race. We have had seminar participants tell us that race is an erroneous and irrelevant categorization because, as they say, "We're all part of the human race." Many native born Americans in the work force today were raised to think that being color blind was the way to overcome prejudice. With claims that they treat everyone the same and deal with others as individuals rather than members of a category, these well meaning people deny a reality that any person of color will affirm. Race matters.

Racial groupings are generally associated with observable physical characteristics such as skin color, eye shape, hair texture and bone structure. In the United States, race, which is most often associated with skin color, is a salient and powerful diversity dimension. Although progress has been made in equalizing opportunity, access and civil rights, especially in the last 35 years, the 300 year old legacy of discrimination continues to result in unequal treatment for African-Americans. In addition, people of Asian, Hispanic and Native American ancestry also face prejudicial treatment. Few people of color can be found in board rooms, executive suites or other bastions of power and the media continues to emphasize negative stereotypes about non-white groups.

Although no team can be expected to undo past wrongs or fix societal inequities, understanding can be gained and positive relationships can be built in a racially mixed team when co-workers face and discuss some of their differences. In one team, for example, the sharing of different perceptions and reactions to Spike Lee's controversial film, *Do The Right Thing*, helped colleagues of different races see issues from each others' points of view. The discussion served as an icebreaker into previously taboo territory and legitimized discussing race, a difference the team had previously politely ignored.

> Questions for the team:
> - How do we acknowledge and deal with racial differences on the team?
> - How are opportunities impacted by race?
> - Do racial differences ever get in the way of team relationships? If so, how?

Physical Ability

Different physical-ability levels will also be present on the team. Some members will be ablebodied, while others may be physically challenged. Some will be able to benchpress 250 pounds, while others will have much less physical strength. A team member may need the help of a hearing aid, crutches, or a wheelchair. In some circumstances, these physical-ability differences can impact teamwork. Incorrect assumptions are sometimes made about the capabilities of employees with physical challenges: "We can't ask her to do that. She can't see the bar codes." Or expectations of ability can be based on gender or size: "Have Dave carry these boxes out. He looks like a defensive lineman." In addition, ablebodied employees who have had little contact with anyone with a physical disability may, because of discomfort, avoid contact with staff members who have some impairment.

Even when motivations are positive and the intent is helpful, assumptions can be limiting. Darrell, husband of one of the coauthors, walks with the help of forearm crutches because of a paralysis due to a spinal injury sustained in an auto accident years ago. He had a recent experience that illustrates this point. While using the stamp vending machine at his local post office, he was continually "coached" by a woman behind him in line, telling him where to put the money and which buttons to press. He thanked her politely, telling her he'd used the machines before and was familiar with the procedure. She continued giving him suggestions, though, so he assumed she was in a hurry and wanted to rush him along. He was surprised to see that when he completed his transaction and walked away, she did not step up to the machine but also walked away. Her motivation was apparently only to offer assistance. So what's wrong with being helpful? Move this scenario to the work arena for a moment. What if she were Darrell's boss? What if she were making a hiring or promotional decision about him? What kinds of projects would she give him? Which assignments might she assume to be inappropriate for him? Although behaviors on the surface might appear beneficial, the underlying assumptions might be limiting.

Finally, adaptations may be called for in order to enable a physically challenged employee to work on the team. A TDD line may need to be added or a rearrangement of work responsibilities may be required to accommodate an individual's special needs. A team member may be asked to change work stations or schedules to fully utilize the contribution of an individual with a physical limitation. These changes can have varied effects on the team, from quick acceptance and an it's-no-big-deal attitude to grudging resentment of and irritation at any changes.

Questions for the team:
- How do we deal with the physical challenges of any team member?
- What adaptations have we made and what has been the response?
- How included do team members with physical disabilities feel?
- How can we ensure full inclusion for team members of all physical abilities?

Sexual Orientation

Sexual orientation is still another dimension in which team members may differ. Some will be heterosexual, while others may be gay, lesbian, or bisexual. Some will openly discuss their sexual orientation and others will not. How a team deals with this dimension can be a telling test of the team's openness to differences. What does it cost a team when an individual feels, as a focus-group participant once shared, that he has to hide who he is to succeed in his organization? What happens to workgroup camaraderie when a gay or lesbian individual does not feel free to bring a same-sex partner to company social events or even to talk about social activities or vacation plans? How do trust and teamwork suffer if individuals judge a teammate's lifestyle as morally inferior?

On one team, the manager was open with her staff about the fact that she was a lesbian. She invited her team to a reception celebrating her commitment to her partner in the same way a heterosexual boss would invite the staff to a wedding reception. Not only did the team give her their support and good wishes, they were there for her a year later when the relationship ended. Although she didn't talk about her breakup much at work, they understood that the pain she was experiencing was the cause of her mood swings, and they rode through the tough period without taking things personally. Had she not been free to share her lifestyle with the team, her behavior would have been much more difficult for them, and without their understanding and support, she would have had a harder time being "there" at work, focused and present.

> Questions for the team:
> - How open are team members about their sexual orientation?
> - How comfortable are people of different sexual orientations working together?
> - What can we do to make the team environment comfortable for all members?

HOW EXTERNAL DIMENSIONS OF DIVERSITY INFLUENCE TEAM BEHAVIOR

In addition to internal dimensions, each team member is formed by external influences such as social factors and life experiences. While individuals have more control over these factors, they too exert a significant impact on behavior and attitudes.

Religion

Once considered a Judeo–Christian country, the United States is rapidly becoming home to people of many other religions. The populations of Muslims, Hindus, Buddhists, and Bahais are growing in cities across the country. In Los Angeles, for example, there are more Buddhists than Mormons. Religion gives many people a basic set of values and rules that guide their lives. The Ten Commandments, the Golden Rule, and the Noble Eight-Fold Path are examples of these teachings.

Religions also prescribe observances, rituals, and holidays that may be at variance with one another. Seventh Day Adventists and observant Jews who consider Saturday the Sabbath would not work or go to company functions on that day. A Muslim employee who prays five times a day would not be available for lunch staff meetings because of noon prayers. Non-Christian team members might be less than enthusiastic about Christmas decorations in their work sites. In one client organization, Southeast Asian employees were upset when offices were changed and furniture moved on the first day of their new year, which is considered a very unlucky day for such changes. In another case, a supervisor whose religion forbade celebrations refused to allow her team to hold birthday parties, causing much resentment, conflict, and morale problems in her group.

> Questions for the team:
> * What needs and practices of team members' religions affect our work?
> * What adaptations do we need to make so we don't exclude any member because of religious practices or beliefs?

Marital Status

"I never hire anyone who is single," proclaimed a seminar participant in one of our sessions. When asked why, she responded with a laundry list of assumptions she had made about single peoples' lack of responsibility, commitment, work ethic, and dependability. Although her stereotyping is extreme, nevertheless marital status does connote different things to different people. On some teams married people are assumed to be less available for travel assignments or overtime. Marital status is also perceived differently for men and for women. Stereotypes tend to endure regarding this double standard. Married men are seen as more stable and dependable, while married women, particularly in their childbearing years, are seen as more of a risk than their single counterparts. The stereotypic assumption is that women may go on leave because of pregnancy or may not be willing to transfer or take on projects that involve travel because of their spouses. In more organizations than we can count, pregnant women have told us that they withheld news of pregnancy until it became absolutely unavoidable. All of them were fearful of the consequences, and in many cases, their fears were justified. On the other hand, single individuals may complain about being overburdened with assignments and treated as though they had no life or responsibilities outside of work.

> Questions for the team:
> - Are there differences in treatment based on marital status?
> - What assumptions are made about men and women who are or are not married?
> - What do we need to do to open dialogue about this issue?

Educational Background

One of the frequent complaints we hear in organizations has to do with preferences about educational levels. "They hire college interns rather than promoting experienced workers from within" and "All they care about is a college degree, not what you know" are commonly heard. Differences in education, either in level (a high school diploma or an MBA, say) or type (an engineering degree versus a liberal arts education) can create divisions among staff. How easy is it for the human resource team members, who have liberal arts educations, to talk with the engineers who have had more technical training? Are people with certain levels or types of education excluded or preferred? Are comments made by a high school graduate given the same credence as suggestions made by a college graduate? Is there support for employees who want to augment their education in ways other than taking college courses?

In one organization, the lack of a formal college education has been an issue for the department manager who, even with her 20-plus years

with the company, excellent rapport with the staff, and continued demonstration of competence, has been repeatedly reminded that she has
no college degree. While her nondegree status increases her credibility
with her own employees, who feel she understands them, she is limited
in upward mobility in the organization and as a member of the management team, where her suggestions and input may be given less credence than her degreed colleagues.

> Questions for the team:
> - What are the team's assumptions and expectations
>   about education?
> - How well do people of different educational back-
>   grounds interact with one another, and listen to and
>   hear each others' input?
> - How can we make sure that team members of all
>   educational backgrounds are full participants?

Income

"You are what you eat" states an old saying about nutrition. We could
paraphrase it for our society to say, "You are what you earn." Much of
an individual's esteem may come from the numbers on his or her paycheck. Disputes over existing salaries or small cost-of-living raises, re-
sentments over job reclassifications or rivalries among team members
concerning opportunities for overtime may have less to do with the
actual dollars involved and more to do with the symbolic value of income. These differences can play havoc with team cohesion and cause
time and energy to be spent on non-work-related debates.

In addition, the income levels of the team members' families of
birth may have provided or prevented opportunities, such as travel or
education, that may give some staff members advantages over others.
They can also influence team members' level of comfort with one another. In one manufacturing organization that was having a problem
with a high rate of product defects, the lead man on the line was invited
to a meeting with managers to discuss ways to solve the problem. The
team leader had never been to a meeting with "suits" before and was
intimidated to be in a setting where others clearly had a different income level. Knowing he had information they needed to solve the problem, the "suits" paid full attention to his input and suggestions. What
resulted was an identification of the cause of the problem and a solution

that worked. None of this would have been possible if either side had allowed the difference in income to block their interaction.

> Questions for the team:
> * How do differences in income show themselves and affect relationships on the team?
> * How does income influence performance?

Parental Status

Having children generally means that these team members have outside responsibilities and time commitments that may affect their ability to participate in team activities. If a member coaches a Little League team, he may not want to put in overtime on a project. A colleague may be called away to pick up a sick child from school right in the middle of work on a tight deadline. A single parent may be thought to have less flexibility for travel assignments. Finally, those employees who do not have children may also have unacknowledged outside responsibilities— caring for an ill parent, leading a scout team, or volunteering on the board of a nonprofit organization.

Many working parents, especially women, opt for a flex-time or part-time position at some point early in their children's lives. One young professional with an MBA decided to switch to a half-time position after the birth of her first child. As a top-producing professional, she gave the organization more than the required 20 hours of work each week, getting excellent reviews from every direction. She was therefore shocked when, at performance-review time, she did not get the top rating. The reason was that, despite her exemplary performance, the unwritten rule held that no flex-time employee could get top marks. She argued and lost. However, by the next year's review, the organization had changed its norm regarding part-time workers and, after much discussion, decided that performance was the only basis for evaluation. Not only did she get top marks, but the way was paved for future working parents.

> Questions for the team:
> * What are the assumptions about employees who are and are not parents?
> * How can we make sure that opportunities and responsibilities are doled out fairly with regard to parental status?

Appearance

We're taught not to judge a book by its cover, but we do. Beauty is definitely in the eye of the beholder, and preferences differ from culture to culture. What is seen as appealing and appropriate in one culture may not be in another. This diversity factor is often commented upon in training sessions, especially with regard to weight. It is no secret in this society that many negative assumptions exist about people who are considered overweight. A consultant recently spoke of a bright, capable executive who stopped him in the hall one day to ask a painful question. Concerned that her plain face and stout body were obstacles to moving up, she asked if he really thought she could ever be considered for the post of chief executive officer (CEO) because of her looks. She knew, as most of us do, that job opportunities are sometimes offered or withheld because of appearance.

> Questions for the team:
> - What are the subtle (and perhaps not-so-subtle) norms about appearance on the team?
> - What appearance factors seem to make the most difference on the team?

Personal Habits

Differences in personal habits such as smoking and drinking can be the catalysts for relationship building or dissolution on teams. Smokers often become a cliquish group because of their shared experience in taking smoking breaks outside the building. Exercisers may "aerobicize" together after work or go to the same health club in the morning before coming to work. Beer drinkers may form close ties through get-togethers that leave out their teetotaling co-workers. Finally, any substance-abuse problem can impact not only individual and team performance but safety as well.

> Questions for team:
> - What personal-habit differences do team members bring that affect team relationships or cooperation?
> - Do any personal habits adversely affect productivity?
> - How does the team treat members who make use of the employee assistance program to help deal with a substance-abuse problem?

Recreational Habits

Fishing? Bowling? Crafts? Aerobics? Off-road racing? Basketball? Gardening? Golf? The recreational preferences of your teammates bring still another piece to the diversity puzzle. In one organization, most of the major decisions were made on fishing trips that only a few team members attended. In another, playing golf was an unstated but clearly understood requirement for promotion into the management team. In still others, camaraderie builds among those who share an activity week after week or who can talk together about a favorite sport or hobby. Again, these differences can form relationships. They can also shut people out.

> Questions for team:
> * Are there preferred recreational habits on this team? If so, what are they?
> * What happens to those who have different interests?
> * How can recreational habits be cultivated or expanded to increase team cohesion?

Geographic Location

The areas where team members were raised and where they presently live have a bearing on the group. Whether employees grew up in small towns or large cities, whether in this country or in another part of the world, that environment will influence their perspectives, values, experiences, and awareness levels. One young professional woman from a small town in the Midwest shocked a group in her company when she told them she'd never talked with a divorced person before coming to work there. In one national sales organization, regional differences made for some interesting variations in attitudes about gender roles. Sales managers and directors from the South were more than surprised that there were many women serving in those roles in the western region. In their area, women had not been considered for such positions. In still another organization, when a destructive earthquake collapsed bridges and shut down roads, causing changes in commuting times, distance, and traffic patterns, team members had to adjust schedules to accommodate each others' needs. Friction among staff members resulted, with people complaining about the unfairness of some of the adjustments. "Why do they get to come in late or leave early?" they asked.

Think about your teams. Do people who live closest to the office get all the overtime? Is it difficult to arrange team meetings because members come from distant places? Do members from different parts of the country bring different styles of communicating and points of view to discussions?

> Questions for the team:
> - What geographic differences do we have on our team?
> - What varied views are brought to the team because of geographic differences?
> - How does geography impact the teamwork?

Work Experience

Team members bring a wide range of levels and types of work experience. Old hands and neophytes, those that are computer literate as well as those who are technophobic, engineers and accountants, technicians and typists—employees with such disparate work histories will undoubtedly come together on your team and all can make their unique contributions.

In some organizations, experience within the company is highly valued, while in others it is less important. Teams often prefer some kinds of work background over others. In one public utility, restructuring meant the redeployment of staff to different divisions in order to retain employees. However, former office workers were not warmly welcomed in the field, where construction workers were disdainful of their "soft" colleagues, who had a lot of computer know-how but no hard-hat experience.

> Questions for the team:
> - What different kinds of work experiences do team members bring?
> - What kinds of experience do we value? Which do we discount?
> - What kinds of work experience do we still need on this team? How hospitable is the current team climate for someone with this skill?

ORGANIZATIONAL DIMENSIONS THAT MAKE A DIFFERENCE ON THE TEAM

Beyond the personal and societal influences on an individual's filter are the organizational categories which also make a difference in assumptions, expectations, and opportunities.

Functional Level or Classification

No matter how level-free organizations aim to be, nor how many attempts are made to flatten the hierarchy, there is always some structure that delineates functional levels or classifications. They may be signified by numbers, with everyone knowing that a level 13 is executive management, while a level 7 is clerical support staff. They may be indicated by titles such as team leader, administrative assistant, customer service representative, or sales manager. Whatever the system, differences in level on your team will bore their way into the group's relationships. They may serve as coveted signs of status, indications of pay differentials, or informal sources of power. The important thing to recognize is that these levels may impact the individual's self-esteem and level of participation, as well as team relationships. One organization that regularly referred to its staff as professional and nonprofessional, to signify the difference between those with college degrees and those without, got an instructive piece of feedback. Clerical workers let management know that they resented being called nonprofessional since they considered themselves to be very professional in their commitment and behavior.

> Questions for the team:
> - What different functional levels or classifications exist on your team?
> - How do these differences impact communication and participation?
> - How do teammates of different levels get along with each other?
> - Do we have sufficient diversities of function on our team to adequately reflect viewpoints that must be heard? If not, how can we get them?

Management Status

Closely related to functional level is the dimension of management status. From team leader to CEO, everyone who reviews another's performance and has accountability for other employees has some level of management status. When different managerial levels are present on the team, there may be perceptions of inequality or fears of retribution. There may also be different attitudes toward bosses because of cultural variations. For those from hierarchical backgrounds, respect for authority figures would inhibit them from sharing feedback with managers. However, having management included on your team can also help dissolve the "us versus them" rift that often exists between management and nonmanagement personnel. On one team, this was dealt with when management and nonmanagement team members shared their perceptions of the stereotypes held about each group. Teammates walked away with some different views of their counterparts.

> Questions for the team:
> - How do differences in management status impact team relationships and teamwork?
> - What can each status level learn from the other?
> - How can we work through any communication blocks between managers and nonmanagers?

Department, Division, Unit, and Work Group

What do the sales and marketing departments say about each other? How about customer service and manufacturing? It is not uncommon for there to be images, assumptions, and stereotypes about specific departments or units. Reputations precede departments. Some are well respected as high performers while others are known as troublemakers.

In one organization, the customer service staff was seen as "kiss———" while the construction group had a reputation of being "kick———." These units were at one time separate departments that didn't get along. Although it didn't matter when they functioned independently, now they are being cross-trained and are expected to work together in some short-term team configurations. They have a lot of assumptions to unlearn about one another if they're going to be able to work together, solve problems, be productive, and meet their deadlines.

Questions for the team:
- What departmental or divisional differences are represented on the team?
- What are the assumptions about those differences?
- How do those assumptions impact interpersonal communication on the team?

Union Affiliation

Whether employees are union members or not can add another wrinkle to the diversity fabric of your team. If some team members are union affiliated while others are not, this can result in conflict on the team. If union and management are at odds and both are represented on the team, their distrust may spill over into team relationships. However, we also see where common interest can build significant bridges. We are noticing the bridge building in many southern California companies as union and management team members work together to keep jobs. Their joint vested interests are creating new and important common ground as they create alternatives to out-sourcing. And even without the critical issue of job salvation, having individuals from both sides of the fence work together can lead to improved communication and commitment from both constituencies, as well as increased understanding of sometimes unsympathetic positions.

Questions for the team:
- How does union affiliation of team members affect the group?
- How do we deal with "us versus them" attitudes when they occur?

Work Location

"Headquarters gets all the good stuff." "They always forget about us out here in the remote sites." "We're treated like stepchildren because we're not at corporate." These are the kinds of commonly heard gripes that indicate the impact of work location. Whether you are in the corner office, the executive suite, or the portable trailer in the parking lot can make a difference in your viewpoint and attitude, as well as in the perceptions other people have about you. Work location often influences communication and can be seen as a sign of importance or value.

One team with members from different locations began to splinter over this factor. Each issue, whether designing a resource center or deciding how to spend the organization's philanthropic dollars, boiled down to a conflict between headquarters versus field offices over which locations would benefit most. However, when they realized that this difference was blocking the group's progress, they began finding ways to create solutions that helped the staff at all locations.

> Questions for the team:
> - What work locations are represented on our team?
> - Do any of these differences impact how team members see each other?
> - How do different locations impact communication and work flow?

Seniority

A bastion of the old order in businesses across the country is the value that has traditionally been placed on seniority. Although this is slowly changing in some places, an employee's length of time at the company generally does make a difference on a team. Promotions, schedules, overtime, and other perks are often expected to be doled out on this basis.

Generally, the hierarchy of seniority is adhered to more by mature workers reared in a system where longevity was a plus and by employees from hierarchical cultures, who see age as commanding respect and seniority as a sign of wisdom. In addition, union contracts and organizational policies have traditionally used seniority as a fair way to distribute advantages.

> Questions for the team:
> - How is seniority regarded on this team?
> - What are the rules and norms about length of service?
> - How do team members with different amounts of seniority relate?

Work Content or Field

The kind of work people do brings still another dimension. Plumbers and social workers probably see things differently. Lawyers and engineers would probably bring divergent views, as would secretaries and computer programmers. Each type of work has a subculture of its own, which tends to give people a methodology for working with problems. The accountant would most likely approach a situation in a different way than the assembly-line supervisor; the engineer might draw a diagram, while the marketer might start with focus groups. In one biotechnology organization, a manager revealed that her most difficult diversity barrier was one of work content. As a nontechnical human resource professional, she found communicating with engineers to be her foremost challenge. Sometimes they just didn't understand each other. In addition, each type of work may have its own status within the organization.

> Questions for the team:
> - What kinds of work do people on this team do?
> - How well do people who do different kinds of work get along with and understand and listen to each other?

DESCRIBING YOUR OWN FILTER

Each dimension of diversity contributes elements to your identity and your filter. How you see yourself and others and how they see you is powerfully influenced by your dimensions. Depending on your life experience and development, some dimensions will have had a bigger impact on you than others.

Think of yourself growing up and developing through your lifetime. Consider each of the diversity dimensions and its impact on you. Select three of these dimensions from within each level of diversity that seem the most important in forming the person you are now. Write down the most important values or rules you learned from each; then write about the effect this dimension of diversity has had on your life and work. For example, if gender is an important dimension and you are a woman, you might have been taught that women should be nonassertive and nurturing and that you should always act like a lady. The impact may be that you are great at maintaining productive relationships at work, but you haven't been promoted to management because you are seen as a supporter rather than a leader. Or, for another example, if ethnicity is an important dimension and you are a recent newcomer to this society, you may have different cultural norms than most others in the organization. You may have been taught to call bosses Mr. or Mrs., to be obedient to your elders, and to drop your eyes when talking to people in authority. At work, the impact may be that you are seen as unassertive and meek and may be overlooked for raises or promotions. It may also mean that you are sought after as a valued team player. Analyze your own filter using Worksheet 2–3 that follows. Once you've filled it out, ask yourself a few questions.

- What are your major influences?
- How do they impact your work life—positively and negatively?
- When do any of these influences cause conflict within you?
- How do you resolve those internal differences?
- When do they create conflicts with fellow team members?
- What is your most interesting lesson from this analysis?

Once you've completed your chart, share your analysis with some of your teammates as you discuss:

- What similarities and differences are there among you?
- What can you add to each others' analyses?
- How can the team capitalize on all its members?

As our mentor John E. Jones, Ph.D., used to say, "Awareness precedes choice." Completing the "Analyzing Your Diversity Filter" chart is a critical first step in self-awareness that can lead to greater understanding among team members. But to fully understand how your various diversities impact teamwork, utilize the next chart, Worksheet 2–4, "Dimensions of Diversity: Same and Different."

WORKSHEET 2–3

Analyzing Your Diversity Filter

Directions: Select within each of the four layers of diversity the three most important dimensions in your own development. What values and rules did you develop because of that dimension, and what has been its impact on your life and work?

Dimensions of Diversity	Values and Rules Developed	Impact on Life and Work	Potential Impacts on Team (Positive and Negative)
Personality Traits e.g. Spontaneity	Free-flowing, idea-generating style preferred	Shoot-from-the-hip style	Makes me an energetic contributor and brain-stormer; also makes me impatient with those who are slower and sometimes not thoughtful enough about ideas
Personality Traits 1. _____ 2. _____ 3. _____			
Internal Dimensions 1. _____ 2. _____ 3. _____			
External Dimensions 1. _____ 2. _____ 3. _____			
Organizational Dimensions 1. _____ 2. _____ 3. _____			

WORKSHEET 2–4

Dimensions of Diversity: Same and Different

Directions: Select five of your closest co-workers or work associates. Write their names on the diagonal lines at the top of the chart. Analyze each person to see whether they are the same as or different from you in each of the diversity dimensions, marking *S* for same and *D* for different.

Work Associates

Diversity Dimensions

Personality					
e.g., Loyalty					
Internal Dimensions					
Age					
Gender					
Sexual Orientation					
Physical Ability					
Ethnicity					
Race					
External Dimensions					
Geographic Location					
Income					
Personal Habits					
Recreational Habits					
Religion					
Educational Background					
Work Experience					
Appearance					
Parental Status					
Marital Status					
Organizational Dimensions					
Functional Level/ Classification					
Work Content/Field					
Division/Department/Unit/Group					
Seniority					
Work Location					
Union Affiliation					
Management Status					

After completing Worksheet 2–4 ask yourself a few questions and discuss your analysis with a trusted colleague.

- Where do you have more similarities? Differences?
- Which dimensions make the most difference in whom you are drawn to? Relate best with?
- Which people might you be shutting out?
- Which aspects seem relatively unimportant?
- Consider an individual with whom you have a difficult time working. Which dimensions are the same and different? Which seem to be the source of your difficulty?

Then you might want to share your insights with the whole team, discussing the following:

- Which dimensions bring us together?
- Which have the potential for causing divisiveness?
- How do these differences enrich the team? If you aren't capitalizing on them, how can the team do so?
- What obstacles are there to including everyone on the team?

As we've previously stated, large-group discussions may be uncomfortable to staff members who are from cultures that prefer more privacy. Small-group discussions may be a step on the road toward comfort, with more openness on the team. Now review Worksheet 2–5.

Once you've rated the degree of difference on the team, consider how well the team utilizes these differences to increase effectiveness. For example, you may find that there is a wide range of personality styles that results in energy and camaraderie on the team. On the other hand, the range of differences in education level may cause some members to be shut out at meetings or feel undervalued if they think preference is given to college degrees over experience on the job.

Compare your ratings with those of your teammates, focusing on the following questions:

- Where do your perceptions of the degree of variation agree and disagree?

WORKSHEET 2–5

Assessing the Impact of Diversity on Our Team

Directions: Think about each dimension of diversity and rate the degree of variation on the team by checking the appropriate column. Put a + in the last column, if you feel the degree of difference is put to good use by the team; put a – there if it is not well used or if more diversity is needed to move the team forward.

Degree of Variation

	1 Little difference	2	3	4	5 Great deal of difference	+ or –
Personality						
Different styles and characteristics						
Internal Dimensions						
Age						
Gender						
Sexual Orientation						
Physical Ability						
Ethnicity						
Race						
External Dimensions						
Geographic Location						
Income						
Personal Habits						
Recreational Habits						
Religion						
Educational Background						
Work Experience						
Appearance						
Parental Status						
Marital Status						
Organizational Dimensions						
Functional Level/Classification						
Work Content/Field						
Division/Department/ Unit/Group						
Seniority						
Work Location						
Union Affiliation						
Management Status						

- Which differences does the team use well? Which ones does it not use well?
- How is this shown operationally?
- Where differences are not used well, what is the impact? How or where is the team hurt? Be as specific as possible.
- What changes in the way the team manages its differences might help improve team performance?

If you are a team leader, you might also want to make a large chart of the dimensions and ask the team members to indicate the degree of sameness or difference that exists on the team. Members rate, on a scale of 1 to 5, how similar or different they are as a group regarding each factor. For example, if everyone has the same level and type of education, they would rate that factor a 1 (low diversity). If team members come from 10 different countries or nationalities and speak many different languages, the team might rate a 5 (high diversity) on ethnicity. Once the rating is done, the team can discuss what difference the presence or lack of diversity makes for the team and which dimensions seem to be the most critical in terms of teamwork. Or you can have team members work in small groups to come up with their top three—those dimensions that seem to make the greatest difference on your team. It would also be important to discuss how these differences are demonstrated and how they affect teamwork and productivity. As you lead the discussion, be sure to focus both on the pluses and minuses. Just having an open, nonconfrontational discussion about these differences begins to show the team that differences aren't good or bad; it's how you manage them that counts.

KEEPING YOUR OWN FILTER CLEAN

The final aspect of dealing with your own piece of the diversity puzzle is to become aware of the ways in which your own filter colors your opinions about and attitudes toward others. As human beings, we tend to gravitate toward what is familiar and predictable because it is comfortable. We also tend to shy away from and mistrust what is different or what we do not understand. Diversity rattles the cage of complacency and may make us apprehensive. It also brings us into contact with new groups that we don't understand. When there is a lack of knowledge, we fill the void with assumptions.

It is these attitudes and assumptions about others who are different from us that often form barriers to productive work relationships and effective teamwork. Once we are aware of our assumptions and attitudes, we can question them and make conscious choices about how we want to think of and behave toward those who are different. Worksheet 2-6 can help you clean your filter by giving you a chance to examine your assumptions, modify them so they are more accurate, and keep them from forming obstacles in your work team.

Some dimensions of diversity make more of a difference to us than others. For example, if management status is a dimension that makes a difference for you, you may hold, or have heard others make, generalizations about managers such as:

- They don't care what we think.
- They only worry about pleasing their bosses, not listening to us.
- They don't have any understanding of what we do.
- They ask for our opinion, then do what they want anyway.

Once you've come up with your list of assumptions, see if you can refute them. Do you have any examples of managers who aren't that way or behaviors that are unlike your statements?

Once you've written your examples, talk with other teammates, sharing your assumptions and examples that disprove them.

This chapter has given you a chance to explore the many aspects of diversity that you and your co-workers bring to the team experience. These differences make for rich variety, but it is for each team to work with those differences to form the most effective, productive combination of elements. Diversity can lead to both creativity and conflict. Succeeding chapters will give you information and processes to increase your ability to capitalize on diversity and to deal effectively with the difficulties it may present.

WORKSHEET 2–6

Keeping Your Filter Clean: Confronting Your Own Assumptions and Expectations

Directions: Chose five dimensions that make a difference in your relationship with co-workers. Then write down some of the expectations and assumptions you have about others who are different from you in that aspect. Finally, in the far-right column, give examples of behaviors that disprove your assumptions.

Diversity Dimension	Assumptions and Expectations	Examples that Disprove Assumptions

Chapter Three

How Diverse Teams Work

"If you have always done it that way, it is probably wrong."

Charles Kettering

The shift from hierarchical organizations that manage by control to ones that encourage, enable, and expect employees to make decisions and solve problems has been underway for the last few decades. Getting this grassroots involvement to happen through a team structure has been a more recent emphasis, which has brought greater focus on group dynamics. What makes a team productive? How does a team function optimally? And, more relevant today, how does the diversity of team members impact the group's output? Answering these questions requires a look at how teams function.

THE FOUR DIMENSIONS OF TEAM BUILDING

Some teams run like well-oiled, meticulously maintained dynamos, while others clunk along, sputtering and choking, barely getting ahead. Yet the "clunker" and the "Rolls Royce" teams have something in common. They share four dimensions in which teams operate. Understanding the four dimensions is an important step in knowing how to lead your team to success.

Task: Focus on the Product

All teams are organized to produce something. Whether the product is as tangible as a report or a machine part, or as intangible as improved communication or increased morale, it represents the team's reason for existing and forms the basis for its goals and objectives. This task focus is one critical cornerstone of the team. When team members under-

FIGURE 3–1

The Four Dimensions of Team-building
A Model of How Teams Function

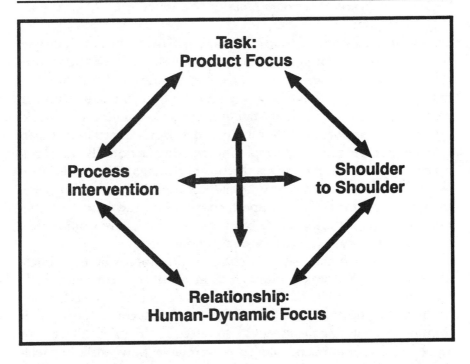

stand clearly what their task is and are committed to it, they can set
their course and organize the sequence of their work. When tasks are
unclear or when there is lukewarm enthusiasm about accomplishing
the articulated goals, productivity and progress suffer.

One administrative team saw its task perfectly. In order to keep this
health care institution alive in the increasingly competitive '90s, it needed
to devise a new and more effective marketing strategy. Team members
were clear about the task they were focused on and were committed to
coming up with a plan that would produce results. Meeting over a period of months, they redesigned the services they provided, added new
ones, and found effective ways to communicate their offerings to their
potential customer base. Their clarity and commitment to the task gave
them the needed focus so that their energy and ideas were honed in on a
very specific and important goal. Critical questions for teams regarding this
dimension are: What is our reason for being? What are we supposed to be
accomplishing? and What are our goals and objectives as a group?

Chapter 4 is devoted to a deeper explanation of this aspect of team building, giving a variety of techniques for helping teams answer these questions.

Relationship: Focus on Human Dynamics

Because teams are not made up of robots but of living, breathing people, there is another factor, that of human relationships. Some teams work diligently to create harmonious music, while others only produce discord. On your team will be a whole range of human relationships. In some cases, there may be long-standing animosity; in others, co-workers have built strong bonds. Informal leaders can bring team members together or cause the group to split into warring factions. Formal leaders can be the focus of loyalty and respect or antagonism and jealousy. When positive, these human-to-human connections built among team members form the basis for support, cooperation, and team spirit that not only make for high morale but the kind of effective communication and creativity that lead to greater productivity.

In one cross-functional team charged with improving the climate of tolerance in the organization, all team members were passionately committed to the task. What they were less devoted to was each other. Each meeting became a grueling session filled with conflict, which left team members asking themselves, "Do I need all this grief? All we do is argue." It took months and many process interventions, including relationship-building activities, to get the group to coalesce and feel like a team. It also took strong facilitation to keep them listening to each other without judgment and to help them continually refocus on their common ground. Critical questions for the team to consider regarding this dimension are: How well do we communicate and get along? How well do we support one another, especially during difficult times? and What are our rules for how we want to treat one another?

Chapter 5 offers help regarding this dimension of team development.

Shoulder to Shoulder: Working Together

"Foxhole buddies," "in the trenches," and "through a few wars" are common phrases that express the comrades-in-arms feeling that develops among team members who work together to achieve results. The shared experience can develop a bond, a common ground that brings people closer together. This feeling that "we're in it together" is often strength-ened by adversity. A common enemy, obstacle, or deadline can often bring a group together quickly. No matter how different members may be, a shared task can give them a way to come together and develop a connection that forges team spirit.

On one team that had been growing slowly but was constantly plagued by self-doubt and weak relationship bonds, the turning point came when they had a specific task, that of producing a companywide newsletter. Spending two days in a workroom grouped around three computers going at once, the team hummed. The energy was palpable as they got excited about their product, relied on each other for help, and could see real, tangible progress. They developed columns and cross-word puzzles on the spot as their creation emerged before their eyes. "This was our best session yet," one member commented, getting many nods from teammates. "We got so much done." This avenue is the es-sence of building teams through working together shoulder to shoul-der. Questions for the team to think about regarding this dimension are: Where do we need to work together? Where are we interdepen-dent? and Where can we help each other?

Chapter 6 can help you answer these questions.

Process Intervention

Teams don't grow only when members work side by side. They can also be built through intervening in the mechanics of how a team works together. Creating special learning experiences outside of the regular work of the team at retreats, training sessions, and team meetings is useful for relationship building, developing understanding, and conflict resolution that might not happen in the process of working together on the job every day. These interventions can be used to jump-start a new group, break through a communication block in more mature teams, or stimulate growth on a team at any stage. For example, a work-group may need to learn how to make decisions; hence, a workshop on using a decision-mak-ing matrix might be called for. Another team could be blocked by friction, divisiveness or lack of trust among members, so a sequence of trust-build-ing exercises could be implemented at regular, weekly team meetings.

In the previously mentioned team that was working on increasing tolerance, conflicts were obstructing progress on the results. Process in-terventions were necessary. First, the team created a list of the norms by which they wanted to operate. Then each session's task was preceded by an activity that had team members share attitudes and feelings with others in the group, thereby breaking down some interpersonal barriers and building common ground. Then, during discussions, when polarization seemed imminent or when egos began to get bruised, the facilitator would stop the discussion and have members share responses to such statements as:

1. Right now I feel . . .
2. I feel listened to when . . .
3. I feel discounted when . . .
4. What I need from others on this team is . . .
5. I need to be more tolerant of . . .

These process interventions helped group members overcome interpersonal obstacles and build stronger connections with each other.

In another example, a team that had poor participation and productivity at staff meetings changed the format and got better results by structuring more interactive communication processes and by rotating the leadership of each meeting. Weekly staff meetings that had once been boring and dominated by one-way communication became lively sessions where real views were aired, problems identified, and solutions generated, all in an environment of shared participation.

To take a look at this aspect of teamwork requires asking questions such as: Where are we blocked in our task accomplishment or in our relationships? What is keeping us from achieving our goals and creating barriers in communication? and How do we deal with conflicts that emerge on the team?

Chapter 7 discusses this dimension and gives many techniques for improving the way a team works together.

Table 3–1 will help you see how each aspect of team functioning is played out in the activities of the team's work.

TABLE 3–1

Teamwork in Four Dimensions

Dimension	Team Activities
Task: Product Focus	• Clarifying purpose and mission • Setting goals and objectives • Solving production problems • Scheduling tasks • Action planning • Assigning responsibilities
Relationships: Human-Dynamic Focus	• Getting acquainted • Sharing reactions, views, and feelings • Resolving conflicts • Giving emotional support to each other • Giving and getting feedback • Sharing information about personal styles, preferences, and expectations
Process Intervention	• Learning team processes to improve communication, problem solving, and decision making • Observing team behavior • Facilitating meetings • Participating in retreats and team-building sessions • Assessing and discussing how the team works
Shoulder to Shoulder	• Cross-training; peer teaching • Working interdependently to accomplish tasks • Giving tangible support by helping each other • Solving production problems together • Facing challenges and overcoming obstacles

ASSESSING YOUR TEAM'S FUNCTIONING

Teams, like individuals, need to assess how they are doing. The information gained through this checkup is of value when used as a springboard for group discussion. In this way it is similar to the biofeedback process. By giving individuals information about their bodily responses such as heart rate and blood pressure, biofeedback enables them to begin to control functions that were previously perceived to be automatic. Group feedback works in much the same way for the team. Sometimes the "biofeedback" may be a pat on the back that validates the team. At other times, it may be a kick in the rear that forces the team to do some things differently. In either case, assessing the team and then sharing the feedback can be catalysts for team growth. Getting information about the team's strengths and weaknesses focuses members' attention on both and begins the process of strengthening the weaker areas. Worksheet 3–1 can give your team valuable information about how it is doing and where it may need some development.

Give yourself 3 points for each item you marked Almost Always, 2 for those marked Sometimes, and 1 for Almost Never; then add your total points. The higher your number, the better your team is doing in each of the four dimensions of teamwork. However, the most important information may be your scores in each of the four dimensions. Take a look at which has the highest and lowest scores and those with only 1 point. These may help you identify your team's Achilles' heels, the places to begin working on strengthening your group.

This assessment is most valuable when all team members take it and share their responses with each other. Group members can discuss their similar and different perceptions of team strengths and weaknesses. This joint-feedback session can then lead to working on ways to develop the team or to addressing obstacles uncovered.

Another way for the team to assess its functioning is by using the Worksheet 3–2, "Team Busters" checklist. This 20-item checklist identifies behaviors that, if present on your team, inhibit productivity and effectiveness. The most helpful way for you to use this tool is to have members complete the checklist and then share their reactions. However, it can also be used as an anonymous feedback tool, with the leader collecting completed checklists and giving the team information about the group's collective data. The anonymity of this is a plus on cross-cultural teams, where self-disclosure might be difficult.

WORKSHEET 3–1

Assessing the Team's Functioning
A Feedback Tool

	Almost Always	Some-times	Almost Never
1. We are clear about the goals of our team.	___	___	___
2. We help each other out when needed.	___	___	___
3. I can count on my teammates to pull their share of the load.	___	___	___
4. We have processes that help us get past obstacles when they occur.	___	___	___
5. Work is organized in a way that helps get the job done efficiently.	___	___	___
6. People on the team are clear and direct in communicating with each other.	___	___	___
7. I need to work with others to get my job done.	___	___	___
8. We spend time talking about how we're working together.	___	___	___
9. We spend time working on ways to increase our productivity.	___	___	___
10. We have effective methods of dealing with conflicts when they arise.	___	___	___
11. I have responsibilities and tasks that are shared with other team members.	___	___	___
12. We spend time learning how to work together more effectively.	___	___	___

Scoring: Almost Always 3 points
Sometimes 2 points
Almost Never 1 point

Total

Task: Focus on Product	Items 1, 5, 9	___
Relationship: Focus on Human Dynamics	Items 2, 6,10	___
Shoulder to Shoulder: Focus on What We're Doing	Items 3, 7, 11	___
Process Intervention: Focus on How We're Doing It	Items 4, 8, 12	___
	All items:	___

WORKSHEET 3-2

Team Busters

Are any of these behaviors present on your team? Check any that you have experienced or seen in the past few months.

_____ 1. Complaints about schedules and deadlines

_____ 2. Ethnic, racial, or gender slurs or jokes

_____ 3. Reluctance to work with people of other groups (racial, gender, ability, etc.)

_____ 4. Talking about problems away from rather than at team meetings

_____ 5. Lack of clarity about team goals, objectives, and tasks

_____ 6. Unresolved conflict between team members

_____ 7. People working in isolation, having little contact with other team members

_____ 8. Unequal participation in team problem-solving and decision-making sessions

_____ 9. Confusion about roles and responsibilities

_____ 10. Lack of fun and camaraderie among staff

_____ 11. Little understanding of the work and frustrations of others on the team

_____ 12. Little attention paid to how we are working as a group

_____ 13. Insufficient knowledge or skill to do the job on the part of any team member

_____ 14. Lack of support for one another

_____ 15. Irritation with teammates who perform different functions

_____ 16. Intolerance of the views of other team members

_____ 17. Weak commitment to the team's goals

_____ 18. Gossiping and backbiting

_____ 19. Frequent "us versus them" comments

_____ 20. Lack of effective ways to deal with team obstacles and conflicts

Scoring

    Each of the items falls into one of the four dimensions of team building.

    Circle the numbers of the items you checked in the lists below:

Task Focus	Items 1, 5, 9, 13, 17
Relationship Focus	Items 2, 6, 10, 14, 18
Shoulder to Shoulder	Items 3, 7, 11, 15, 19
Process Intervention	Items 4, 8, 12, 16, 20

Then share the items you circled with your teammates. The more items you circled, the more team obstacles you may have. Discuss the following questions:

- Which items did team members check most?
- Which of the four aspects of team building present the most difficulties?
- What are the consequences for teamwork? For work-group cohesion? For productivity?
- How can we work on overcoming these team busters?

Succeeding chapters focus on each of the four dimensions of team building and offer tools and processes for developing aspects of each dimension.

DIVERSITY VARIABLES THAT IMPACT TEAM FUNCTIONING

- A teammate nods and says he understands, then proceeds incorrectly.
- A co-worker talks on and on, never getting to the point.
- A team member won't tell you when there's a problem.
- Some group members never speak out in meetings to make suggestions, yet you know they have some good ideas.
- A colleague pretends everything is fine, when you know she is upset.
- One member of the group comes unglued when meetings don't start on time.

Are these just irritating occurrences? Could they be examples of personality issues? Is there just a communication problem? These kinds of differences may be the signs of diversity variables on your team. Although the most obvious difference in a pluralistic group might be seen in teammates who don't speak the same language, native or otherwise, there are other, more subtle differences that can seriously impact how effectively your team works. These are the variations in cultural values

FIGURE 3–2

Diversity Variables that Impact Teamwork

Egalitarian ⟷	Hierarchical
• Equal status for all • Informal relationship with boss • First-name basis • Expectation that all individuals have a right and responsibility to participate and share ideas	• Respect for authority, chain of command • Formal relationship with boss • Titles, formal forms of address • Expectation that ideas and suggestions come from the boss
Direct Communication ⟷	Indirect Communication
• Direct and to the point • Preference for specificity • Explicit and clearly stated	• Subtle, more circuitous communication • Preference for general, vague language • Implicit, hinted at, or suggested
Emphasis on Individual ⟷	Emphasis on Group
• Rewards, credit, and responsibility assigned to individuals • Pride in being singled out • Individual accomplishment and initiative prized	• Shared responsibility and accountability • Embarrassment at being singled out • Individual accomplishment and initiative discouraged, downplayed
Linear/Logical ⟷	Lateral/Intuitive
• Sequential ordering of thoughts • Problem solving done by following an organized, step-by-step method	• Circular and meandering thought process • Problem solving done in a spontaneous, less ordered manner
Task Focus ⟷	Relationship Focus
• Top priority: getting down to business • Emphasis on work and information pertaining to tasks	• Top priority: getting along with others • Emphasis on building human-to-human connections
Confrontation in Conflict ⟷	Preference for Harmony
• Interpersonal problems directly and openly dealt with • Discussing differences seen as productive • Ignoring differences seen as counterproductive	• Interpersonal problems ignored or smoothed over • Tension and conflict avoided • Discussing differences seen as disruptive, counterproductive
Change Oriented ⟷	Tradition Oriented
• Progress and improvement through change • Innovation and betterment valued • Desire to fix things	• Change seen as disruptive • Order and stability valued • Desire to adapt to status quo
Strict Time Consciousness ⟷	Elastic Time Consciousness
• Time = money • Priority on promptness and meeting deadlines • Brisk pace	• Time spent on enjoyment as well as on task accomplishment • Deadlines not treated as top priority • Relaxed pace

and preferences each team member brings to the group. The range of differences in cultural values that may be present on your team is shown in Figure 3–2.

Each team member brings a different set of preferences and values in these areas. Team members' places on each continuum will depend on their own unique cultural software. Each team member is a product of his or her four layers of diversity—personality and the internal, external, and organizational dimensions. A female immigrant from Colombia who is a claims processor may have a very different style, approach, and perspective from her teammate, who is an African-American male and a manager of human resources. On the other hand, they may have many similarities in their values and preferences. These differences can make for creativity and dynamic problem solving when valued and utilized. Witness the case of a Japanese manufacturing firm in the United States that discovered a problem. High-tech equipment was disappearing, and it seemed to be an inside job. A team of managers was called together to solve the theft problem. All of the managers were American-born Caucasian males, with the exception of one Japanese-born manager. The American managers' unanimous solution was quick and to the point and came out of the American value of individualism. "Reward the whistle-blower and punish the culprit" was their suggestion. The lone Japanese manager, being from a more group-oriented culture, had a very different solution. "Reward the teams that have no theft," he offered.

However, these differences in values can also create problems when cultural variables are not understood, as was the case when a holiday party flopped. A new owner of a manufacturing company wanted to reward his hard-working production employees, most of whom were fairly recent immigrants from Mexico and Central America, so he decided to treat them to a Christmas party. He spared no expense in the holiday dinner-dance he planned at a local hotel, to which all employees and their spouses were invited. You can imagine his chagrin when hardly anyone showed up. When his irritation and disappointment subsided, he decided to investigate the reason for the lack of attendance.

Asking a "cultural interpreter"—a third party who could speak Spanish and who understood the cultural background of the employees—to investigate the reasons for nonattendance produced some insightful information. The staff explained that most of them had never been to such a fancy event, their wives didn't have the appropriate clothing, and they were afraid they would embarrass themselves or their host

by committing some social faux pas. Telling the boss directly or refus-
ing the invitation would have seemed ungrateful and an affront. Rather
than put themselves or him in an awkward position, they chose not to
attend. It seemed to them that this was the course of least resistance and
the best way to preserve everyone's dignity.

Had the boss known more about the culture and preferences of his
employees, he might have planned a different kind of celebration. Perhaps a family picnic or a barbecue after work would have been a more
successful team experience for his employees.

How can you know all of these things? you might wonder in frustration. The short answer is, you can't. But you can create experiences
that allow people to talk about their values differences and share their
preferences. This helps accomplish two important steps in bridging cultural gaps. First, it increases understanding about differences. Second,
it builds relationships among people so they are more comfortable telling each other about problems or obstacles that crop up.

Worksheet 3–3 is one way team members can build this understanding and connection.

Compare your bar graph with your teammates', sharing similarities, differences, and ways these can be strengths and weaknesses for
your team. Which differences could produce problems? One way to
share this information with the team is to select the one dimension that
could cause the greatest conflict, then create a large graph showing the
different responses of team members on that one continuum. Similarities and differences then become visually apparent and give the group a
jumping-off point from which to begin discussing their team's joint
profile.

Clearly these eight variables impact relationships among team members. But how do they affect the functioning of the team as a whole?
Let's take a look again at the four dimensions of how a team works. For
example, for those who have a strong task focus, it is important to realize that some team members will be much more committed to the task
if they've first developed a relationship with their co-workers. However,
this view may be different from that of team members who have traditionally seen time spent on relationship building as a wasteful diversion
from "real work." These individuals may not understand that the "soft
stuff" of relationship building can be an investment that will pay big
dividends in loyalty and commitment down the line. Conversely, those
who place a premium on relationship over task need to realize the importance of following an organized sequence of tasks and adhering to

WORKSHEET 3–3

Diversity Variables on the Team

Directions: At the top and bottom of each column are pairs of opposites. Find the point in each column that represents where you are and fill it in with a fine-line marker to that point. You'll end up with a bar graph that shows your pattern of preferences.

Egalitarian	Direct Communi- cation	Emphasis on Individual	Linear/ Logical	Task Focus	Confronta- tion of Conflict	Change Oriented	Strict Time Con- sciousness

Hierarchical	Indirect Communi- cation	Emphasis on Group	Lateral/ Intuitive	Relation- ship Focus	Preference for Harmony	Tradition Oriented	Elastic Time Con- sciousness

schedules. Not doing so would undoubtedly create irritation and frustration among teammates who expect such a focus, possibly leading to impaired relationships.

Team members with a more hierarchical orientation may find it extremely uncomfortable for the boss to roll up his sleeves and work alongside them. They may also find it difficult to give the boss bad news, yet in a collaborative and team problem-solving environment, full staff participation is called for. It may be important to explain the reasons for needing to know about problems and mistakes. Those from more individualistic orientations may need to structure tasks, give feedback, or share praise with groups rather than on an individual basis to get the most out of more group-oriented co-workers.

Finally, the process interventions used to improve team dynamics and functioning may be uncomfortable and a foreign experience for some team members. Activities that ask people to share feelings may be difficult for men who have been socialized to be strong, rational, and in control of their emotions, or for individuals from cultures that do not value self-disclosure ("The best counsel is my own"). Participating in learning experiences that may uncover educational deficits ("I don't want anyone to know I can't spell") or vulnerabilities ("I'm very nervous about speaking in front of the group") may be difficult for others.

What each team member brings to the group in the form of background, values, preferences, and past experiences will color his or her contribution to and view of the team and co-workers. Together, this combination of backgrounds, values, and perspectives forges the team's ability to make progress on its tasks, to form productive relationships, to work shoulder to shoulder, and to manage its process so that it can achieve its desired results. The next chapter helps you explore in greater depth the task-focus aspect of team building.

Chapter Four

Task Accomplishment
The Raison D'être of Teams

"No wind blows in favor of the ship that has no destination."

Montaigne

T he primary reason for forming teams is to accomplish tasks that meet performance objectives. The best teams can provide a morale boost, fun, cohesion, increased job satisfaction, and a greater sense of involvement in the life of the organization. But all of those perks are secondary benefits. The main stage, front and center, is to accomplish tasks that bring desired results. A clear purpose, joint accountability, performance standards, and a realization of carefully de-lineated goals and objectives serve as a team's lifeblood, giving a diverse group a natural place and reason to build common ground. This task accomplishment can't happen without agreement on fundamental values, a clear mission, relevant goals, and well-defined objectives.

VALUES: THE CRITICAL UNDERPINNING

Of all the factors that can derail a team's efforts to achieve results, that of values differences is the most fundamental. Agreement at the values level is what brings commitment to the task. An overlap in values is a precursor to all decisions involving very real and potentially divisive issues such as resource allocation, prioritization of goals and objectives, expectations about how to behave together, and almost anything else connected to team performance. Although values are certainly critical underpinnings of team objectives and decisions, they are not always articulated as the key factor around which team norms are defined. Even when they are, these conscious and articulated values often get

81

pushed aside amid conflicting choices, expedience, or the reality of lim
ited resources. In some cases, exuberant professionals campaign for personal preferences rather than adhering to stated organizational values as
a reliable guide in making hard choices.

Discussions on values are a little too abstract for some people's tastes.
It is important, therefore, to help team members understand that every
day, all day long, they make value-based choices. Not all examples are as
clear-cut as the one we're about to describe. A year ago, we did a workshop for a government agency that asked us to structure a day in which
participants could focus on values. Attendees were asked to list their
top five life values and rank them from 1 to 5, with 1 being the highest.
In the case of all 20 participants, values 1 and 2 involved performance
on the job and commitment to family. Although the language used to
describe these top two choices may have differed, and there was no
unanimous agreement on which was more important, work or family,
in some way everyone stated those as the top two choices. As a follow-
up to the discussion of their lists, we pointed out that our real values are
seen in our actions. We then asked the participants to analyze where
they actually put their time.

That experience led to some surprises and a very rich discussion,
which culminated with an insightful question by one man who had
listed family as number one. He mused, "If family is so important to
me, why am I rarely home? And why, when there is a conflict between
commitment to family and deadline on the job, do I almost always pick
the job?" He joked that his wife also wanted the answer to that question, but the issue clearly had touched a nerve. This participant had a
lot of company in that room, and what started out as an abstract exercise about values became a meaningful discussion with real dilemmas.
For example, if "quality is job one," as Ford likes to say, but other organizational values are efficiency, productivity, and profits, when do you
send parts back that don't meet quality standards, particularly when
flaws are not obvious? If team members value time with family but also
value meeting a deadline for a client, what gives? And under what circumstances does the answer to that question change? These conflicts
will occur in work groups because, while the team values many things,
those values themselves often conflict and force people to make choices.

How does the government-agency example transfer to your work
groups? On your teams there will be values that everyone verbally es-
pouses. If you are leading or facilitating a team, some time in the life of
that team, and preferably sooner than later, you need to start a discussion

about team values. The old aphorism "Talk is cheap" comes to mind here. This discussion will enable team members to explore concretely what they base their decisions on, what their potential value conflicts might be, and whether they act on the values they espouse. They will also see where they already have an overlap in values and where they can build on their common ground. None of the values that dominate team discussions is inherently better than any other. But it is very important to see where differences exist because therein lie the potential trouble spots, and the resolution of these differences will impact the team's results.

Recently we had an opportunity to work with a group that decided to see what their values were as a way to get to know team members better and to see how individual differences might impact team performance. Their task was to have each member pick his or her top 10 values and discuss the similarities and differences they noticed among themselves. After they did that, we put each team member's number one value on a flip chart. They were amazingly different and offered such variety as financial security, duty to family, inner peace, and loving relationships. When all seven team members looked at each of their answers, they were shocked and amazed at the variety and lack of agreement. The follow-up discussion was very fruitful, however. They started by defining what those values meant to them, with an eye toward finding overlap in the concepts each value implied. The consistent thread was the desire to find common ground, even if the stated values were very different. For example, someone on the team volunteered that financial security was a good start toward inner peace and serenity. Another person offered the view that duty to family can help in meeting obligations in the workplace because of the strong commitment implied in the word *duty*. As the discussion proceeded, team members created more common ground than would ever have appeared on the surface. More than anything, it gave team members an opportunity to size up their own values and create ways to make room for everyone. It was an exchange that helped team members learn more about one another and how they could work better together. The most helpful part of the discussion centered on their differences. They looked at potential problems, such as when duty to family might conflict with work deadlines and how that conflict might erode a sense of trust or accountability on a team. The discussion ended not with a resolution about the hierarchy of an individual's values, but rather with an awareness that values do matter, that values are fluid, and that team members will handle the differences best with open discussion and understanding.

But this discussion would be much tougher if the goal is reaching agreement on team or organizational values rather than individual values and how they might impact teamwork. Most teams, for example, would subscribe to values such as making a high-quality product, providing excellent service, and maintaining efficiency in delivering both product and service. But there are times that the very efficiency that would demonstrate excellent service in meeting a deadline might violate the high quality both you and the client would want to see in the product. Which value reigns supreme in this case?

Our clearest, most recent example of this dilemma involved a cross-functional team in an organization that manufactured machine parts. A clear split in values appeared between quality-assurance people whose top value was a high standard of excellence, and line supervisors, whose responsibility to turn out products in a timely manner made volume and efficiency their top choices. This conversation led to a discussion of ethics, customer service, and respect for self on the job—all over a values conflict between what matters most, meeting deadlines or high-quality work. In the best of all possible worlds, you get both. On high-performing teams, these Hobson's choices in values are discussed and battled out, which leads to a guiding rationale for making these choices. We offer a technique to aid the process.

The following strategy is a diagnostic tool that will help the team prioritize its values and determine what matters most. The challenge in selecting these values is this: Although all 30 stated values in the checklist may have merit, in the context of real team functioning, people have to make choices. In choosing some values, others will automatically fall by the wayside. In truth, values change with context, circumstances, life stage, and experience. They can change moment to moment. However, the team is more productive and its experience more satisfying, harmonious, and enlightening if it makes some values sacred and agreed-upon in the context of working together.

This is a multiple-part process. Begin by using the tool, Worksheet 4–1.

Once each person has prioritized his or her own values, the team needs to conduct a discussion that focuses on the following questions:

- What was hard about making these choices? What was easy?
- In general, what values do you most want to see reflected on this team? For what reasons? (As team

WORKSHEET 4–1

Values: The Critical Underpinning

Directions: One way to structure effective, productive team dynamics is to discuss and decide upon a set of sacred values that your team is willing to subscribe to. Below are some commonly expressed team values. Please check the eight that you'd most like to see on this team and rank them from 1 to 8, with 1 being that which is most important to you.

_____ Responsibility (joint and/or individual)	_____ Accomplishment
_____ Involvement in decision making	_____ Satisfying relationships
_____ Competence	_____ Creativity
_____ Meaning	_____ Self-worth
_____ Autonomy	_____ Self-expression
_____ Recognition	_____ Leadership opportunities
_____ Personal and professional growth	_____ Financial security
_____ New and different experiences	_____ Diversity
_____ Collaboration on common tasks	_____ Career mobility
_____ Harmony or an absence of conflict	_____ A sense of belonging
_____ Competition	_____ Shared fun and experiences
_____ Meeting deadlines in a timely manner	_____ Peace and serenity
_____ A high standard of excellence	_____ Good health
_____ Status, position	_____ Loyalty
_____ Stimulation from challenge and change	_____ Duty to family
_____ Other _____	

members give responses, the team leader may list the values, but it isn't necessary to list the rationales.)

- Where do the responses indicate similarities and differences about the team's value preferences? Where might our differences show themselves and lead to conflict in the real work-group choices we make every day?

- Since making hard choices is part of the values-clarification process, what is your number one value? (The facilitator definitely lists each of these.) Based on the collective responses, where are we compatible? What trouble might these responses suggest?
- How can we make our differences more compatible?

Each team needs to anticipate these conflicts, do its best to see that all team members' values are reflected, minimize potential divisiveness, and be mindful of the fact that values, however subtle, do matter very much.

The next step in the values strategy is to ask participants to go back to the "Values" checklist, look at the 30 listed values again, and change the context in which they choose their top eight. This time they are asked to put an *I* (for individual) to indicate value preferences outside of work. The goal here is to see how priorities change and which values come into conflict between work and home. In the example in which one woman checked "duty to family" as her number one individual value, we talked with that group about the consequences that her choice might have on the team and the stress for her when she is pulled between opposing values in different parts of her life. These value conflicts will indicate volumes about issues of personal commitment to the job, of integrity, and of stress when employees feel they violate their best selves when they go to work. As one individual dramatically expressed it, "Working here corrodes my soul." He is no longer in that corrosive environment. In organizations, and on teams, the degree to which people feel their prime individual values can be expressed in the work environment is the degree to which a team can count on real loyalty and commitment from its members.

As we stated at the beginning, values are not static. They change regularly depending on any number of factors, but it is very important to at least go through the exercise of articulating what matters most to us as a team and as individuals because these values impact team performance and commitment. If you are on a team in which diverse ethnic and cultural groups are represented, this becomes even more important. Issues such as loyalty, harmony, and duty to family are sacred in various ethnic groups. If loyalty to family is very strong, does that carry over to the workplace? And if it does, is greater loyalty given to the organization as a whole, to the direct boss, or to peer group members?

Under what circumstances might the answer to that question be significant? The issue of harmony is another one worth looking at. Most human beings prefer to work in a group that functions harmoniously. However, under what circumstances might harmony become a minus for the team rather than a plus? A discussion about harmony, and at what cost, is worth having, as is a follow-up discussion about how dealing with differences doesn't have to result in conflict. The opportunities for creating understanding about value differences are endless. Some value preferences may also be indicators of opposing positions, such as pro-life or pro-choice, while others may be due to cultural differences, such as a preference for direct confrontation versus a greater comfort with smoothing over differences. These variations are important to explore because misperceptions, or incorrect interpretations about people's behavior may be made based on these cultural values. When they are, it presents all involved with a chance to learn, grow, and adapt.

THE TEAM'S MISSION: A COMPASS THAT CHARTS ITS COURSE

The team's mission is formed by the meshing of organizational and individual values. It can be described as the compass that charts the team's course, and it spells out the team's reason for being. Following are two examples, one of an overall organizational mission statement and the other a statement for a team within the whole.

The Los Angeles Commission on Assault Against Women (LACAAW) states that it is a feminist organization that has as its mission the elimination of violence against women and children and the empowerment of women to make constructive, healthy choices in their lives. At one time we were LACAAW board members and served on its board recruitment team. We had a separate mission, which was to recruit board members who would not only generate revenue to pay for services LACAAW wanted to provide, but also reflect the overall demographic composition of the community so that any woman in our service area would feel comfortable using LACAAW's programs. Our group was only one of several teams functioning in various ways to support the overall organizational purpose.

LACAAW is an example of a nonprofit agency that is faithful to its mission. But mission statements are just as necessary in the corporate world. We have included an example of one of these too. You'll see below that one of our clients has some clear business objectives. Notice how the mission statement for its diversity task force supports its broader business objectives. Developing a culture in which tolerance and respect prevail, becoming an employer of choice, and attracting and retaining high-achieving associates, support the four business objectives. The work of the task force is measured against its mission statement, and all choices made regarding diversity in the organization are designed to nurture the business objectives in a variety of ways.

Organization's Business Objectives
- Increase market share
- Continuously deliver on our customers' expectations
- Be the employer of choice for a high-achieving team of associates
- Achieve the profitability expectations of investors

Task Force's Mission Statement
This initiative seeks to create a culture of tolerance and respect, which provides a climate that supports the business objective to be an employer of choice, able to attract and retain a team of high-achieving associates supporting an environment where people can flourish.

Creating a Mission: An Artful Process

On diverse teams, choosing from a variety of artful group processes is a good way to get participation and commitment to the mission. Because language fluency is often an issue on diverse teams, and because other cross-cultural norms, job experiences, or education levels may impact a team member's willingness to contribute to the discussion, we have designed some processes that rely more on intuitive, creative thinking and less on verbal skills—more right brain than left. There are four kinds of approaches designed to help a diverse team define its mission. They are:

1. Visual art
2. Performance art
3. Construction art
4. Language art

Visual art. Among the most successful, effective techniques we have used with teams are those that involve visual art. The first, a collage, was fun and involving for all people present. We asked participants to bring magazines and newspapers from home to our mission-definition session, and we provided the materials for people who had neither. We then asked all participants to cut out articles, words, headlines, or pictures that reflected their perception of the organization's mission. Often, people brought their own ethnic newspapers in different languages. That was a fun and fascinating experience that stimulated people to talk to one another and get to know each other better. In addition to a lot of space for people to spread out, you will need scissors, glue, and small pieces of construction paper. On a small team, each team member can use a piece of 8½-by-11-inch construction paper, filling it with images that describe what he or she sees as the overarching purpose of the team. After about one hour for selecting, cutting, and pasting, team members present and discuss their respective collages. Each can then be taped to the wall. When everyone is done, the team leader or facilitator asks the group to discuss what it heard. The leader can list major themes and help the group decide on its overall purpose, based on the data collected and the contributions of everyone involved. By consolidating these themes in a central place, building a coherent mission statement is a natural step. As you can see, this process takes several hours. It is particularly effective at retreats, where time is less of a factor than at the work site, where people juggle meeting deadlines with continuous work responsibilities. If there is no retreat building in sight for you, but it is time to dust off your mission statement and you'd like to try this, you can break the process down into parts. In one session, you can cut and paste; in another, you can share. And finally, you can discuss, disagree, define, and decide what your mission will be.

In some organizations, when teams exceed 9 or 10 people, facilitators opt for butcher paper on the wall. All participants are asked to paste their contributions on the butcher paper, then look at the whole effort and see if they can see themes. Again, the team leader facilitates a useful discussion. The butcher-paper idea was used at an LACAAW session with 75 to 100 people. It was a very practical and energizing tool for garnering communitywide input and support for the organization's mission. It is a tool that can work equally well in small and large groups, and it works especially well with teams that are in need of goodwill and a common, uplifting experience.

Another visual-art tool involves giving small teams within the larger team several colored markers and some chart paper. Their task? To draw a visual image that reflects the mission of the team. Discussions are held about organizational and team values, with an eye toward discovering how the small team can support the larger organization in meeting its goals. When each small team is finished presenting its view of the mission, a whole-team discussion is held in which participants discuss what they saw and then synthesize all perceptions to achieve consensus on what the overarching purpose is. The process is designed to be fun, stimulating, energizing, involving, and results oriented. We have yet to see it fail to meet all of these criteria.

For all of the previously mentioned reasons, visual-art is a good tool to use during the most lethargic part of the day. We used the drawing of a visual image that reflects the mission of the team at a professional organization of our colleagues recently. It was the last activity of a full-day workshop, on a Saturday, no less. Everyone was tired by 3:45 PM. We gave directions to a listless crowd, and participants in each of the four small groups just sat there as though they were frozen. Slowly they unthawed. The energy built and by the time they left at 4:30, they were as fresh and vital as they were at 9:00 AM The visual-art techniques pay many dividends in team building and team accomplishment. They also add variety to your facilitation design. As a bonus, they incorporate right-brain creativity as a way to help define your team's mission, and they show the powerful effect of working together to deliver a tangible product.

Performance art technique.   Performance art takes a little more time to plan and organize. It involves developing a skit or a role play that indicates a group's perception of what the group's mission and purpose should be. The caveat here is what the Wallaces' *Book of Lists* refers to as people's number one fear: speaking in front of groups. Some people will be nervous about the "performing" aspect and not see this as an opportunity to work together on a joint project and have some fun exploring meaningful issues. One thing that can help reluctant participants is to clarify the purpose and give very clear directions.

First, divide the team into subgroups. This is critical in order to compare the perspectives of different team members. In groups of four or five, have each small team create and present a skit or role-play situation no more than five minutes in length that illustrates its perception of what the group mission should be. Mostly, this performance should enable the viewer to identify the group's suggested top values and priorities and to have a real sense of what the team and the organization stand for.

At the end of each "performance," discuss the following questions with the larger team:

- What did you like or enjoy about the content of this presentation?
- What are the major themes and values the members depicted?
- Based on these major themes and values, how do you think this group defines the mission of our team?
- How is this group's view of our mission similar to yours?
- Is there anything they omitted that's important to you? If so, what?

After all groups have given their presentations, the whole team can have a discussion about the process itself as well as the content. Ask the participants what they thought of using this technique to define their mission. Structure your questions so they look at both the pluses and minuses of performance art. You may hear pluses such as "It was an unconventional way to explore our mission" and "We got a different result than we would have by a more traditional method," while a minus might be that some people are shy, felt intimidated, and didn't contribute. Focus on how their participation, interest level, and commitment changed throughout the process. Get them to articulate the reasons for those changes. When you're through discussing the process, talk about the content itself. Concerning content, start by seeing where they are in agreement about what their real purposes are. They can also use the discussion to resolve some of their differences. To help them do so, as team leader you need to look at all resources, time lines, and trade-offs involved in following one path instead of another. With clear directions and the promise that substance is far more important than form, you can have a good time and reap rewards with this technique by bringing a variety of perspectives and some levity to noteworthy issues.

Construction art. For those who like to build, plan, or design, this technique is a natural. You'll need sets of Tinker Toys, Legos, Lincoln Logs, or any construction materials. The task, as in the two previous approaches, is for small teams within the large team, or for one team of between seven and nine people, to engage in building a structure that illustrates how the collective unit defines the purpose of the team. Among the topics for discussion are values, work content, and interpersonal processes for getting the job done. Issues such as those brought up in the performance-art approach can be discussed. In addition, the team can look at its own process. When you have only one team constructing its visualization of the mission, the facilitator can be a process observer and give feedback at the end about what he or she saw in the team dynamics. It is instructive to focus on each person's contribution to the whole. For example, who organized the team? Did one person take charge? Did some people give ideas that they felt were ignored? Before they started building, was time spent on planning how the team would operate? Who was especially good at asking challenging questions during the discussion of goals, roles, and values? Who supported the ideas? Did anyone play devil's advocate? If so, what did the group gain? If not, what did the group lose? Giving feedback in this way is very helpful in teaching the group about its own process. It probably is best given after the group talks about how it sees itself, what it did well, and where it could improve.

After this experience, you end up not only with information about how a team works together, but also with a product in the form of some newly built structure that teams often revere. We have had team members return the next day to take pictures because they knew their objet d'art would eventually be dismantled. It seems to leave participants with a shared experience and a tangible symbol of pride and belonging.

Language art.   Of all the artful mission techniques, only with the language-art tool are written words the dominant part of the group's outcome. This technique asks the team or subteams to come up with a jingle and/or motto that reflects the mission. The jingle itself is clearly a language tool. Like the other art techniques, this too involves spontaneity and creativity. By creating a jingle, team members have to think about and discuss their purpose. The biggest caveat in the jingle and motto is that participants have a hard time understanding the difference between the two. Explain that a jingle is a quick, clever, catchy lyric about a product, whereas a motto is a more straightforward statement. So, for example, the mission at McDonald's, might be to serve food quickly and efficiently with consistency of taste at a reasonable price, so its jingle is "You deserve a break today." Mottoes, on the other hand, are more direct. Ford's emphasis on excellence is shown in its motto, "Quality is job one"; Westinghouse's focus on innovation is shown by its saying, "Progress is our most important product." A team discussion similar to those previously described is conducted after jingles or mottoes are shared; the discussion helps the team identify the common themes, values, and goals depicted.

Each of these techniques will help your team define its mission. They will also add energy and vitality to the process while allowing your diverse team members—in fact all team members—to fully participate.

GOALS: CLEAR, COLLECTIVE, AND COMPELLING

Goals are the articulated values of the work group, according to our colleague John E. Jones. We also remember something else John told us about himself years ago, when he turned 42. He had accomplished all the goals he had set for himself at that time and was depressed because he had not yet identified any new goals to take their place. Of course, a few months later he developed a whole new set of aspirations and expended a lot of energy on moving toward their accomplishment. What we (and John) learned from that experience is the importance of having goals. They add value, meaning, and importance to life, a reason to get up in the morning. A team is a living organism just like an individual. It too needs purpose and meaning.

Goals are the team's primary vehicle for articulating and implementing the meaning behind the mission. Team goals show up as performance objectives. The process of setting goals may need to be a little different on a diverse team than with a team where everyone is reared in a homogeneous environment. To understand the relationship between goal setting and diversity on your team, begin by answering the following questions.

1. *What kinds of diversity do you have on your team and how are they acknowledged?* For example, what is your team's gender ratio? How about the number of women in nontraditional jobs, specifically? Will the answer to either of these questions cause women to feel intimidated or excluded and, as a result, give less input or commitment? Further, is anyone on your team hard of hearing or unsighted? What kind of accommodations do you make at your meetings, such as making sign language translation available? Also, what religious groups are represented on your teams? For example, do you consider that prayer times for Muslims or the High Holy Days for Jews are not good times to hold sessions where the primary goals and direction for the team are delineated? Do some working parents

(probably more mothers than fathers) need flexible schedules to meet the demands of parenting? If so, are you cognizant of this when you plan sessions where goals and objectives are defined? How many different languages are spoken, and how many ethnic and cultural norms are displayed on your team? What is their impact on team participation and productivity? Does the mix of these rich differences ever cause conflict that erodes work energy? Does everyone on your team speak up and participate? If not, are any of the reasons cultural?

Right about now, you're probably thinking that having to consider these variations on a theme is a royal pain in the neck. And if you're like some team leaders we've worked with, you're also wondering, Whatever happened to the practice of "When in Rome, do as the Romans do"? You have a lot of company if your view is that the responsibility of employees coming to the team is to adapt to existing norms. There is a strong belief that the team leader can't be expected to know about and accommodate every whim and uniqueness of each team member. In reality, even if you wanted to, you wouldn't always be able to.

But there is another truth here as well. While people will not always have every individual need and preference responded to and accommodated, it sure doesn't hurt to at least find out about those aspects of people's lives and practices that are very significant to them. If you do so, and indicate respect and honor toward these uniquenesses, people will work with you and go the extra mile for the team effort. Showing respect for these needs changes the whole environment and dynamic on a team, whether or not people always get their needs met. In fact, our experience has been that team members don't always expect to be accommodated, but they appreciate the effort. Certainly, regarding goal definition, it is important, before you even think about going through the process, to look at the composition of your team, identify the diversity variables, and plan accordingly as you seek input. Doing so will send a strong signal that each person's contribution matters, and it gives you the best chance of tapping the talents of everyone.

2. *Are these goals subscribed to by all team members?* While the overall organization has goals and objectives, your team also has its own mission and goals to which people need to subscribe. The best way to avoid either apathy or sabotage is to include and utilize feedback and suggestions from all team members. When goals are finally articulated,

state them in a way that reflects the views and desires of everyone on the team in some fashion. Having a tent big enough to include everybody will go a long way toward getting agreement and participation.

3. *Are the goals meaningful?* What is the relevance of these goals to people on the team? Will anyone in the world, country, local community, or organization be better off because of what your team does? And how will each team member's life in this organization be better or different because of your work together? As the late Magdeline Coughlin said about her goal to create a leadership program at Mt. St. Mary's College, "If you ask me to give my all for a chain of hot dog stands, forget it. But if you ask me to develop a leadership program for women, now you've got me." Each person will define meaning differently. For some, a chain of hot dog stands may be meaningful. But the point is, there has to be some outcome that is perceived to be beneficial in order for the goals to be meaningful. Here are a few examples of goals that matter.

When Chrysler had the goal of increasing customer satisfaction, it received the suggestion to create built-in child car seats. Does that idea add meaning to anyone's life? You bet it does. Just ask parents with young kids who get tired of dragging car seats around. Chrysler waxes poetic about convenience, and it's right in this case. Also, when Jane Evans talked about her goals as CEO of Monet Jewelers, she talked about how great it felt to help working women be able to buy moderately priced jewelry that would accessorize their outfits, help them look professional, and build their esteem. Until she rhapsodized about that intent, we hadn't looked at costume jewelry as all that meaningful. We do now. Meaning always lies in the eyes of the beholder, but as a team leader or facilitator, your task is to lead a discussion of goals so that their meaning becomes clear and apparent to those charged with the task of making them a reality.

4. *Are the goals flexible enough to be adapted and concrete enough to be measured?* Working with several diversity task forces at a large insurance company brought a new slant to this question. The initial goal of a professional development team was to increase the chances for advancement and promotion in the company. As the team investigated the issues and came face-to-face with changes in American business, the insurance industry, and its own company, it was very clear that advancement or promotion for a large portion of

employees in this era is close to being obsolete. The goal of investigating and creating solutions to issues regarding the lack of traditional promotional opportunities had to change to become meaningful and relevant in the context of 1990s organizations. The goal instead became one of developing a continuous-learning organization, where all employees have chances to learn new skills, to expand their job functions, and to bring new vitality to their work. The vehicles for doing so revolve around training conducted in a variety of formats. The proposed crown jewel is an assessment center that will evaluate skills and competencies, and a leader lab that will groom any interested employee for greater leadership, whether in a traditional, formal role or one that is informal.

The concrete measures of this goal are numerous, but the decision to proceed is pending the accumulation of further data that will give a detailed cost-benefit analysis that may or may not suggest the expenditure of resources. That analysis, of both the assessment center and leader lab, will help the organization determine whether or not they would provide a good return on the investment. If implemented, an employee-satisfaction survey will measure attitudes and performances and see what, if any, of these changes can be attributed to the assessment center and leader lab. This organization will be prepared (and so should yours) to make midcourse corrections as the team gains new information, changes personnel, loses or gains resources, and adapts goals. As goals evolve, so should your measurement criteria.

5. *Is the goal defined in the same way, even in the same language, by all participants?* This question is an easy one to test. Just go around to the various team members one at a time and tell them you're asking a question for an experiment about goal clarity. You want them to articulate the top three goals and priorities of the team. This can be easily done at a meeting by having them write their three goals on 3-by-5-inch cards. The degree that you hear the same language, ideas, and concepts repeatedly that is the degree to which your team members are unified in their goal definition. If instead you get the Tower of Babel effect, meaning people are not literally or figuratively speaking the same language, that tells you that goal confusion, rather than goal clarity, exists.

6. *Can the goals be broken down into small pieces so victories can be celebrated and tasks less overwhelming? Is the connection between goals and objectives understood?* Any goal worth accomplishing on most

teams is complex enough to involve substantial changes. It is important not to be daunted by the overwhelming nature of the task. Taking a whole issue and breaking it down into bite-sized but accomplishable pieces gives the team a sense of progress, movement, and confidence in its ability to break through inertia and bureaucracy.

A few years ago we worked with a hospital's executive staff whose goal was to increase revenues. The staff's objective—the concrete manifestation of its goal—was to design a marketing plan aimed at creating some profit centers. Among the objectives that would help in accomplishing that goal was the formation of a new entrepreneurial venture that would bring in expanded psychiatric health care treatment and services. Another objective was to reach out to the local community by offering a series of wellness lectures in the evening which would theoretically bring people into the hospital and position the hospital as an organization that encouraged proactive health care. There were other objectives designed to be revenue producers. Some worked well; some less well. But all were designed to help the hospital meet its goal of generating revenues and were clearly understood as such.

When you work with your own team and you have clearly defined goals, breaking them down into smaller pieces will help your team set some clear objectives that can be timed, measured, and altered as needed.

7. *Do effectiveness criteria measure end results as well as gains from the process itself?* Clearly, the most important reason for forming teams is to achieve goals, solve problems, make decisions, refine processes, change systems, or investigate questions and issues, all for the betterment of the organization and its profits. Team effectiveness ultimately hangs on not only whether or not these things get done but done well. But in addition to meeting these performance goals, it is also important to evaluate the process itself. How do team members change along the way? How does their commitment and tenacity in pursuit of team goals change? What new skills have they picked up? What new awarenesses have they gained? How much more politically savvy are they? And what difference might this new sophistication make? What would they do differently next time? These are the kinds of changes that can come about from the process of working on a team. The ultimate question is, What difference does any of this make to the team, specifically in meeting its targets, and to the organization as a result?

To use a stage metaphor, the mechanics of how a team works together may not be front and center, but it is certainly in the wings. The
process itself matters because it significantly influences what happens
on stage. If team members are left to process their gains, losses, and
changes individually rather than as a team, or if they don't process them
at all (which is usually the case), you will lose the opportunity to help
them grow from their collective experiences. The lessons the team learned
from each task accomplished should be extracted and applied to future,
similar scenarios. It's the rich harvest from all the seeds that have been
sown. Process matters, not just in problem solving but interpersonally
as well. The total experience will all flow back into the accomplishment
of subsequent tasks.

You can move the team forward by spending a little time exploring
what worked and what didn't. Some sample questions you might ask
are the following:

- What did you like best about being involved in this
  project?
- What contribution are you the most proud of as an
  individual? As a member of this team?
- What's the most important insight you gained
  through this experience? How might that translate
  to other team projects?
- What would you do differently next time?

If you have people on the team who are reluctant to speak up due to
cross-cultural norms, lack of confidence, different educational levels, or
organizational politics, it may help to break team members up into
smaller groups, where they can talk more comfortably. You can follow
that small-group sharing with a whole-team discussion to hear about
people's attitudes, experiences, and realities. You can then elicit and facilitate the team's learning from these individual experiences. Worksheets 4–2 through 4–5 will function as tools that will enable your team
to learn and grow as it effectively defines its mission, goals, and objectives.

WORKSHEET 4–2

Goals: Charting Our Course

Directions: Respond to each of the following statements by filling in the blanks.

1. I understand the overall mission of our team to be:

_____

_____

_____

_____

2. On our team, I find meaning and purpose in the following issues:

_____

_____

_____

_____

3. As I look at our mission and any unresolved issues that can impede our team, the following goals are important to me:

_____

_____

_____

_____

Utilizing the worksheet "Goals: Charting Our Course" is an important starting point in helping team members see that the team does have a charter, a reason for being. It is worthwhile talking about the overall picture before focusing specifically on your goals.

As a backdrop, you may want to discuss how your team's mission can support the larger organization's purpose, while defining clear goals gives the team its own distinct meaning and rallying cry. Notice that you will proceed in question 2 to a discussion about what team members find meaningful in their work.

Question 3 then asks each participant to think honestly about conditions as yet unaddressed that may warrant energy and team commitment and create an impact on the whole organization. Two recent examples are:

1. To remove barriers to excellent customer service and to improve interactions between staff and their internal and external customers.
2. To reduce defective products and eliminate waste by improving the packaging process.

The questions in "Goals: Charting Our Course" are relevant for any team discussing and creating its direction. From a commitment standpoint, you need the involvement, agreements and support of all participants. From a diversity standpoint, there may be some impediments to full participation. Consider the possible issues that may influence discussion and involvement on diverse teams:

- *Status Position.* Cultural influences and other diversity factors such as age, formal position, gender, and years on the job may keep some people from giving their opinion, or may keep some opinions from being listened to. Participants may see it as disrespectful and inappropriate to offer feedback when dealing with bosses or co-workers who are older, for example, or with team members who have more education, better English skills, or a higher position.
- *Education.* Sometimes people who have less formal education are inhibited in expressing their viewpoints or making contributions. We've seen this on some problem-solving teams dealing with customer service in health care. When you have a good cross section of hospital personnel, usually no one challenges physicians. These cultural influences are sometimes multiple. People don't challenge physicians, not only because of education, but also because of status, position, and gender.

- *Work Experience.* On cross-functional teams, sometimes people have a hard time seeing how the expertise of staff from marketing, engineering, management, and the union can create a mission that reflects all these disparate interests. With team members from so many different parts of an organization, goal-setting sessions may resemble the parable of the six blind men and the elephant. One may be touching the trunk, one the side, and one the tusk. Although they are all feeling the same animal, it surely doesn't seem the same.

There may be other diversity issues as well. A task force designed to investigate flexible benefits or flexible schedules, for example, may face conflict in making recommendations when the team includes people with differences in parental or marital status, stages of life, age, or time with the organization.

All of these viewpoints and experiences will enliven the mix and make the discussion more complex. Just remember (and sometimes it's hard to do so) that all the different ingredients included in the stew add texture and taste even while they make it more difficult to stir. If you know this ahead of time, you expect it and are prepared. Once you have finished discussing the responses from "Goals: Charting Our Course," you are ready to identify the goals that result from that discussion using Worksheet 4–3 shown below.

WORKSHEET 4–3

Goal Clarification
(Example)

Our team's mission is: to create an organization where employees can flourish and to become the employer of choice.

The goals that most clearly arise from our mission are:

Goal 1	Goal 2	Goal 3
to create a more inclusive, open climate in which all employees can utilize their full talents in the workplace.	to develop all employees through a continuous-learning environment that emphasizes training in many formats.	to increase communication among employees at all levels of the organization so that information is accessible and good rapport is the norm.

No team should focus on more than three goals at a time. You can, however, have teams focus on multiple goals if you divide into subgroups. In any case, prioritizing the goals is critical. Once you determine whether you'll work as one team or as subteams, select and prioritize your goals and begin defining performance objectives. Worksheet 4–4 will give you the opportunity to articulate performance objectives, and state conditions or behaviors that are specific and measurable.

WORKSHEET 4–4

Defining Clear Goals and Objectives

Directions: In the boxes below, write the current goals of your team. After you have written the goals, define the specific performance objectives that arise. Follow the example shown below.

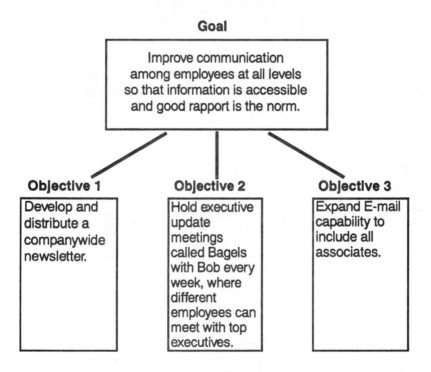

Once you have defined your objectives, complete Worksheet 4–5 for each one.

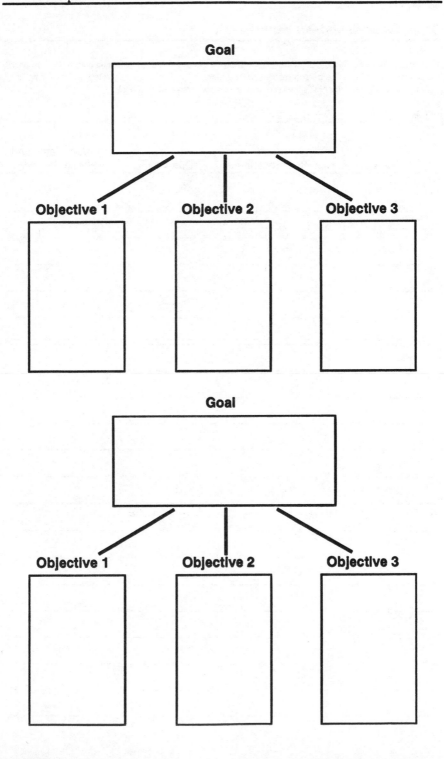

WORKSHEET 4–5

Task-Accomplishment Worksheet

Directions: Write the specific objective below. Then list the tasks needed to accomplish it. Next to each task, write the name of the person responsible, the date the task is to be completed, and the name and phone number of any other individual you need to contact in order to do the job.

Objective:_____

Task	Person Responsible	Due Date	Contact Name and Phone Number

Once the team starts working on its objectives, results won't happen unless names and dates are tied to every suggested activity. There will undoubtedly be a lot more investigations and information gathered than will actually be part of the team's final plan, but clear objectives mean that milestone dates are given all along the way. It has been our experience that dates with short lead times are extremely helpful and energizing because they tend to create more urgency and accountability. And while not every meeting will be one for making major decisions or determining direction, a few of those high-stakes meetings or milestones need to be sprinkled throughout the process to create a sense of movement and importance.

Whether you are working with ongoing teams or with a task force in long-term processes, a tight deadline helps keep people involved and energized. You can create this by juxtaposing a variety of run-of-the-mill working meetings against more formal, performance-oriented, "you will present for feedback" meetings. This little team-building trick of the trade helps to keep fires lit that otherwise might blow out from exhaustion, overwork, or too many places to focus.

Once you go about working on achieving the objectives, you will be making progress toward a successful conclusion that ultimately involves measuring your results. Did we do what we said we were going to do? Did we do something that mattered to the bottom line? To our customers? To our employees? Were the results worth the effort? Did this process make us more profitable or efficient? Did we change or stray from initial objectives? If so, what are we evaluating now?

Having well-defined measurement criteria is one of the most important parts of any team-building work. The measurement-oriented questions you can ask yourself as you embark on any team-building process are:

1. How will we know if we are successful at achieving our goals?
2. What will change and/or improve?
3. What are the concrete manifestations of these changes?

These criteria need to be talked about and determined before a team begins to embark on its journey. It is the ultimate report card that keeps the team honest; it holds the team's feet to the fire.

How will things be different or better? These kinds of up-front questions and discussions are extremely important. They can infuse your journey with meaning and import. If you can't come up with measurable criteria that indicate success or disappointment, don't even start down the path. And if, in the process of discussing this criteria after a goal has been articulated, there's no energy around the discussion or no vision of a different organization or product when visualizing task completion, maybe the team is pursuing the wrong goal. Apathy is a good indicator that you're not on the right path.

There are several ways to work effectively with diverse teams in helping them develop measurement criteria. One that works very well (and de-emphasizes language skills when you have multiple languages on the team) is to have people break up into small groups within the team and draw pictures on chart paper showing how the organization's product, service, climate, or other factor would will be different if this team is successful. Stress that the groups must be as specific as possible. Sometimes groups like to combine pictures and words; that's fine. The key is that they have a picture of how something is different after all your collective energy is expended.

You can have each subgroup present its diagram and when you've seen them all, a whole-team discussion can focus on similarities and differences among the group criteria. In fact, this is a variation of the performance and visual-art approaches discussed earlier. After seeing the diagrams, you can then discuss as a team which measurement criteria you want to adopt and which you want to avoid. The key is having them stated clearly and unequivocally. It is important to have some way to indicate change. It is possible to use data such as absenteeism, turnover, exit interviews, product returns, numbers of complaints registered, or written/verbal feedback from customers.

But as we previously suggested, make sure you determine ahead of time what you're looking for. And don't be afraid to be creative. We remember working with a group years ago that was charged with the task of improving morale in the organization. One of their measurable criteria focused on the cleanliness of the restrooms. They believed that in an organization where people felt ownership and commitment, employees would take pride in the plant. One of their indicators of pride was cleaner restrooms: (1) Towels and extra toilet paper would not be strewn all over the basins and floor; (2) loose grains of soap would not be caked on the tile counters; and (3) less graffiti would be found on restroom doors. We chuckled when they came up with this because it was unconventional. We gave them a few questions to think about, but the team believed in their indicators and it worked for them. They did not quantify this criteria in dollars and cents, but they did link cleaner restrooms to pride, commitment, and loyalty. The hard core among you may ask what difference any of that made to the bottom line. The answer is, we don't know. Some measurements can have a dollar figure attached to them, and in terms of overall productivity and results, we highly recommend financial measurement. It speaks the primary language of most organizations. Having said that, we will also say that much of the human-resource work we do is based on hunches or assumptions that aren't always backed up with numbers. Anecdotal data about increased pride, improved morale, or decreasing alienation can result in renewed commitment, greater tenacity, and more concentration on tasks at hand. But ultimately these measurements, while provable through pre- and posttest interviews and observations of behavior on the job, require an act of faith by those in the organization who intuitively believe that a satisfied employee is a more loyal, devoted, and productive one. For some, this evidence is enough; for others, it isn't. To help your team determine its evaluation criteria, Worksheet 4–6 may be useful to you. Once each team member has filled this out, then decide as a group what your measurement criteria will be.

WORKSHEET 4–6

Measurement Criteria: Holding the Team's Feet to the Fire

Directions: Think about the outcomes you want your team to achieve as you embark on your specific objectives. Fill in each of the four sections below, being as specific as possible.

A. List four specific outcomes indicating improved product or process on the team or in the organization:

1. _____

2. _____

3 _____

4. _____

B. List four impacts of these outcomes on the organization, especially in relation to strategic objectives:

1. _____

2. _____

3. _____

4. _____

C. List four indicators of better interpersonal relationships on this team:

1. _____

2. _____

3. _____

4. _____

D. List four team productivity gains from improved communication among us:

1. _____

2. _____

3. _____

4. _____

As you look at leading a team toward the accomplishment of its work, focusing on a definition of values, mission, goals, objectives, and measurement criteria is vital. If there are no performance objectives and no clear purposes to rally around, then there's no real reason to have the team in the first place. Once you determine that teamwork is the best way to accomplish your tasks, these tools can be helpful. And since all teams are diverse, make sure you know your players as you use or modify these processes to get the results the team is capable of and that both you and the organization demand.

Chapter Five

Relationships
The Ties that Bind

"Satisfaction depends on the network of enduring and dependable human relationships that has been at the heart of human evolution for millions of years."

Hamburg and Hamburg

hen asked about the biggest barriers to team accomplishment, employees enumerate a laundry list of factors, from personality clashes and conflicts to communication blocks and hidden agendas. Most of the obstacles cited are human rather than technical, with roots in the relationships among people. What's more, these barriers produce consequences in daily interactions on the team. Positive and supportive work relationships not only result in clearer, more accurate communication, facilitates task accomplishment, but also increases morale, esprit de corps, and commitment.

BUILDING TRUST: THE FOUNDATION FOR PRODUCTIVE TEAM RELATIONSHIPS

Think of the best team relationships you've experienced in work groups. Undoubtedly, trust was at the base of them. In fact, these relationships could probably be characterized by statements such as the following:

> "We could count on each other."
> "We listened to each other."
> "We could speak our minds freely, without fear of reprisal."
> "We had each other's best interests at heart."

109

"No one was out to get anyone else."
"There were no hidden agendas."

This kind of trust builds slowly, through a series of shared experiences in which expectations are met, belief in each other is validated, and individuals find they can depend on the predictability of each other's behavior. It is the basis for honest, direct communication and for healthy team relationships. You know when it is present. You also know when it is broken or begins to erode. Take a look at a list of trust eroders on Worksheet 5–1 and see if any of them are present on your team.

WORKSHEET 5–1

Trust Eroders on Your Team

Directions: Put a checkmark in the *Me* column next to any behaviors you have shown. Put a checkmark in the *Others* column next to any of these behaviors you have seen others do.

Me		Others
_____	Not coming through on a commitment	_____
_____	Breaking a confidence	_____
_____	Changing the rules without telling anyone	_____
_____	Saying one thing, doing another	_____
_____	Withholding information	_____
_____	Talking behind someone's back	_____
_____	Giving false information	_____
_____	Avoiding an individual or group	_____
_____	Forming or belonging to cliques	_____
_____	Making us versus them comments	_____
_____	Making slurs or jokes about other ethnic, racial, gender, or other groups	_____
_____	Gossiping	_____
_____	Other:_____	_____

Share your responses with other team members, focusing your discussion on the following questions:

- Which of these behaviors have been shown by others on your team?
- Which have you shown?
- Describe the effects of these behaviors on your team, recalling as many specific examples as possible.
- What can you and other team members do to rebuild trust once these behaviors have happened?
- How can you prevent these trust erosions in the future?

One way to build trust is to talk openly about this essential building block of teams and share both helping and hindering behaviors in the group. Using Worksheet 5–2, the team can spend time in a meeting, brainstorming and listing on a chart how you build trust and how you erode it. Then the group can discuss the major barriers to trust and begin creating ways to overcome them. If team members are uncomfortable talking about "bad news," having small group discussions first may help.

WORKSHEET 5–2

Trust on Our Team

Directions: List as many ways as you can think of that trust is built and eroded on the team.

Ways We Build Trust	Ways We Erode Trust

On one team the staff identified lack of contact with each other as a major obstacle to trust and openness on the team. To remedy this separation that prevented the interaction they needed in order to really know each other, they planned regularly scheduled staff meetings that would bring the team face-to-face with one another on a consistent basis.

In another case, a team made up of both American-born employees of many backgrounds and an equal number from Asia was having a difficult time coming together as a group. There was polite interchange but standoffishness and wariness on both sides. Off-the-record comments were heard from each group about the other. Remarks such as, "They don't understand us or our ways," "I don't know when yes means yes and when it means no; why don't they just tell me?" and "They're so cliquish; they always stick together" were common.

The manager was astute enough to realize that these trust busters were signs of a growing rift and that the underlying mistrust probably wouldn't remedy itself on its own. He decided to hold some team-building sessions focusing on understanding cultural differences. Employees were initially cool to the idea and approached the first session about as eagerly as they would a dose of cod liver oil, figuratively if not literally holding their noses. However, bit by bit they were drawn into the content through interactive exercises and a nonconfrontational approach in the sessions. By the end of the second get-together, staff members who had barely said more than good morning to each other were opening up to one another, sharing their personal histories and prejudicial assumptions and asking each other about their respective cultures. While there are no easy fixes in breaking down barriers between groups or individuals, this intervention helped the team make progress in chipping away at some of its trust obstacles.

Another method of helping a group develop trust is to give team members an opportunity to assess themselves around four trust building concepts: (1) interpersonal interactions, (2) risk-taking behavior, (3) problem-solving processes, and (4) openness to diversity. When team members have open and honest communication with each other, feel free to take risks, work together to solve problems rather than point fingers, and value differences, then trust grows. The questionnaire in Worksheet 5–3 gives you and your teammates a chance to assess your group in these four areas.

WORKSHEET 5–3

Trust Building on a Diverse Team

Directions: Respond with a checkmark in the appropriate column.

	Almost Always	Some-times	Almost Never
Interpersonal Interactions			
1. Team members come through on commitments.			
2. Confidences are kept on this team.			
3. "My word is my bond" is the motto for team members.			
4. We admit mistakes when we make them.			
5. Co-workers give me feedback about my behavior.			
6. I give teammates feedback that can be helpful.			
7. We let each other know if we're upset.			
8. When someone breaks trust, we talk about it.			
Risk-Taking Behavior			
9. Engaging in cost-benefit analysis is our norm and results in intelligent risk taking.			
10. When someone on the team takes a risk that doesn't work out well, we help him or her learn from the experience.			
11. People feel free to try new things.			
12. People are encouraged to express honest thoughts, feelings, and reactions.			
13. Team members have the freedom to do things their own way.			
14. Trying something new is rewarded on the team.			
Problem-Solving Processes			
15. Our team uses processes that get the team to work together and minimize divisiveness.			
16. We focus on "how to fix it" rather than "who broke it."			
17. Team members share ideas openly and freely, without fear of criticism.			
18. All team members contribute in problem-solving processes.			
19. "Way out" ideas are welcome in problem-solving sessions.			
20. Team members bring their "parking-lot ideas" into the meetings.			
Openness to Diversity			
21. People mix easily together, regardless of their differences.			
22. Differences of ideas or opinions do not create animosity among team members.			
23. When people use "we" and "us," they are referring to the whole team.			
24. I have close relationships with teammates who are very different from me.			
25. Ridicule about other groups and people is nonexistent on this team.			

Once you have completed the questionnaire, take a look at what it says about your team's trust level. Discuss your responses as a team. In which of the four areas do you have Almost Always checked the most? This indicates that these trust-building behaviors are alive and well. Where do you have checkmarks in the Almost Never column? How does the absence of these behaviors harm the team? What is keeping them from happening? What cultural factors might influence how trust is demonstrated? Look at the items on this questionnaire again. Which of these behaviors are most culture-bound and might pose the most discomfort for someone not reared in the United States? What can you do as a group to reach agreement on a few key barometers of trust on your team? How can you work toward achieving these conditions?

SELF-DISCLOSURE: ONE AVENUE TO DEVELOPING TRUST

Psychologists tell us that self-disclosure—sharing our thoughts and feelings with others—is essential for mental health. It is also a foundation for building trust and understanding. We tend to trust people who confide in us, who explain the reasons for their behavior, and whose motivation we can understand. However, for many individuals this kind of sharing is extremely threatening. Sharing our feelings makes us vulnerable. One abused child explained this eloquently when asked why she never cried, as other children did. This wise-beyond-her-years eight-year-old replied, "If I cry you'll know what hurts me; then you can hurt me too." There's a piece of this little girl in all of us that sometimes makes it difficult to be open and share some of our deepest feelings.

In addition to this general human phenomenon of fear of vulnerability, there are cultural factors influencing people's willingness to self-disclose. In some cultures, especially in much of Asia, it is considered wise to keep one's own counsel. Anyone telling his or her thoughts is looked at as stupid. From the other side of the globe an old Yiddish proverb warns, "Never show a man your whole knee." Even in the United States, we're taught that it's not wise to "wear your heart on your sleeve."

A caution here is in order. Inappropriate self-disclosure does not help a team and can even be harmful. Teams are not self-help groups, and team meetings are not intended to be therapy sessions. However, relevant self-disclosure can build trust, open relationships, and strengthen bonds. The key is to be discriminating in what is shared. Information that pertains to the team's work and personal insights that impact behaviors on the team are valuable.

The following activity on Worksheet 5–4 is an example of a way to create an opportunity for appropriate and relevant self-disclosure on the team.

WORKSHEET 5–4

Sharing Perspectives on the Team

Directions: Pair up with someone on your team (preferably someone you don't know well), and take turns responding orally to each of these open-ended statements. You may go straight down the list or you may take turns selecting an item that you both respond to. You do not need to write anything. Let your responses be spontaneous.

1. What I like best about being on this team is . . .

2. I'm most frustrated in the group when . . .

3. I feel most part of the team when . . .

4. I try to include others by . . .

5. I feel left out on the team when . . .

6. One strength I bring to the team is . . .

7. A major problem or obstacle on our team is . . .

8. I work best with people who . . .

9. I'd be a better team member if . . .

10. Our team works best when . . .

11. Our team gets blocked when . . .

12. One thing I wish others on the team knew or understood about me is . . .

13. I'd be happier on this team if . . .

14. An accomplishment of the team I'm most proud of is . . .

15. Getting ahead on this team means . . .

16. I get nervous on the team when . . .

17. I'm most stimulated and energized on the team when . . .

18. One of the smartest moves we made was . . .

19. One of the biggest mistakes we made was . . .

20. Something I'd love to see our team accomplish is . . .

   Once you've shared your responses with your partner and listened
to his or hers, discuss the experience. What was it like to divulge this
information to your co-worker? How did it feel? What happened to the
two of you in the process? How did you feel about your partner before
you started? How do you feel now? What did you learn about your
partner? About yourself? What did you have in common? What does
the team gain by this process?

   A variation of this activity can be used at team meetings by selecting
one or two of these open-ended statements (or some of your own making) and using them as a warm-up at the beginning of the meeting.
Each team member is asked to share his or her response in turn until
everyone has had a chance to participate.

GENERATING COMMITMENT TO EACH OTHER

When you consider people you work best with, 10-to-1 there is a strong
bond of loyalty and mutual support between you. No doubt you've
been there for each other through thick and thin. None of us goes
through life alone and almost everything we want to accomplish requires the help and cooperation of others. How do you generate this
kind of interpersonal commitment among diverse individuals? Helping
team members understand and cultivate mutual support is one way.

   A colleague of ours, Natasha Josefowitz, writes in her book *Paths to
Power* that all of us need three kinds of support in our lives: "a shoulder
to cry on, a brain to pick, and a kick in the pants." Developing commitment to each other on a team means both getting and giving these
kinds of support. Worksheet 5–5 is a way to analyze the support you
give and get. It will also help you find ways to increase the mutual
helpfulness on your team.

   As you think of the three kinds of support, jot down the names of
your teammates who give you each kind of support. Who is your "shoulder to cry on," someone you can go to to pour your heart out, someone

who will listen to your problems and tales of woe without judgment? Who is your "brain to pick," someone whose clear thinking, analytical ability, and problem-solving skills can help you through a dilemma? Finally, who gives you a "kick in the pants," a well-needed voice of reality, a tough question, or a sobering piece of honest feedback? Write down the names of co-workers who help you in each of the three ways.

Then do the flip side. Who on the team do you give these kinds of support to? For whom are you a shoulder, a brain, or a kick?

WORKSHEET 5–5

Developing Mutually Supportive Relationships on the Team

Directions: Write the names of teammates who fit in each category.

Type of Support	Teammates I Get Support From	Teammates I Give Support To
"Shoulder to cry on"		
"Brain to pick"		
"Kick in the pants"		

Adapted from Natasha Josefowitz, *Paths to Power*

Once you've done your analysis, share it with some of your team-mates. Whose name comes up over and over? Whose name is missing? How diverse is your support system? Does it span many of the diversities mentioned, from personality differences to variations in dimensions such as race, physical ability, educational background, and work experience? Do you get as much support as you give, and vice versa? Where are there holes in your support grid? Are there kinds of support you need but can't get from co-workers? Where else can you get it? How can you be more supportive to colleagues?

It is important to remember that there may be some diversity-related influences at work with regard to building mutual support. Cross-gender relationships might be awkward for staff members who are from cultures that don't view male and female roles as equal. Also, some people may be sensitive to the potential for rumors when a man and woman develop a helping alliance. In addition, it may be difficult for some team members to ask for help. Whether because of gender socialization ("Real men can do it themselves") personality characteristics ("I should be able to handle this alone"), or cultural factors ("It is inappropriate for me to ask my boss for help"), there may be diversity-related inhibitions that block some team members from giving and getting support. However, if relationships on the team are to be strengthened to help get the job done, individuals need to assist each other. Finally, it's important to let supporters know they're on the list of people you relied on by acknowledging their help and thanking them. One way to do this is to spend five minutes on a closing activity at the end of a team meeting by having each member salute a co-worker for help given in the past week or so.

WHEN PROBLEMS REAR THEIR UGLY HEADS

No matter how supportive the relationships, nor how well intentioned the team members, problems will arise when human beings work together. Having these problems is not an indicator of how effective or ineffective the team is; however, the way in which they are handled is. Often individuals need help in working through these one-on-one relationship glitches that, if left unattended, will sabotage teamwork, impair communication, and damage cohesiveness. These seven steps will build your interpersonal problem-solving skills, which reinforce teamwork.

1. *Decide with whom you need to speak about the problem.* This requires identifying and then talking with the person or persons most responsible and accountable, those who have the greatest investment in the problem's solution. If you have an issue with another team member, it does no good to talk about the problem with a buddy in your car pool or over lunch but never confront your teammate. Decide who is responsible for the glitch and who has the power to make the changes necessary to fix it. If this is a difficult behavior for team members not reared in the United States, using cultural interpreters or mediators, or meeting in an informal surrounding might be your best bet. Straightforward discussion can be difficult in these cases.

2. *Describe the problem situation or behavior.* Be specific and objective in explaining the issues. Stick to descriptions of behaviors and situations and avoid blaming behavior, which produces defensiveness. Vague descriptions such as "an attitude problem" or a "failure to communicate" don't help. Be clear in zeroing in on specifics—the garbled phone messages, the unfinished tasks, or the safety violations, for example—that are the issue.

3. *Explain the problem's effect on results.* Productivity, relationships, work flow, and the bottom line are issues you might focus on, showing how the problem impacted these areas of teamwork. Pay particular attention to results that matter to your teammate. If he or she takes pride in quality, you might show how the problem results in a shoddy product. If you have a profit-sharing bonus plan, you might emphasize the cost-saving benefits of eliminating the obstacle.

4. *Offer solutions, stressing the benefits to your teammate.* Make solutions specific, delineating changes in procedures, a different system, or steps that need to be taken to correct the problem. Then stress how these changes would benefit your listener by focusing on issues that matter to him or her.

5. *Listen to other ideas and suggestions.* View your teammate as a partner in this problem-solving process and be ready to get input from him or her. What ideas or suggestions might he or she contribute to improving the situation? Incorporate these into your own plan and work toward a mutually satisfying solution, one that is the product of your joint discussion.

6. *Jointly make an action plan.* The end result of your problem-solving discussion should be an action plan that spells out the steps that need to be taken and clearly defines responsibilities. The who, what,

when, where, and how need to be clear and mutually agreed upon, with each of you having responsibility for some steps.

7. *Arrange a follow-up meeting.*   Don't just leave the process at the solution stage. Set a time to check in with each other to see how the solution is working and to make midcourse corrections where necessary. Also, agree in advance on a way to let each other know about hitches you encounter as soon as they happen.

Using Worksheet 5–6 will help you prepare yourself for your interpersonal problem-solving encounter.

WORKSHEET 5–6

Interpersonal Problem-Solving Worksheet

Directions: Begin by filling out the responses to the questions below. Then, one on one, discuss with your teammate how to solve the problem.

1. With whom do you need to speak?

2. What is the specific situation or behavior that is problematic?

3. What is the effect of this problem on productivity, work flow, relationships, and/or the bottom line?

4. What solutions are you suggesting in terms of specific procedures, systems, and steps? What are the benefits to your teammate?

5. How can you solicit your teammate's ideas?

6. What is the plan you and your teammate have made jointly?

7. When will you and your partner in this process meet to follow up? How will you signal each other if problems crop up?

BALANCING INDIVIDUAL FREEDOM
AND JOINT ACCOUNTABILITY

Is your team a choir or a group of prima donnas? Do team members care more about winning the pennant or about being named most valuable player? Do you function as an orchestra or a group of soloists? Perhaps your team is both, at times feeling like a cohesive unit, at others like a group of individuals all "doing their own thing." This duality is one of the ongoing tensions on any team. It may be a particularly critical balance to preserve on a diverse team, where members may have distinct preferences for either individualism or collectivism and may be on one end of that continuum or the other.

Some cultures, such as that of the United States are more individualistic, seeing each person as a separate entity responsible for his or her own behavior and making choices based on his or her own needs, desires, and preferences. Other cultures, such as those in Asia and parts of Latin America, are more collectivist, seeing the group rather than the individual as the basic unit. Actions, decisions, and choices are based on conformity to group norms and attention to the good of the group rather than on any one person's desires. This fundamental difference may show up on your diverse team.

In addition to cultural factors, personality differences such as a need for inclusion or a desire for solitude will impact responses. Some people are lone wolves; others are social butterflies. The following questionnaire on Worksheet 5–7 will give team members a chance to assess how they balance this duality.

WORKSHEET 5–7

Individual and Group: Maintaining the Balance

Directions: Think of yourself on the team as you respond to these statements. You have 10 points to distribute between the two choices representing the degree to which this choice is true for you. The scores for the two choices in each item can range from 5=5 if both choices are equally true for you to 10=0 if one is entirely true and the other entirely untrue for you.

1. I'm happiest when:
_____ a.   I'm working on my own.
_____ b.   I'm working jointly with others.
2. When it comes to rewards:
_____ a.   I don't want mine tied to the performance of others.
_____ b.   I want mine to be for teamwork and joint accomplishment.
3. When things go wrong:
_____ a.   I'm willing to be held accountable for my mistakes.
_____ b.   I expect the team to be held accountable for its mistakes
4. I like:
_____ a.   to proceed with my own ideas.
_____ b.   the creativity that emerges when the group works together.
5. I see my work as:
_____ a.   independent and separate from the team.
_____ b.   part of a bigger picture of the team's work.
6. Group work and joint decisions:
_____ a.   make me impatient.
_____ b.   are enjoyable for me.
7. When working in a group:
_____ a.   I feel held back.
_____ b.   I feel comfortable and secure.
8. Being singled out for praise:
_____ a.   makes me feel positively acknowledged.
_____ b.   is embarrassing and uncomfortable for me.
9. Working as a group:
_____ a.   takes too much time.
_____ b.   is worth the investment in time.
10. I like it when the team gives me:
_____ a.   freedom and independence to do things my own way.
_____ b.   support, nurturing, and guidance.

Add your total points for:
_____ *a* responses   =   Individual Orientation
_____ *b* responses   =   Group Orientation

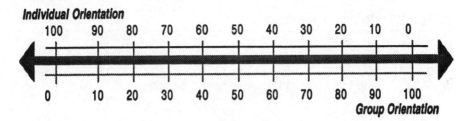

Individual Orientation

Mark your score for each orientation, individual, and group, on the appropriate line. Then connect your marks. The point where your line crosses the continuum represents where you are regarding your orientation. The closer it is to the left, the more you are oriented toward individual freedom and responsibility. The closer it is to the right, the more you prefer group collaboration, accountability, and productivity.

Once you have completed your profile, share it with your teammates. You can even make an enlargement on chart paper and have each team member mark his or her point on the continuum with a different-colored marker. Then discuss your orientations, both the similarities and differences. How does your combined team pattern serve as a strength for the team? As a weakness? Where are there potential conflicts? How can your differences in orientation be used productively by the team? This may lead to a discussion of the tasks and projects your team is working on, with clear application to maintaining an effective and appropriate balance. Using Worksheet 5–8, the team leader can facilitate the discussion, getting the team to chart tasks, projects, and responsibilities of the team regarding individual or joint accountability. Some tasks will fall at the extremes, while others will require a combination of individual and group responsibility.

There may not be automatic agreement on where to place certain projects or assignments. These differences of viewpoint should produce a worthwhile discussion and give the group a chance to deal with their differences in a very concrete way.

WORKSHEET 5–8

Accountability for Team Tasks

Directions: List the team's tasks, responsibilities and projects on the appropriate line on the chart below. More individual responsibilities would be listed toward the top, group tasks toward the bottom.

Individual (Alone)	(e.g.) Time cards
↑	
	(e.g.) Quality assurance reports
↓	
Group (Joint)	(e.g.) Consensus decisions

If team members have a highly individualistic, antigroup orientation, Worksheet 5–9 may open some eyes.

WORKSHEET 5–9

Group versus Individual
A Group Experience

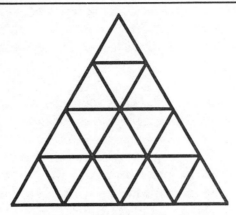

How Many Triangles Are There?

Directions: First, work on your own and without talking to anyone come up with your answer to the number of triangles in the figure. Then, in small groups with other teammates, come up with a group response.

Now compare with other groups, having each group share both its group answer and its range of individual answers. Mark the results in the table shown below.

Group	Group Answer	Range of Individual Answers
1		
2		
3		
4		

Discuss as a team what this activity tells you about the results produced by groups as compared with individuals. What are the advantages of each group and individual work? Under what conditions might each be preferable on the team? (Note: the total number of triangles is 27.)

Evidence exists that teams can, and frequently do, produce a superior product. But that outcome presumes a hospitable climate.

CREATING AN INCLUSIVE
ENVIRONMENT ON YOUR TEAM

An inclusive environment is like an umbrella that is large enough to cover everyone so that no one is left out in the rain. That kind of atmosphere is created when team members accept and value each other, no matter how different they are. Creating this tone is the responsibility of the whole team, not just the formal leader. The following eight tips may help you in that process.

1. *Structure opportunities for sharing and self-disclosure.* Building the relationships that bind a team into a cohesive group and that tie each individual to the whole happens when people have shared vulnerabilities and have been accepted by one another. While sharing and confiding can happen naturally, because of the demands and hectic pace, on most teams it doesn't necessarily happen that way. Employees need both a chunk of time carved out for that purpose and processes that stimulate self-disclosure. Set aside time at team meetings for relationship-building activities or engage in a team retreat, where you can spend time getting to know each other. We are frequently asked about making time for relationship building because, in the opinions of many, attention to interpersonal dynamics is soft stuff and a much lower priority than doing the job, meeting the deadlines, and being held accountable. We can tell you that the investment in relationship building pays dividends. The feedback we get consistently from groups is that they weren't too sure about the time invested in relationship building when we did it. They were impatient and wanted to just get on with the job. But the trust, cohesion, and affiliation built by those experiences paid dividends down the road, when the tough issues emerged. What got people through the conflict and difficult times was their early investment in relationship building. The many processes explained in this book, especially those in Chapter 7, offer activities that give structure to team sharing.

2. *Increase understanding about cultural differences.* Cultural differences that are not understood can be the source of disruptive conflict and interpersonal bitterness that can erode team harmony. When differences in cultural programming are understood, there is less chance for behavior to be misinterpreted. Direct eye contact won't be seen as aggression, and downcast eyes won't be interpreted as

deceitfulness. Saying yes when meaning no won't be interpreted as lying but as a desire for harmony or respect for authority.

Team members can learn about the differences in cultural programming before they cause misunderstanding by participating in cultural-diversity training sessions, seeing films about cultural differences and sharing some of their differences with one another. The books, films, and activities listed in the resource section at the end of the book give you materials to use in learning about these cultural differences. If your team has participants from different cultures, you can make use of their differences by having team members respond to such open-ended statements as the following.

- The difference between how things are done here and how they were done in my native country is . . .
- One norm (in this organization, country, team, or office) that is hard for me to adapt to is . . .
- The biggest difference between my culture and American culture is . . .
- I don't understand why . . .
- One thing I'd like you to understand about my culture is . . .

3. *Make opportunities for team members to teach each other.* Beyond teaching about general cultural norms, team members can be "cultural informants" for each other. On one team, a member from Iran taught the group about Noruz, a Persian holiday that celebrates the spring equinox. In another case, group members asked one of their African-American co-workers which label she preferred, black or African-American. She explained that black was a label given by others, while African-American was a term that came from the group itself, so she preferred to be defined as African-American. In a third example, a gay team member explained why he preferred the term sexual orientation to sexual preference. Orientation connoted an inborn characteristic such as size or eye color, while preference implied a choice.

4. *Demonstrate flexibility for differing needs and preferences.* Actions speak louder than words, as the saying goes. How the team responds when differences cause inconvenience will send a loud and clear message about how inclusive your environment is. One hospital administrative team had traditionally held executive staff meetings on Friday afternoons. However, its new director of nursing was an Orthodox Jew whose Sabbath began at sundown on Fridays. In the

winter she needed to leave the hospital by 4:00 PM to be home before sundown. The team quickly changed its meeting time to Thurs-
day afternoons. On another team, meetings were never scheduled
until all members had checked the date to be sure it was no one's
holiday.

5. *Explain the unwritten rules.*   Although few staff members ever read
the organization's rules and policies, they quickly learn the ropes by
observing behaviors. Breaking these unwritten rules is what gets
people into trouble. Not adhering to the norms or "how it's done
around here" can be the quickest way to be shut out of the team.
One way to avoid confusion and embarrassment when someone
unwittingly breaks a rule is to make the rules public. On one team,
the manager made it a standard practice to have old-timers brief
new-hires on the informal rules. She'd get them together for a staff
meeting and have the old hands tell the newcomer about "what's
not in the employee handbook," focusing on such topics as:

- What they don't tell you at new-employee
  orientation
- How things really get done around here
- The informal rules about how to act and what to do
- What gets you ahead and what holds you back
- The biggest "kiss of death" here

   This session helped them understand and adapt to the culture
of their new team. It also minimized the discomfort of being the
new kid on the block.

6. *Demonstrate that you value differences.*   When someone suggests a
radical point of view, do eyes roll? When the group is coming to
closure on an issue but someone blocks consensus, do people get
irritated? When disagreement exists, is there frustration? These are
the times when valuing differences is tested. On one team that had
worked for months to solve a particularly difficult organizational
problem, this value was put to the test. Just as the team was ready to
finalize its solutions, one team member expressed his reservations
about supporting and committing to one of the plans. The team's
response was anger: "How could you pull the rug out now?" "Why
didn't you say anything before?" "Your lack of support will sabotage
the plan!" Once over their frustration, they listened to his objec-
tions, saw merit in them, and ultimately scrapped this part of the
plan. Had they tried to bully him into conformity, they might have

silenced an important piece of information and ignored a glitch in their plan, since he had given voice to a position that undoubtedly existed elsewhere among the troops. He had been willing to tell the emperor he had no clothes. The good news was that he felt enough trust to share his view. Had there been a greater level of trust, however, he could have helped the team more by sharing his reservation earlier.

7. *Work toward mutually satisfying resolutions to conflict.* When conflict arises, the response is usually to ignore it and hope it will go away or to meet it head-on with an ultimatum. Neither of these approaches results in successful long-term outcomes. A third approach is needed. When differences cause conflict, they need to be acknowledged and addressed. They also need to be resolved in a way that works for both parties, or they will continue to erupt in new forms.

On one team, a mandatory meeting was called. Members could choose to attend the morning or afternoon session, but they needed to sign up for their preference. One team member was angry because he had reserved his spot in the morning time slot, but had been asked by his boss to switch with one of his colleagues, who could not attend the afternoon session because she had children to pick up at day care. He was irritated because he felt she should have signed up early if she wanted a particular session. She was upset because she expected cooperation and understanding from her co-worker. The group's solution was to have each person negotiate any switches individually, without interference from the manager. In that way team members would need to rely on each other and take responsibility for their own needs and preferences.

8. *Play together.* Finally, teams can build camaraderie through shared experiences that are social rather than work-related. A summer picnic, a holiday party, birthday celebrations, or a bowling league can bring some levity and fun to the work group. Fun can be enjoyed in other ways as well. Some teams buy lottery tickets together, others have regular TGIF get-togethers, while others have a monthly lunch. Whatever the activity, remember to consider everyone on the team. Does the activity go against anyone's strongly held beliefs, such as buying lottery tickets for someone who believes gambling is a sin? Does it exclude anyone, such as a Saturday picnic that would not be acceptable to an Orthodox Jewish or Seventh Day Adventist team member? Does it require an ability not shared by all, such as a bowling league that could exclude a quadriplegic team member?

Respond to the checklist in Worksheet 5–10 to see how well your team is developing an inclusive environment.

WORKSHEET 5–10

How Inclusive Is the Team Environment?

Directions: Check any conditions that exist on your team.

_____ We have structured opportunities for sharing and self-disclosure.

_____ We have ways to increase team members' understanding about cultural differences.

_____ We create opportunities for team members to teach each other.

_____ We demonstrate flexibility for differing needs and preferences.

_____ We explain the unwritten rules to new team members.

_____ We value differences.

_____ We work toward mutually satisfying resolutions to conflict.

_____ We play together.

Strong interpersonal bonds on teams are made, not born. The more a team works to create these trusting, caring, and supportive relationships, the greater will be the results in productivity and satisfaction.

Chapter Six

Shoulder to Shoulder
In the Trenches Together

O ne of the cornerstones of team building is the unity of purpose and cohesion that is built when teammates work together on tasks and share in the sense of joint achievement. The back-slapping, hair-tousling, champagne-dowsing locker-room scenes of winning football teams have their counterparts in the beams of joy on the faces of team members who have just achieved a goal. That deep satisfaction comes from working long and hard together, overcoming obstacles, and working through problems, an experience that only those involved can know and one that gives the group a sense of cohesiveness.

For a group to function as a cohesive and productive unit, its members need to build common ground and interdependence. On a diverse team this may require structuring interactions that break down barriers between groups and bring people of different backgrounds and experiences together for greater creativity and productivity.

An incident from a non-work team can shed some light on this point. This is the case of the integrated Girl Scout troop. As an elementary-school student, one of the authors was very excited to have graduated from Brownies and become a real Girl Scout. Since her elementary school was racially mixed, so was the troop. In what she thought was an enlightened nod to shared decision making and self-direction, the troop leader gave the girls a chance to choose their squads, the subgroups in which they would work to achieve merit badges. Each girl was asked to list the four or five other girls she wanted to be grouped with. It doesn't take a rocket scientist to figure out what the squads looked like: There were black squads and white squads.

Were the girls inherently racist? Probably not. They were, like most humans, more comfortable with those who were like themselves. Did this division cause any animosity or conflict on the troop? Not at all. Everyone got along well, both one-on-one and squad-to-squad.

What's the problem, then? Simply this: The leader missed a golden opportunity to help the girls get so much more out of the experience. Who knows what they could have learned from each other or how much richer their merit-badge projects could have been if they had the mix of different experiences and perspectives to draw upon. Perhaps a few bricks could have been removed from the wall of prejudice that separates the races in our society if the groups were mixed so the girls could have formed cross-racial bonds.

What can we learn from this group of young girls? A few realities about interactions in diverse teams come to light.

1. *Like attracts like.* Generally, individuals tend to gravitate toward those who are like them in some significant way. Whom do you sit by at meetings? Probably one of your buddies, someone you feel comfortable with. If you had to pick several people to work with you on a project, whom would you choose? Undoubtedly you would choose co-workers with whom you had a shared history, those you knew you could get along with easily and depend on to come through. This trust is generally reserved for those who have a track record with us, and often those are people who are similar to us.

   One seminar participant asked why Latinos always stick together. As an American of Mexican descent, she was bothered by this clannishness of newer arrivals from south of the border. In response to her question, we asked her whom she had chosen to sit next to at this session, where managers from throughout her organization were assembled. A knowing smile crossed her face. She answered her own question when she realized she'd taken a seat next to one of the few people in the room she knew.

2. *People are unaware of their biases.* Most of us don't get up in the morning and ask ourselves whom we can discriminate against that day. Nor do we make blatantly stereotypical comments or overtly prejudicial decisions. Biases and preferences are usually unconscious and the result of the powerful "second-hand smoke" effect of societal stereotypes that bombard us daily. When we make decisions, we often think we are acting from free will and independent thinking. "I want to decide whom I work with." "I know who is best for the job." "I don't want anyone telling me whom to select." However, our choices are rarely independent of external influences, and our assumptions reflect many unintentional biases.

   One team member spoke of an incident in which he came face-to-face with his own biases. When he met a new teammate who'd just been hired, he was full of reservations about this new man's competence. Here's the reason: The new hire was an immigrant from Poland who spoke with a thick accent. All the "dumb Polock" jokes that had made the rounds a few years ago accumulated in his unconscious. He expected a dolt to show up. Then they began to work together. He was amazed to find that his Polish teammate spoke seven languages and, what's more, caught on to the work in no time. "I learned so much from him," he said. "He was one of the most intelligent human beings I've ever met."

3. *Interactions generally need to be structured.* Left to our own devices, we will generally continue to interact with, spend time with, and depend on the same people because interacting across diversity groups doesn't always come naturally. The mixing may need to be engineered intentionally by such moves as altering groupings, redesigning work flow, moving offices, or assigning individuals to projects. These structured groupings give people a reason to interact with those they might not have worked with otherwise. It also breaks down the barriers between groups.

One cross-functional team had the task of opening up communication in the organization by getting rid of barriers to both the upward and downward flow of information. Since the major obstacles seemed to be at the midmanagement level, having both managers and nonmanagers on the team was vital. Not only did members from the two groups bring different perspectives, but they also began to break down some of the stereotypes that existed in both camps. Had individuals from both groups not been brought together on the team, they might never have changed their views nor have begun to overcome the positional hurdle that was at the heart of their team's problem.

4. *Change may cause resistance.* Ruts, even the most boring and dull, are comfortable for us. We know the old tried-and-true ways are predictable, and what is new and different may be frightening. If we are not threatened by change, we often balk at it because it causes inconvenience. Restructuring work interactions, reconfiguring groups, or changing the way projects are handled may cause team members to resist initially. This digging in of heels is a normal, predictable response.

However, change can also bring stimulation and energy. Once people get over their initial balking and begin working on a common goal, the freshness of the new can give the group a real boost.

PREVENTING THE GHETTOIZATION
OF THE GROUP

Like the Girl Scout troop, many teams divide into subgroups that begin
to form their own identity. It might be the smokers who take breaks
and lunch together outside, the native Spanish speakers who find comfort in speaking their own language, the women who commiserate about
the "second shift" they work at home, or the golfers who compare their
scores after every weekend. There's nothing wrong with teammates finding connections with each other because of common interests and experiences. However, the team can suffer when these groups begin to
solidify and exclude others. We've heard employees complain that the
real decisions are made on the golf course, not in team meetings. We've
seen teams splinter over language differences because people feel left
out and talked about when co-workers speak another language in their
presence. We've heard stories of teams whose members have nearly come
to blows when ethnic subgroups have been in conflict.

As long as team members see each other as categories rather than as
individual human beings, there is danger of "ghettoization." Conversely,
the more people work together, build one-on-one connections, and find
common ground, the less apt the team will be to splinter into warring
camps or isolated subgroups.

There are two steps you can take to prevent this potentially destructive phenomenon.

1. *Pay attention to groupings.* Keeping your radar out to detect
    ghettoization at its early stages is key. Notice whom team members
    work with, take breaks with, and eat lunch with. Keep a watchful
    eye so that these "natural" grouping patterns don't lead to isolated
    clumps of staff members.
2. *Give people reasons to interact.* Since cross-group connections might
    not occur naturally, you may need to intervene. Requiring staff to
    get input from others; sending co-workers to seminars, conferences,
    or training sessions together; or putting them on committees to-
    gether are examples of legitimate reasons you can create for people
    to interact with different colleagues and build common bonds.

GUIDELINES FOR STRUCTURING
WORK-RELATED INTERACTIONS

Getting people to work together on tasks and projects makes sense when their joint effort can produce a better product than any one individual's work. Interdependence needs to be a requirement of task accomplishment; otherwise working jointly is artificial and counterproductive. However, often the group that is literally thrown together to accomplish a task is not made up of the right people; hence, the frequent disappointment with joint products. The skepticism about group productivity is illustrated by the often-quoted quip that says a camel is a horse put together by a committee.

One way to bring some clarity to the structuring of work-group interactions is to look at the variables involved. If the purpose of work-group interactions is to accomplish tasks, then the first place to start is the task itself. Four types of contributions by team members are required for the tasks to be accomplished: (1) knowledge, (2) skills, (3) experience, and (4) information. If, for example, a team is going to formulate a marketing plan for a new product, a number of areas of knowledge are needed, from understanding the product, its features, and benefits to knowing how to do a marketing plan. Skill in creative problem solving and in positioning ideas would also be called for. In addition, experience with various aspects of marketing would be useful. Finally, information about the marketplace is essential.

The first step, then, is to analyze the project to delineate the task's specific requirements in each of the four contribution areas. The next step is to analyze the available human resources. Who on the team can bring the necessary contributions, and what is the best combination of people? Some team members can make the same contributions, while others will bring very different skills or experiences. The keys are to look at each requirement necessary to complete the task and to assess which team members have similar contributions to offer and which have different ones. Worksheet 6–1 can help you delineate the variables on a particular team task so you can select the most appropriate group to work on the project. This analysis can be helpful when done on your own. However, it is even more effective if it's done together as a team so that perceptions are shared, information is more complete, and agreement on who works on the project is increased. As a bonus, there may also be less resistance to the changes this new configuration may bring about.

WORKSHEET 6–1

Structuring Work-Related Interactions for Task Accomplishment

Directions: First, list all of the kinds of knowledge, skills, experience, and information the task calls for. Then begin listing employees who can make the required contribution. The Same column includes those team members who share a similar kind of knowledge; for example, those who know WordPerfect software. The Different category includes those who have unique knowledge, such as familiarity with less well known programs. The first line in each row is a sample.

Task Requirements	Team Members' Contributions	
	Same	Different
Knowledge Statistics _____ _____ _____	Theoretical—Bob, Martha, and Mike	Organizational—Raquel
Skills Interviewing _____ _____ _____	English only—Jane, Ari, and Sid	Other languages—Rosana and Kim
Experience Training _____ _____ _____	Customer service—Susan, Efran, Young, and Taylor	Diversity—Faye
Information Organizational structure _____ _____ _____	Formal—Vince and Diana	Informal—Randy

Once all team members are listed in any area where they can contribute to the task, you are almost ready to begin assigning groupings. There is one more variable to consider, and that is the willingness of each staff member to participate. The stronger the individual's motivation, the greater his or her contribution is to the task. Two factors influence individual willingness to participate. The first is interest. Which team members have a particular interest in the content of the project? Who wants to learn more about this area? Who sees this experience as an asset to career development and increased visibility?

The second aspect affecting team members' motivation to work on the task is time availability. Which team members are able to make the time commitment the project would require? If the task requires overtime or travel, which employees are able to adapt to such demands?

By clearly putting issues out on the table, the team can make the most effective decisions about the composition of task groupings so they suit both the project's requirements and the team members' needs.

VEHICLES AND VARIATIONS FOR BRINGING PEOPLE TOGETHER

No team's work requires everyone to work together all the time. Projects, tasks, and operations have varying requirements, so the number and mix of team members will vary as well. Some tasks are enriched by the mix of varied ideas and input that comes from the whole group, while other tasks can get bogged down when too many cooks have their hands in the soup. Let's take a look at some ways you can bring people together on tasks and projects at different levels.

Total-Team Tasks

Using the combined time, energy, and resources of the total team on a task or project is costly. Therefore, the involvement of all team members needs to be utilized judiciously for those aspects that call for the full range of diverse views, knowledge, and skills brought by the collected group. It is also important to consider the benefits of total-team involvement, and there are four important ones: (1) cohesiveness, (2) commitment, (3) creativity, and (4) communication.

Shared experiences only build common ground and cohesiveness for those who participate. In addition, having partial-team involvement or leaving some members out means that those not participating have little stake in the work, nor do they have sense of connection to those who do. Another reason for including all members is to widen the range of ideas and perspectives for a more complete picture and more creative problem solving. Finally, there are times when the whole team needs to get or share information together, such as when hearing some critical news or communicating progress on aspects of their separate projects.

Tasks in which the whole group could be involved might include:

1. *Brainstorming.* Free-flowing idea generation as part of a problem-solving process.
2. *Consensus decision making.* A group task that calls on the judgments, opinions, and values of all group members to come to a jointly agreed-upon decision, either through discussion or by using a decision matrix. (An excellent explanation of the process of using a decision matrix can be found in John Arnold's book, *Make Up Your Mind.*)
3. *Goal setting.* Deciding on priorities and setting direction for the team through group discussion and prioritization.
4. *Action planning.* Delineating a sequence of tasks, assigning responsibility for each, and creating a time line for the project.
5. *Evaluating.* Comparing results against objectives, giving input about the outcomes of a project and analyzing the lessons learned.
6. *Celebrating.* Enjoying fun and social events.
7. *Team training.* Participating in workshops and seminars as a whole team.
8. *Team building.* Experiencing group activities, such as retreats, that focus on developing team cohesion.

Small-Group Tasks

Many aspects of team projects can be done more efficiently if divided among small groups of team members who have expertise in particular areas. These tasks generally focus on more specific segments of the job, such as the following:

1. *Researching.* Investigating to find needed information, facts, or figures. This might include research about markets, competitors, or new methods of producing widgets more quickly. It could also involve

archival research using company records or publications.

2. *Data gathering.* Getting input from staff or customers through written or oral feedback.
3. *Peer coaching and training.* Sharing knowledge with and teaching skills to one another.

Individual Tasks

Finally, the following tasks can be more efficiently accomplished by individuals working alone:

1. *Implementing.* Following through on specific action items.
2. *Writing.* Compiling information and analyses and composing written documents such as reports or instruction manuals.
3. *Individual training.* Participating in specific, individual learning experiences.

TABLE 6–1

Bringing People Together on Tasks and Projects
Variations of Groupings

GROUPING	TASKS
Total Team	• Brainstorming • Consensus decision making • Goal setting • Action planning • Evaluating • Celebrating • Team training • Team building
Small Group	• Researching • Data gathering • Peer coaching and training
Individual	• Implementing • Writing • Individual training

FOCUS ON COMMON GOALS AND
BUILD SHARED EXPERIENCES

For the team to develop cohesiveness, it needs a continuing focus on both common purposes and common experiences. Attention to the group's achievement of its joint goals is maintained both by setting those goals and by monitoring progress as a group. The activities for goal setting described in Chapter 4 offer a variety of processes the group can use to clarify its purpose and come to agreement on priorities for action. Progress checks that keep the team members' attention fixed on their collective goals can be done in four ways.

1. *Graphs and charts.*   As the saying goes, a picture is worth a thousand words. Graphs and charts provide visual depictions of the team's progress. A graph can show month-by-month figures for customer satisfaction or sales revenues. Or a thermometer can be filled in to show advances toward a sales target, for example. Visual depictions have the advantage of working effectively in a multilingual environment.
2. *Progress reports.*   Individual team members, managers, or groups within the team can give updates on tasks completed or outcomes achieved, discussing the gains made with the team.
3. *Results feedback.*   The group can also see progress when information from outside the team is fed back. Managers of departments within the organization that are internal customers might give the group information on the impact of a new procedure, for example. Or customer-service or sales staff might share results from the field.
4. *Intrateam feedback.*   Group members can share their own perceptions about progress toward goals. If, for example, one goal of the team is to improve communication and mutual support, team members can share experiences that have demonstrated an increase in help from other team members. Or the staff can compare its ratings of the team on paper-and-pencil assessments, such as those offered throughout this book.

WHEN TAKING TWO STEPS BACK
DOESN'T SEEM LIKE PROGRESS

Sometimes progress reports show negative results, no gains made, or even backsliding. How can these seemingly negative outcomes be used to help the team? These instances can, in fact, be critical turning points and learning periods for a team. Going through a few battles together and weathering rough times can forge strong bonds among members. The following steps can help the team make every venture a learning experience.

Step 1: Acknowledge successes.   The first step goes against most of our natural reactions, especially when the experience is a disappointing one. The tendency is to catalog all the things we and others did wrong. However, this first step is critical. The team needs to articulate at least two things it did well in this project. Pats come before pans.

Step 2: Analyze the experience.   Only after the successes have been noted does the group proceed to do a full analysis—including what went well, what didn't, and why. Be as specific as possible at this point so the baby isn't thrown out with the bathwater. Even in the most dismal projects, there are generally some effective aspects. The critique aspect of this step may be difficult for team members from cultures that value harmony and respect authority. In such cases, breaking the team into subgroups to discuss these steps and generate information might be more helpful. The critique then is the product of the group rather than any individual.

Step 3: Play Monday-morning quarterback.   At this point the analysis turns to the "so what" stage. Hindsight is 20–20. Knowing what you do now, what would the group do differently if the experience were repeated? What changes would be made in approach?

Step 4: Transfer the learning.   This last step is essential for the application of what has been learned through the experience. What is the next opportunity in which the group can apply this new learning? Perhaps a similar project is waiting or a new opportunity needs to be created. The team then makes a commitment to use its revised and improved methodology the next time.

Worksheet 6–2 gives you a format for team members to use these steps. This method enables the team to be constantly self-improving and self-examining in a positive way. Each experience becomes a dress rehearsal for the next. As Sally Behn, a stockbroker with her own brokerage house in Washington, D.C., so aptly put it, "When I try something new, I call it a pilot." In this way each venture is seen less as a success or failure and more as a potential learning opportunity for the team.

WORSHEET 6–2

Maximizing the Learning from Every Experience

Directions: Analyze a recent team experience by filling in the boxes on the right.

Step 1. Acknowledge Successes	List two things the team did well.
Step 2. Analyze the Experience	Identify specific elements that worked effectively and ineffectively.
Step 3. Play Monday-Morning Quarterback	What would you do differently if you could redo this experience?
Step 4. Transfer the Learning	Where is the next opportunity for the team to apply what it has learned?

PEER TEACHING AND COACHING: BUILDING ON EACH OTHER'S STRENGTHS

In today's organizations, where there is a growing emphasis on cross-functional teams and the breaking down of walls between organizational departments, units, and divisions, peer coaching can offer some clear benefits. On diverse teams it offers yet another method to give people a reason to work shoulder to shoulder with teammates of different groups. Let's take a look at the ways teams benefit from peer coaching.

1. *Greater understanding of the whole process.* When team members who have different functions teach each other, not only do they learn new skills, but they also develop a better understanding of the total process and their part in it. They see what a delay or mistake in one step can mean to the product at a later stage. This knowledge often serves to increase employees' commitment to taking greater care about quality.

2. *Greater empathy for co-workers.* It is not uncommon for team members to be irritated with one another about delays and mistakes. Cross-training gives each trainee a chance to literally walk in a teammate's shoes for a while, to understand the whys behind a frustrating delay or a maddening error. Generally, employees involved in cross-training experiences come back with comments such as "I never realized how stressful their job is" and "Boy, now I see why they have a hard time keeping on schedule."

3. *Increased respect for co-workers.* Generally, employees spend time with co-workers who do similar work—machinists with machinists rather than engineers, nurses with nurses and not lab techs, and so on. Cross-training gives diverse employees a reason to get to know, work with, and develop respect for the skill and competence of co-workers in different areas or fields. As each employee teaches his or her counterpart, each has a chance to be both student and teacher, gaining valuable knowledge from someone who might before have been just another face in the cafeteria or name on the door. Now that individual is seen as a knowledgeable, competent, and skilled colleague.

4. *Increased esteem.* Studies have shown, even with schoolchildren, that the greatest gains in tutorial programs are in the self-esteem of the tutor. In this cross-training experience, each staff member gets to be tutor to a co-worker, giving each the opportunity to demonstrate competence and skill. Realizing that he or she has special knowledge, a grasp of the process, or a skill level that not everyone else has is often a confidence builder for the cross-trainer.

5. *Increased morale.* The individual esteem built through the peer teaching process, coupled with the job-enriching aspect of learning, often translates into a morale boost. Learning something new makes the job more interesting and challenging. What's more, the process of teaching someone else and mastering new processes or skills gives one an increased sense of self-worth.

Peer training works best when there is voluntary commitment on the part of both trainer and trainee. One way to generate this willingness is to allow for self-selection or team selection in the process. The following analysis in Worksheet 6–3 helps staff members delineate the skills and knowledge they and others have, as well as those they would like to learn and/or teach.

WORKSHEET 6–3

Cross-Training Self-Analysis

Directions: Fill in the appropriate information in the boxes below.

Job skills and knowledge I have	Job skills and knowledge I'd be willing to teach

Job skills and knowledge I'd like to learn	Co-workers I'd want to teach me job skills and knowledge

Individual team members complete the analysis, then share the assessment with one another. After doing that, the team can discuss which skills and knowledge need to be learned by a wider number of members. Only then can the group begin designing appropriate pairings for peer teaching.

The best ally a team has is the real work its members need to do together. The organization and the individuals who work in them both benefit from being foxhole buddies.

Chapter Seven

Group Process
Human Engineering to Keep the Team on Track

Good bridges don't just happen. Neither do good teams. Both are "engineered."

Anita Rowe and Lee Gardenswartz

The thrill and the challenge of teamwork comes in large part from the realization that disparate people can come together to achieve work-related goals of varying complexity, importance, and impact. Melding a group of individuals of both genders, with different ego strengths, and with a multitude of competencies, ages, backgrounds, values, races, ethnicities, religions, geographic influences, and lifestyles is not for the faint of heart. Building common organizational ground amid these vast and sometimes intractable differences to improve team performance in pursuit of accomplishing objectives is what teamwork in diverse work groups is all about.

Dealing effectively with all of these disparities and creating a sense of overlap and purpose, particularly on task-force or problem-solving teams with short lives, takes considerable skill and understanding of human nature. It is through understanding both the human dynamics and the goals of a particular team that team leaders can most effectively exert their influence and intervene at strategic times with appropriate tools to engineer results that warrant an organization's expenditure of time, money, and energy.

For this reason, Chapter 7 is dedicated to making team leaders, managers, facilitators—anyone who builds and works with teams—the *human engineers* that can alter work-group dynamics and productivity. How well teams function, how productive they are, is largely a function of their internal dynamics. In the life of all teams, there will be road

145

blocks, resistance, conflict, varying levels of commitment, impasses in how to get the job done, and even changes in team membership. Through all of these variables, the human engineer is needed to keep the team moving down the track. On diverse teams, some of the human challenges may be even greater. With this reality in mind, let us show you the group-process technology you need to keep your pluralistic work team on track and on target.

For starters, let's acknowledge that the umbrella purpose for team functioning is to accomplish the goals and performance objectives the team sets within the context of a larger organization. As Katzenbach and Smith, in their book *Wisdom of Teams,* say "Performance . . . is the primary objective while a team remains the means, not the end." The accomplishment of those objectives occurs on teams that function in one of three ways:

1. *Investigate an issue and make subsequent recommendations.* Gathering information about things like the cost and capabilities of a new information system is an example of investigative functions. So are a cost-benefit analysis of shortening the turnaround time on product delivery, and discovering how other health maintenance organizations are forming partnerships to prevent duplication of services and carve out centers of excellence in the health care industry. Investigating an issue can be done by a work team if the issue is localized. However, if it affects the entire organization, it usually requires a short-term task-force team comprised of members representing different functional units within the organization. The task force determines what questions are investigated, evaluates the answers received, and usually makes recommendations that clearly delineate expected gains and losses, depending on the choices made.

2. *Solve problems.* All teams encounter and solve problems in the course of their work. Some teams will be formed specifically for this purpose. The kinds of problems to be solved can center on interpersonal interactions, reporting relationships, role redefinition, systems refinement or modification, product development, product modification, delivery systems, customer-interface issues, strategic planning, global competitiveness, resource allocation, or ways to cut costs and increase profitability. The list of problems to solve in every organization is endless. Effective, ongoing teams deal with these either proactively, in anticipation of problems, or reactively, as a damage control measure. On cross-functional or other short-term teams, the formation of the team may be a clear response to a current crisis, in

which case the parameters are usually defined. It is important to realize the need for flexibility in the scope of team exploration because as issues get uncovered and discovered, the problem solving paths may lead to seeking information in domains that were not necessarily part of a team's original charter. There needs to be an initial understanding that if parameters need to be expanded, they can be. The *Exxon Valdez* oil-spill experience provides a useful example of the kind of complexity and elasticity required in problem solving. Immediately after the spill, cleaning up Alaska's Prince William Sound was the central problem. However, in truth it was only one part of a larger issue that clearly needed attention. Beyond prevention of further spills and public-relations issues designed to minimize the hemorrhaging of customers and Exxon's reputation, the company's criteria for selecting ship captains and its performance-review systems could stand to be looked at and refined. Had a task-force been asked to focus on how best to clean up the spill, it would eventually run into issues involving consumer affairs and public-relations, and performance-review or hiring criteria. Your teams will find similar overlaps and complexity as they solve problems together; hence, the importance of clear but flexible parameters.

3. *Make decisions.*   The third overall function of teams is to make decisions that will impact and change the organization. The scope of the decisions will vary. At the executive level, perhaps an ongoing group of top-level staff wrestles with options about how to trim expenses 20 percent for the next fiscal year. As they comb through some unattractive choices, they make the decision to downsize because they think they can get the biggest bang for their cost-cutting buck by amputating human resources they deem expendable. That's a decision that can be made in part at the executive level; however, while the amount to be cut may come from the top, decisions about actual positions lost or expenses cut can be made at lower levels by the teams themselves.

Another example may involve training personnel. Let's say a team knows it needs to get team members trained in total quality management (TQM) principles. It is not uncommon for a team to look at several options. The first might involve the cost of bringing in external consultants to work with the training with TQM principles. The second might result in bringing in external consultants to train the Organization Effectiveness (OE) department so it can work with other departments or teams. And third, it is also possible to send people to public seminars or classes at local universities. These three choices are the kinds of options that teams could and should discuss. The team can then make a decision that it feels is in its best interests.

There are many issues that teams experience all the time to improve quality, customer service, or product reliability. But ultimately, no matter how specific you get on these issues, facilitating, leading, or participating on a team means you will be working toward accomplishing some important purposes by performing one of three functions: (1) investigating and recommending, (2) problem solving, or (3) decision making.

Once you acknowledge the overall functions that repeatedly get played out on teams, the most important competency involves understanding the human dynamics of teams.

EGO AND AFFILIATION: THE UNIVERSAL NEEDS

Norman R F Maier, author of *Problem Solving and Creativity in Individuals and Groups,* and his colleague Rick Roskin have each spent a lifetime teaching at the University of Michigan and writing about the behavior of people involved in group problem solving and decision making. Among their simplest and most profound contributions is the idea that for people to function productively in groups, their ego and affiliation needs must be met. Abraham Maslow, in a slightly different context and a slightly different way, said that all human beings have needs, among them the need for esteem and belonging. Similar thought, different language. For the skilled team leader or facilitator, the realization that all human beings need to feel good about themselves and to feel connected to one another permeates choices about meeting design. These needs are acute in organizations in which people often feel isolated and alienated. Team membership is a good place to get these needs met. Although the needs may be universal, how those needs are met will vary depending on the diversities your team members reflect. The importance of structuring teams so that esteem and belonging needs are met cannot be overstated. Feeling valued and connected impacts the following behaviors:

1. *Sense of trust.* Team members need to feel that what they say at least merits consideration, and they need to trust that they will not be

overlooked, ignored, or discounted because of the diversities they bring. Think about your team. If people are openly gay or lesbian, does that automatically bring disadvantage to their comments? Do people's eyes roll when they speak? If someone speaks with a thick accent, can you trust that people will really work hard to understand, or do people discount him and perceive him to be stupid because he doesn't speak English well?

Another aspect of the trust issue comes up repeatedly on every team with which we work: confidentiality. It needs to be addressed explicitly because violating confidence is a sure way to be an ego and affiliation buster. There has to be a sacred commitment that what people say in the meeting stays in the meeting, and that who says what is never leaked. Of course, there will be a time to communicate with other parts of the organization or to report progress on a certain issue. The team should collectively decide what is to be communicated. Honoring the confidentiality agreed upon does more to move trust forward than anything we can think of, and if trust is violated, it is very difficult to repair. The concept of honoring your word as an indicator of trust is a mainstream American view. Trust will have to be discussed and negotiated cross-culturally.

2. *Willingness to risk.*   On teams where people feel like they belong, they can discuss sensitive issues such as promotional policies or exit interviews without being afraid of being perceived as insensitive or racist. For example, it may be a risk for white males to say that they perceive reverse discrimination since diversity has become a factor in hiring and promotion, while it may be equally risky for black males to say that in spite of talk about a more inclusive organization, nothing has really changed. Each may bemoan the amount of talk backed up by very little action. Can this discussion between whites, blacks, or others on your team take place in nonthreatening, nonconfrontational ways? If any team member is afraid to bring something up, that will limit a team's ability to do its best, most creative work together.

3. *Mutual respect and accommodation.*   On teams where esteem and belonging needs are met, someone who is a Jehovah's Witness is not afraid to say, "I don't celebrate or attend the traditional holiday or birthday parties." Another example of respect may be seen in someone who is of Chinese ancestry and is unafraid to bring up the Chinese New Year, or someone of the Eastern Orthodox religion discussing her celebration of Christmas on January 7 rather than

December 25. On a team where respect abounds, team members who are clueless about cultural holidays will ask sincere, genuine questions and willingly learn about one of their co-worker's traditions. If a particular diversity issue impacts the mechanics of the work group, it should be discussed. If not, simple information sharing and interest is helpful. The tone you don't want to convey if you are trying to create an effective pluralistic team is one that broadcasts, "How can I be expected to learn and honor everyone's holidays? It's just too much, and after all we're here to work, not deal with all these differences." We do hear a variation of this theme frequently, and it is important to understand the cost, in a pragmatic, business-driven way, of ignoring things that are important to your team members. Any time you have to hide pieces of yourself because others aren't interested in learning about or accommodating your uniqueness, you become a little less open and lose chances for relationship building. Understanding and commitment wither. When people have to check who they are at the door, then the team gets only a small part of the talent those team members have to offer. Both individuals and the company are cheated, and so are those employees who never know what they've missed.

If you agree with the idea that ego and affiliation needs are important in terms of encouraging functional, production-oriented behavior on teams, then the question for a team leader is, How can you foster the perception that getting to know one another is a social and productivity lubricant rather than frivolous attention to relationships?

For starters, we suggest that on any new task force or team, and at intervals on existing work teams, as the human engineer you need to come in and revamp, retool, redesign, or reinforce the human dynamics on the team. We offer a series of tools here for very different purposes. At the beginning of a new team's formation, the quickest way to create opportunities for meeting esteem and belonging needs is to take the group through some get-acquainted processes. You can adapt or modify any of them to suit your teams, based on their productivity goals and how they need to work together in the process of getting the job done.

The "Being a Productive Team Member" tool is a good opener when teams are fresh and forming, or it can be an appropriate retooler on a mature team, when it reaches plateaus. In the latter case, this tool gives the enduring team members a chance to look at each other anew and see how they can help everyone get their needs met. In either case, new

WORKSHEET 7–1

Being a Productive Team Member

Directions: In each of the quadrants below, respond with the appropriate information. Then share it with other team members. The first line is an example.

	What I Bring to the Team	What I Need from the Team Experience
As a Human Being	Sense of humor, intensity	Support, new experiences
As a Member of This Team	Knowledge, content expertise, commitment, enthusiasm	Loyalty, a chance to grow, the opportunity to create something meaningful

team or old, give team members about 10 minutes to fill out this form
and then have people share this information in pairs or threesomes.
When you give them directions, explain that they will be sharing this
with other team members so that no one feels betrayed or surprised.
Once they've had about 15 minutes to share information in small groups,
then you can engage team members in a meaningful discussion. Some
of the questions you might ask are:

1. How did you feel about filling out this form?
2. If parts were difficult to answer, what made them
   so?

3. Were there differences in what you bring as a team member and as a human being? If so, what were they?
4. What similar needs were brought up by others in your group?
5. Were there any specific needs that people have that would be hard for you to deliver? If so, what are they?
6. Based on your discussion, how do you feel about being a member of this team?
7. What makes you optimistic that the team can achieve its goals?
8. Is there anything you heard that causes concern? If so what?

On a diverse team, particularly a newly formed group with no history and little trust, your opening comments will be critical. You'll want to put this activity in the context of working together to achieve important results while you also enjoy your team members in the process. These comments may provide the rationale for people who are more private to engage without feeling threatened. It is ultimately easier to solve the difficulties you will face, and give the support that will be needed, if you know one another and understand each other's needs both individually and collectively. Ask people to be as honest as they can be, but realize that mainstream American culture is much more open than most other cultures, so some participants might be reluctant. Your best bet is to serve as a model by honoring individual differences. That may mean accepting whatever degree of openness people demonstrate and realizing that, for some, the openness will come slower.

After the group discusses this grid, the most important question you can ask is the following: Based on the discussion we just had, what team norms should we develop or agree upon that will help us be productive and have some fun in the process?

As team leader, you may write the suggestions on a flip chart. Norms such as "Come through on commitments when we make them" usually come up, as does "Be open to all suggestions and ideas rather than dismiss them out of hand."You will most likely end up with some good suggestions from the team, but if you don't, that's OK too. Tell them to file the question away and that you'll revisit it down the road. A process for group norm setting will be given later in this chapter.

Worksheet 7-2 is another tool you can use to help team members get to know one another better, thereby improving working relationships and output.

WORKSHEET 7–2

Who Am I?

Directions: In the spaces below, write your responses to each open-ended statement.

Topic	My Answer
The most important skills and competencies I bring to this team are:	
My best team experience distinguished itself because:	
I am sometimes leery of team experiences because:	
What I value most about our company is:	
I was reared in: (location)	
The most enduring lesson my parents gave me is:	
My joy in life comes from:	
A life-changing experience for me was:	

The "Who Am I" tool is a way for team members to get a better sense of themselves and those they are working with. The risk is that, cross-culturally, this may be too revealing for some people. On the other hand, the first four items are directly related to work, and the last four offer teammates a chance to monitor what they disclose while still getting to know people as human beings.

You can have people share their responses in pairs or small groups to protect those who find this too revealing. When you detect less reluctance, you can also have people put their names on their sheets and tape them on the walls, leaving them for a time so that everyone can eventually read all of them. You can offer team members a chance to comment by focusing on surprises as well as common ground. It would be interesting in a whole-group discussion to talk again about which questions were hard to answer and why. You also need to focus on similarities and differences and on observations or lessons learned. Applying those lessons to team performance is ultimately the purpose of this exercise.

The focus of this tool should be on its application to the functioning and productivity of the team. With that in mind, the most important part of your discussion and the least risky part cross-culturally, comes from the "best team experience" and "unpleasant team experiences" topics. Our suggestion is that you draw a line down the middle of your flip chart so that it looks like Worksheet 7–3.

WORKSHEET 7–3

Team Experiences

Best	Unpleasant

Then you can have people brainstorm as a whole group the items they've already talked about in the small groups regarding factors that make the experience a good or unpleasant one. They can also add to the list. The relevant part of this discussion is its application to the team experience you're about to embark on or are already involved in. The following questions may help the discussion:

For newly forming teams:

- What do our most distinguished team experiences have in common?
- What does this suggest about the norms we establish on our new team?
- Are there behaviors or practices we should avoid?
- If members are leery of team experiences, what is the root cause?
- What does this suggest we should do or not do on our team?

For already existing teams:

- Do we have any of those experiences or characteristics listed under best team experience.
- What do we have going for us that makes us a potentially high performer?
- Are there any practices we should change or modify to increase our performance standards? To improve our interpersonal dynamics?
- Which factors that caused unpleasant experiences exist on our team?
- How can we extinguish or avoid these saboteurs?

The outcome from either of these tools is that people will know each other better, even those who think they already know each other well. On new teams, members will no longer be cardboard cutouts; they will have real distinctiveness. Beyond knowing each other better and knowing what each person needs, you will also have a heightened sense of how interpersonal dynamics impact team relationships and productivity. It's a good starting point for growth.

THE HUMAN DYNAMIC: CREATING
AN INCLUSIVE ENVIRONMENT

Norman Maier, Rick Roskin, and Abraham Maslow have told us in different ways that people who function in groups need to feel valued, respected, strong, whole, and contributing, while also getting a sense that their presence matters. If they can't be present at a task-force meeting or they aren't on the assembly line two days in a row, team members would notice, care, and show interest in reaching out to help when support is needed.

Does this kind of caring show itself on every team? Not in our lifetimes. Do you have to have it to get the job done? Probably not. But will it grease the relationship wheels of teamwork and make getting through the sticky issues easier? Without a doubt. Besides, the fact that it doesn't happen on every team is irrelevant to you. It can happen, at least to some degree, on your team if you use techniques and tools that give teams a chance to learn, grow, collaborate, introspect, and self-correct so that they meet or exceed their productivity goals.

One of the most important tools you can provide, which will also clarify group expectations that team members have of one another, is to determine group norms at the outset. The norms can definitely be revisited and revised, but they are an essential tool early in the life of any team.

WORKSHEET 7–4

Establishing Norms on Our Team

Directions: On the lines below, list the behaviors you'd like to see as the norms by which this team operates.

Behaviors I'd Like to See on This Team:

1._____

2._____

3._____

4._____

5._____

Behaviors I'd Like Us to Avoid:

1.＿＿＿＿＿＿＿＿＿＿＿＿＿＿＿＿＿＿＿＿＿＿＿＿＿

2.＿＿＿＿＿＿＿＿＿＿＿＿＿＿＿＿＿＿＿＿＿＿＿＿＿

3.＿＿＿＿＿＿＿＿＿＿＿＿＿＿＿＿＿＿＿＿＿＿＿＿＿

4.＿＿＿＿＿＿＿＿＿＿＿＿＿＿＿＿＿＿＿＿＿＿＿＿＿

5.＿＿＿＿＿＿＿＿＿＿＿＿＿＿＿＿＿＿＿＿＿＿＿＿＿

Start new teams out with this tool early in their operation. If this follows a discussion of the "Who Am I?" tool, the pump has already been primed to look at what works on teams and what doesn't. This norms-setting tool gives each team member a chance to identify individual preferences. Once each person makes his or her own list, people pair up or form small groups or, depending on the number of team members, you may discuss the whole group's responses together. However you divide the group for discussion purposes, in the end, as team leader, you can write people's responses on the flip chart:

Establishing Norms for Our Team

Like to See	Like to Avoid

Have all team members give their suggestions; once you have written them on the flip chart, have a group discussion and decide which ones matter most. Your final list should not be longer than a dozen items because it's too hard to monitor more behaviors than that at one time. Regarding diversity, consider such issues as time consciousness, participation in meetings, how formally or informally to address people, and ways of dealing with conflict. If some of the cross-cultural issues don't come up, then as leader you need to raise them, where relevant. Some people may be afraid to say things. For example, a tacit approval of racial or ethnic slurs and jokes will not improve teamwork. Allowing jokes at the expense of others can never benefit the overall performance of the team. We have seen teams where there is enough understanding, insight, or political correctness to avoid jokes about most groups, but it appears to be OK to ridicule or scapegoat a few others. If this behavior exists, it needs to be discussed. Once the group decides on the norms, have them typed up for everyone or write the final list on a piece of chart paper and post it at every team session. It will come in handy.

FIGURE 7–1

Sample Team Norms

Active participation by all team members
No side conversations
What's said in the room, stays in the room
Each person speaks for him- or herself
Open, honest communication
Respect for all viewpoints by not discounting others' views
No ridicule of others
Willingness to cultivate a variety of options
Promptness
Each person is responsible for making up what he or she missed
Commitment to deadlines
Attend all sessions

Establishing norms is only the first step. Reinforcing them is a necessary follow-up. We recently facilitated a weeklong advanced diversity training conference with a group of professionals that formed a loose team of learners and colleagues. The group had defined its norms, but we had to revisit them several times during the week to see if they were still valid. Complaints about the noise level during small-group discussions that made hearing difficult, and side conversations that distracted some people while the whole group was having a discussion, needed to be mentioned more than once. The norms may change, but if you want a collaborative, inclusive environment, establishing and reinforcing them is a critical place to start and a promising avenue for growth.

TASK AND MAINTENANCE BEHAVIORS

In order to create and develop a group that does meet its performance objectives, a team has to pay attention to two areas: (1) task behaviors, and (2) maintenance behaviors. Task behaviors are those team behaviors that further the task accomplishment of the group. They are hard-core, performance-oriented behaviors that speak to the issue of getting the job done rather than how people feel about doing the job. Task behaviors aren't focused on feelings or developing relationships. They are about identifying goals and meeting performance objectives.

Maintenance behaviors, on the other hand, look at the way team members do business together and interact in the process of getting their tasks accomplished. If task behaviors focus more on the "what" of accomplishment, maintenance behaviors look at the "how." Both play critical roles in meeting the team's overall objectives. The following task and maintenance behaviors in Worksheet 7–5 are among the most important in creating a productive team.

For example, giving useful feedback in nonthreatening ways may be very difficult for people from the Middle East, Asia, and Mexico or Central or South America. We don't mean to imply that it's always easy for people born in the United States, but if you are from Canada, Western Europe, or the United States, harmony is not valued more highly than discussing real differences or giving useful feedback. Another example of a behavior that might be very difficult in parts of the world where culture is collectivist and where assertiveness wasn't taught for an entire decade in the '80s, as it was in the United States, is clearly stating what you need from others.

Read all the items on the list carefully. Once everyone has responded to the checklist, team members can discuss those behaviors they see in meetings and those they don't. Part of the discussion should include behaviors that the team could use more of and how those behaviors can be encouraged. Pay particular attention to ways of fostering behaviors that may be difficult for some people, either because of culture or any other diversity dimension. This checklist can also be used by having one team member at a time act as a process observer who gives the team feedback or by having all members discuss the progress made by the team as a whole at the end of a session.

Since every team member will be better at some of these behaviors than others, ask each person to pick out his or her three most difficult task behaviors and three most difficult maintenance behaviors, and have

WORKSHEET 7–5

Identifying Behaviors Necessary for High Team Performance

Directions: Put a checkmark next to those behaviors that the team seems to have in abundance. Then put an *X* next to any behaviors that may be impacted by culture or other diversities on your team.

Task Behaviors	Maintenance Behaviors
_____ Asks clarifying questions	_____ Encourages the participation of others
_____ Shares information	_____ Gives useful feedback in nonthreatening ways
_____ Initiates discussion	_____ Offers support of various kinds
_____ Proposes possible solutions	_____ Listens to the viewpoints of others
_____ Brainstorms options	_____ States what is needed from other team members
_____ Summarizes the content of the meeting	_____ Demonstrates an openness and willingness to risk different points of view
_____ Finds out the facts	_____ Observes interactions of fellow team members' behaviors in the group
_____ Identifies clear goals and objectives	_____ Suggests that team deals with disagreement and revisits the norms
_____ Determines action plans	_____ Gives group feedback about behaviors on the team
_____ Diagnoses problems	_____ Relieves tension
_____ Sets up monitoring and evaluation processes	
_____ Assigns tasks	
_____ Volunteers for tasks	

WORKSHEET 7–6

Improving Performance on the Team

Directions: Pick no more than three task and three maintenance behaviors where you could improve. Based on the behaviors you pick, fill in the data below. The first line in each section shows sample responses.

TASK BEHAVIOR

BEHAVIORS	REASON FOR DIFFICULTY	ONE THING I'M WILLING TO IMPROVE IN THIS AREA	ONE WAY IN WHICH THE TEAM COULD ADAPT AND BE MORE FLEXIBLE IN MEETING ITS NEEDS
Brainstorming ideas	It's hard for me to think on my feet	Come to the session with ideas	Have agendas with topics distributed ahead of time
1.			
2.			
3.			

MAINTENACE BEHAVIOR

BEHAVIORS	REASON FOR DIFFICULTY	ONE THING I'M WILLING TO IMPROVE IN THIS AREA	ONE WAY IN WHICH THE TEAM COULD ADAPT AND BE MORE FLEXIBLE IN MEETING ITS NEEDS
Sharing ideas and feelings about behaviors in the group	I'm not comfortable being open. I resist conflict and sharing	Challenge myself to take baby steps in the sharing department; start small and grow	Use suggestion box or buddy system, where there is more trust
1.			
2.			
3.			

all participants go through the process shown in Worksheet 7–6. It is designed to level the playing field and not to stigmatize anyone by assuming that all of us could improve our behavior in some areas. Follow the directions as is, or adapt them to suit your group more appropriately.

After each person fills out his or her own "Improving Performance on the Team" chart, you can ask team members to discuss this in small groups or, depending on team size, you can write each person's name on a flip chart and list his or her most difficult task and maintenance behavior. To see how the flip chart would look, see the illustration below.

Improving Performance on The Team

Team Member	Most Difficult Behavior	Most Difficult Maintenance Behavior

By having team members share one task and one maintenance behavior that they need to improve, and by listing it publicly, you accomplish several important outcomes. They are the acknowledgment that:

- None of us is perfect. We all need to grow.
- The more we know about one another, the more we can help each other grow.
- The more we know about ourselves as a team, in both the task and maintenance areas, the more we can improve our performance.

Once all of this information is on the flip chart, you can ask a few questions:

- What does this say about us as a group?

- Where could we sabotage our own performance?
- How do we need to adapt as a team to ensure the demonstration of all necessary behaviors?

You don't need to go through this process of identifying task and maintenance behaviors formally or on a regular basis. You'll be too busily engaged in accomplishing the task itself. But at some point, and that point is better earlier in the life of the team than later, the group needs to be introduced to this concept. Call particular attention to those behaviors that have cross-cultural implications, such as giving feedback, being straightforward, or sharing feelings. Some of these may be very difficult for people, depending on when and where they were reared or depending on their self-esteem and comfort with the group members. Once you've taught the initial concept and engaged the team in a worthwhile discussion, this kind of self-examining tool can be a very helpful and important maintenance technique. Dust if off every once in a while for diagnosis or when problems present themselves in either the task or maintenance areas.

OVERCOMING DIVERSITY OBSTACLES TO PROBLEM SOLVING AND DECISION MAKING

A team can spend a great deal of time, and should spend at least some, utilizing interventions like those presented throughout this book to help team members know each other well for the purposes of solving problems and making decisions together. But any maintenance or process interventions—in fact any tools and techniques that are used—are not an end in themselves. They are only helpful inasmuch as they result in a team's increased ability to meet its performance goals and objectives. Problem solving is one of the best tools for yielding results. It can also be a source of great fun and creativity and can build confidence and pride in the team's ability to get the job done. The track record a team builds will hold it in good stead in future experiences.

The tools for problem solving we present here are designed to shed light on some of the assumptions we make on diverse teams and to simplify the process in order to find areas of agreement. For starters, we'll share our never-fail way to recognize problems. We call it the OH-OH Syndrome. Simply stated,

$$\begin{array}{rl} 0 & \text{(Objective)} \\ + \; 0 & \text{(Obstacle)} \\ \hline = & \text{Problem} \end{array}$$

This little model looks deceptively simple, but it is usable with any problem you have. Here is a common example from many organizations with whom we work:

> *Objective:* The company wants all employees to feel committed to and included in the organization; it wants to be perceived in the marketplace as an employer of choice with new recruits so that it attracts the best and the brightest.

> *Obstacle:* Diverse groups (e.g., working mothers, older employees, gays, lesbians, and people of color) perceive that they are not being valued or included and have little opportunity to advance and grow.

You could add other objectives or obstacles to this list, but it is an example that gives you a starting point. To use this model, take a problem of your own and follow the steps in Worksheet 7–7.

Once you have had all team members define the problem(s) of the group as they see it, the five open-ended statements are important questions because they will help team members define and see the problems differently. Good problem solving requires an appropriate definition of the problem, and this process can help achieve it. It is important to explore and not assume that the obvious problem definition is the accurate one. Learn from our example. We remember doing a three-day team-building session years ago with an executive team of 18 people. When we collected data for our own planning prior to the session, the consensus seemed to be that the biggest issue on the executive team was communication, or lack thereof, among team members. Executive team members had various objectives they wanted to meet, but the one obstacle that they all agreed hindered their performance was communication.

We started trying to get clearer, more specific information, so we asked a number of questions similar to the five open-ended ones. What emerged from our probe was that the executive director had worked for years with his 17 department heads, all of whom had equal rank. All were competent; all were long-timers in a very stable, small community.

WORKSHEET 7–7

Defining a Problem on Your Team

Directions: Start problem definition by identifying one person exhibiting the OH-OH Syndrome on your team.

```
        0 (Objective) _____

                      _____

  +  0 (Obstacle)     _____

  _____

  =     Problem       _____
```

Once you have filled out the OH-OH Syndrome, complete the following open-ended statements about this issue.

1. You could define this problem as:

    _____

2. This is a problem for me because:

    _____

3. What I would really like to do is:

    _____

4. If I could break all the laws of reality, I would try to solve the problem by:

    _____

5. The problem stated another way might be:

    _____

In an attempt to become more efficient and not have to deal with the questions and responses required from a direct-reporting staff of 17, the executive director picked 3 of the 17 and made them assistant directors.

By the time participants learned of this change in structure, it was a fait accompli. He had never talked previously about his objective of being more efficient, nor about the time constraints, the structure that he thought posed obstacles to efficiency, or the fact that he was playing buffer and advice-giving roles that he didn't want to play. To meet his objective of simplifying his life and making the executive team more efficient, he eliminated the obstacles by changing the structure and limiting the access of 14 department heads who previously had unlimited access. The downsides? Many, as you might imagine. Here's a list of just some of the consequences that would spawn new problems.

1. A key decision was made that affected all participants, but they had no input.
2. Three people were "elevated," leaving 14 disgruntled department heads feeling very inadequate and irrelevant.
3. The 14 who weren't picked were very annoyed about losing access.
4. They were even more upset, although this was hard for them to verbalize and admit, that they weren't picked to be one of the three. They may not have liked the new structure under any circumstances, but since it was operational, they were hurt that they weren't one of the three assistant directors selected.

We could continue listing numerous dilemmas this decision caused. As we worked through the definition of this problem, it became clear that "communication" was not a full or accurate description. Changing the management structure, altering reporting relationships, and not seeking input on a team issue that seriously involved all team members were among the biggest facets of the problem. Once the group discussed the issues, a clear, more accurate statement of objectives and obstacles could be defined. Although in this case the three assistant directors kept their new positions, future key decisions were made differently, and a way for the other 14 people to have some access to the executive director was created.

Correct problem definition is critical. We offer our OH-OH Syndrome and subsequent questions not as a definitive way to identify the problem, but as a nonthreatening purposeful tool for all team members to explore issues and arrive at an accurate problem definition. By using this technique, subtle and less obvious but still critical aspects to problems will emerge.

ASSUMPTIONS AND BLOCKS: SUBTLE SABOTEURS

Identifying the objective and the obstacle is step 1 in problem solving. Not far behind, however, comes the issue of assumptions. Limiting assumptions and expectations can cloud every aspect of problem solving, from the way the problem is defined to how some individuals are involved and even who might be invited to help create the solution. Effective problem-solving teams are usually effective because they invest some time in coming face to face with their assumptions so that participants don't shortchange their own capabilities or those of other team members.

To get a sense of your own assumptions and how limiting they can be, try this problem-solving puzzle, one that has been handed down to us over the years by team members on groups we have facilitated:

> Just before the nurse dies of the effects of an attack, she said, "He did it, the villain!" referring to one of the three doctors in the room. She didn't glance or point in his direction. The doctors were named Green, Brown, and White. Why was Dr. Brown immediately suspected?

The answer to the puzzle is that Dr. Green and Dr. White were both women. If you got that answer right away, good for you. You got beyond a gender/role assumption that many people still make in our society.

Assumptions run so deep that very often we don't even know we're making them. One of us, Lee, shares an example that is instructive, though she is not at all proud of it. It involved a surgery she had a few years ago. A day after the surgery, a nurse came in to check on her. She was still heavily anesthetized, so when this gentle, patient nurse woke her up to check her blood pressure, Lee's uncensored responses came from her deep socialization. The nurse, a very large man, was kind, but what Lee remembers thinking in her semiconscious state is that he was in the wrong job. With his size and gender, he should have been on the offensive line of the Los Angeles Rams, her local team at the time. Days later, when she was awake, conscious, and less under the influence of anesthesia, Lee recalled her assumptions with embarrassment. But the painful truth is that all of us, like Lee, do limit ourselves and others by these kinds of assumptions all the time. To help yourself and your team face them, try the following exercise shown in Worksheet 7–8.

Use the "Diversity Assumptions Impacting Problem Solving on Your Team" worksheet to see what assumptions you are making and how they might be limiting you and the people about whom you are making them.

What is very important regarding assumptions is to look at those that are made about groups of people we work with and groups of which we are a part. You won't necessarily make an assumption about each dimension of diversity, but it's important to come clean when you have one. These assumptions can color the perceptions we have of our team members and can upgrade or downgrade performance expectations. Because we all make assumptions, this exercise can be a humanizer and a leveler. No one escapes, and coming clean about them to the team builds openness and cohesion. While this experience may not necessarily feel good, it can be very enlightening to members of the team. And like all the techniques we've suggested, the issues are not nearly so intimidating or problematic once they are discussed. Assumptions are one way we limit ourselves and others; blocks are the other.

The tool "Blocks to Problem Solving," Worksheet 7–9, will enable team members to come face-to-face with their own limits. The point of assessing these obstacles is not to expect to eliminate them. We all have them, but we need to understand them so we can minimize their limiting influences on our creativity and openness to exploring problems. The first column in the worksheet relates most clearly to the individual personality profile; the middle column, Cultural Blocks, has the most to do with diversity; and the third column relates to organizational factors. To deal with these blocks, have each person write an *M* (for me), indicating personal blocks, or a *T* (for team) for the ones seen on the team, next to each item. After each person makes his or her marks, have discussions in small groups of about four or five people to compare perceptions of the team. It is also important to end the discussion with each member acknowledging his or her toughest block. This is helpful information when solving problems because the blocks will show themselves in the process of working together, and team members can give each other gentle nudges that help each member grow.

WORKSHEET 7–8

Diversity Assumptions Impacting Problem Solving on Your Team

Directions: As you think of the various dimensions of diversity, in the right-hand column write an assumption held by the general public that could impact team members' perceptions of a person from this group as a problem solver.

Dimension of Diversity	Assumption that Might Be Made
Age	Example: You can't teach an old dog new tricks. Older people are closed to new ideas. Example: Younger people haven't had the proper experience to come up with good solutions.
Age	
Ethnicity (e.g., Mexican)	
Gender	
Race	
Physical Ability (e.g., hard of hearing)	
Sexual Orientation	
Marital/Parental Status (e.g., single parent with children)	
Religion (e.g., Buddhist)	
Recreational Habits (e.g., hikes on weekends)	
Educational Background (e.g., college education)	
Work Experience (e.g., union)	
Appearance (e.g., overweight)	
Geographic Location (e.g., rural)	
Personal Habits (e.g., smoking)	
Income (e.g., well-to-do)	

WORKSHEET 7–9

Blocks to Problem Solving

Directions: Becoming aware of one's psychological, cultural, and environmental blocks is an important step in becoming a more effective problem solver. After reading the lists below, put an *M* (me) or a *T* (team) next to any blocks you have experienced or observed in the work setting.

Psychological Blocks	Cultural Blocks	Environmental Blocks
_____ Preference for the predictable and orderly	_____ Values (e.g., reverence for age)	_____ New ideas perceived as threatening
_____ Unwillingness to tolerate ambiguity	_____ Attitudes (e.g., either–or thinking)	_____ Failure to reward innovative thinking
_____ High achievement motivation	_____ Beliefs (e.g., equal justice)	_____ Work environments that do not engender supportive behaviors
_____ Quick success orientation	_____ Behaviors (e.g., promptness)	_____ Workplace that is too hot
_____ Inability to allow ideas to incubate	_____ Preference for reason, logic, numbers	_____ Workplace that is too cold
_____ Valuing sensory perceptions over intuition	_____ Limited emphasis on feelings and intuition	_____ Ringing phones
	_____ Viewing problem solving as humorless and serious	_____ Distracting noises
_____ Fear of failure		_____ Interruptions
_____ Fear of success	_____ Perceptual biases (seeing only what you expect)	_____ Selective perception
_____ The need to be right		

Adapted from James L Adams, *Conceptual Blockbusting*

An *M* or *T* placed by any of the blocks listed in the Psychological Blocks column indicates a person's difficulty in living with the ambiguity necessary to develop creative solutions to problems. These personal tendencies indicated by the psychological blocks would suggest a desire for predictability and stability that might preclude the necessary incubation, chaos, and messiness usually required for creative solutions to complex problems.

The Cultural Blocks listed relate to the assumptions listed in the previous exercise. Do you have expectations, positive or negative, based upon any team member's culture? Do you have a fixed attitude about any team member because he is pro-life or pro-choice? Republican or Democrat? Male or female? Black or Hispanic? Gay or straight? As we stated earlier, assumptions are deeply held and hard to change. But if you acknowledge them honestly, they don't have to limit you.

The environmental blocks speak for themselves. You have undoubtedly been in meetings or problem-solving sessions where beepers, phones, or overcrowding impacted the outcome. There may be others we haven't included, but these distractions can be very inhibiting. Ground rules about interruptions are very helpful.

Once you have looked at the blocks in a general way, focus specifically on the assumptions that may impact your team regarding any of the diversities we've mentioned. Discussing the blocks each team member brings to the team experience can be very instructive, clarifying, helpful, and cathartic. It can also increase your openness and exploration in pursuit of effective solutions.

Once you have identified a problem and spent some time trying to minimize the negative effects of blocks and assumptions, you will be ready to look at how the group makes decisions.

DECISION MAKING ON THE TEAM

Because teams are a conglomeration of individuals with very different decision-making approaches, it is helpful to note people's primary decision-making styles and deal with the differences in a nonthreatening way. These individual styles will influence group decision making. The following exercise in Worksheet 7–10 is a light way to make a point about these differences. It can be used as an introduction to decision making in general or to consensus building specifically.

WORKSHEET 7–10

Decision Making: What's Your Style?

Directions: Think about your general decision-making style. Consider your knee-jerk response when you make decisions ranging from what to order on the menu or where to take your vacation to what you should do first at work when you have 10 top priorities. Place a checkmark by the style that best describes you.

_____ Coin Tosser: leaves outcome to chance or fate

_____ Anguisher: agonizes over decisions, goes back and forth over options

_____ Procrastinator: keeps putting off decisions (à la Scarlet O'Hara)

_____ Decidophobe: paralyzed by the pressure of decision making

_____ Plunger: quick to act, decisive

_____ Systematic Analyzer: methodically weighs alternatives, often using lists and charts

_____ Abdicator: will not accept the responsibility of decision making, leaving it to others

Most people have more than one decision-making style. Look at the seven options presented and decide which style is your dominant one. Then consider both the upsides and downsides of that style.

Dominant decision-making style: _____

Good News about My Style	Bad News about My Style
_____	_____
_____	_____
_____	_____
_____	_____
_____	_____

Now, take a look at how your own style works for you. List any three work-related decisions you've made in the last month. Is there any correlation between the decision-making style you checked and the decision-making style you demonstrated? If so, does it work well? Would another style have been more effective in any of these circumstances?

WORKSHEET 7–11

Analyzing Decision-Making Styles

Decision	Decision-Making Style Used	Result
1.		
2.		
3.		

Now list the decision-making styles of the members on your team. Then compare your perceptions with one another. How consistent are they? What accounts for the differences? What impact might these individual traits have on the team's collective decision making?

Name of Team Member   **Decision-Making Style**

_____   _____

_____   _____

_____   _____

_____   _____

Once you have looked at the decision-making styles and considered the pros and cons of each, look at yourself as a team. Each of these styles has advantages and disadvantages. Think of a time when each would benefit and hurt the team process and results. Then see if all styles are represented on your team. Are there some you need to cultivate more?

CONSENSUS: A PRIME DECISION-MAKING TOOL

One of the ways high-performing teams distinguish themselves is by their refined use of problem-solving and decision-making skills. Consensus is one of the most frequently mentioned, effective strategies for team decision making. It is also often misunderstood and incorrectly used. Creative consensus is best described as a decision-making process that requires the group to develop a decision that all can live with. Reaching consensus effectively is not easy. Issues that warrant consensus should involve decisions that people are very attached to and ones that offer multiple alternatives. Teams utilize consensus most effectively when they are taught how to use it. Begin by having a discussion, for background information, of the generally accepted guidelines about using consensus found in "How to Use Consensus" with your team. Once you have instructed team members on the guidelines, ask them to practice using consensus by utilizing the next tool, "Characteristics of an Effective Team Member on a Diverse Team," Worksheet 7–12. It will not only help them learn to use consensus, but it will also generate a good discussion about what it means to be a good team member. Consensus is best taught using a simulator exercise such as this. Because it is relevant but not real, the experience offers feedback and learning but does not result in long-term consequences for the team.

TABLE 7–1

How to Use Consensus

General Information on Consensus

- Technique for shared decision making that creates a decision all can live with
- Uses diverse opinions for creative problem solving
- Best used when decision requires acceptance, ownership, and commitment
- Avoids creating winners and losers
- Only used when there are more than two alternatives but no "right answer"
- Time-consuming process
- Most effective with small groups, where only those involved with the decision are included

Generally Accepted Guidelines for Using Consensus

- No voting!
- Avoid arguing for your own point of view.
- Focus on points of agreement.
- Do not change your mind simply to avoid conflict.
- Avoid bargaining and coin flips.
- Expect disagreements. Use them to spur the search for alternatives.
- When deadlocked, divide into subgroups.

WORKSHEET 7–12

The Characteristics of an Effective Team Member on a Diverse Team

Directions: In the column labeled Your Ranking, prioritize the following eight characteristics of an effective team member on a diverse team with 1 being the characteristic that is most important to you and 8 the least. Then, with fellow team members, reach consensus on the ranking.

_____	1. An open, tolerant attitude	_____
_____	2. Knowledgeable about cultural norms of different groups	_____
_____	3. Willingness to be held accountable for performance and do what it takes to get the job done	_____
_____	4. Gives honest feedback and input about issues that affect the productivity of the team	_____
_____	5. Expresses ideas clearly	_____
_____	6. Skilled in facilitation and knowledgeable about group dynamics	_____
_____	7. Supportive and responsive to needs of other team members	_____
_____	8. Believes in the mission and goals of the team	_____

Once the team has achieved its collective ranking, the group discusses the experience, using the following questions as guides, in order to maximize the learning.

1. What was your response to ranking the characteristics?
2. Which posed the most difficult choices for you personally?
3. Which differences caused the most conflict on the team?
4. What happened when people gave their rationales for their choices?
5. What did your team do well in reaching consensus?
6. What did you do poorly?
7. What do you need to do better as consensus decision makers the next time around?

8. What part of this experience translated to real organizational life in your work together?
9. What are the implications for you as a team?

This tool is useful for individual awareness and group discussion about important characteristics of effective team members. Since there are no right answers, the value comes from articulating the specific characteristics and the sharing of information among team members. It can be a very effective teaching tool for learning consensus and a great team-building tool for discussing norms.

CONFLICT: VARIATIONS ON A HUMAN THEME

Conflict is a natural, normal part of every team's existence. The difference between high-performance teams and those that are ineffective is that top performers have a process for dealing with it. In fact, how teams deal with conflict separates the proverbial men from the boys. Before we talk about methods for dealing with conflict, it is important to understand that there are some common and predictable but ineffective human responses to conflict, among them anger, pouting, withdrawal, denial, suppression, and sulking. When you overlay the dimensions of diversity on some of these previously mentioned behaviors, it is easy to understand why having productive ways to handle differences is a topic of such import. The human species has never been particularly effective in handling conflict. Our collective history is filled with wars and strife, pogroms and genocide. Our present-day structure for handling conflict on a global scale, the United Nations, achieves debatable results. Thankfully, for your purposes, you only have to worry about conflict on a small scale.

Part of the difficulty may be cultural. Seventy percent of the world's population values harmony more than dealing with conflict, but even here we get mixed messages because the globe is currently dotted with conflagrations. It is into this macro environment that your miniature group will try to find positive ways other than denial, suppression, or violence for dealing with its troubles.

With that sobering reality in mind, let's look at a few truisms about conflict. They will help put resolution of team conflict into focus and into context.

1. *Conflict is a natural, normal part of life.* Over the many years we've been helping seminar participants deal with conflict, we have noticed

their expression of one repeated emotion: fear. In their perception, the terrifying consequences of manifested conflict, however real or imagined, cannot justify the benefit of easing the difficulties. Fear of losing love, job, esteem, friendship, and a host of other things keep people from dealing with issues that need to be dealt with. Part of what team members need to realize is that conflict need not be cataclysmic. Rather, it is a natural, normal part of life. By using to the family structure as a reference point, participants can see that even those who love, value, and cherish one another have their differences. These struggles can result in positive change; they don't have to result in destruction. Perceiving the naturalness of conflict can make the outcomes more durable and the process less fragile and intimidating.

2. *Conflict is neutral.* Another truism about conflict is that it just "is." In and of itself, it is neither positive nor negative. It simply reflects a reality that shows, in the case of teams, different viewpoints, priorities, or choices. What a team chooses to do with conflict, or how it chooses to look at the whole process, will determine whether conflict becomes a plus or a minus. A word to the wise: On high-performing teams, conflict is seen as a gift that gives the team information about central issues that could, if unattended to, derail its achievements. Conflict may be neutral, but viewing it as a catalyst for positive change can make it your team's very good ally.

3. *Conflict is not the sign of a poorly managed team. Rather, it is just a reality of team functioning.* On effective teams, conflict is an indication that differences are acknowledged and out in the open. We always consider acknowledging and dealing with conflict to be one barometer of a healthy team because the group is not denying or burying issues that cause fissures. When you see conflict on the team, your best and most productive strategy is to bring it to the surface in a nonconfrontational tone and simply ask the team to identify the issues. If teams develop a history of doing this and see that they survive, grow, and remain intact, conflict will be less scary and more just the way business is done.

4. *Not all conflicts can be resolved.* This painful truism can be seen from two different vantage points. The first is that not all conflicts have good resolutions, even when agreements are reached or compromises agreed to. Sometimes the alternatives look bleak even though unattractive choices are preferable to an ongoing, destructive reality.

But the other truth regarding this issue is that often, people have invested much more in keeping the conflict going than in dealing with it or in solving the problem. If someone on your team gains power and control by keeping people off guard or by intimidating them, he gains nothing by ending the conflict. Conflicts exist because someone, somewhere gets something out of keeping them going.

5. *Conflict can result from clear communication.* The prevailing belief is that conflict is the result of a lack of communication. In truth, it is most often the result of very clear communication about very real differences. We know a therapist who shared a valuable insight with us. A couple walked into his office for the first time and the husband's body language spoke volumes. He had a clenched jaw, folded arms, and an angry look. The couple came for therapy because, as he revealed, "We're not communicating." The therapist's retort was, "Oh yes, you are. You are communicating very clearly, but not very well." Usually, the conflicts on your team will be the result of very clearly communicated differences in priorities, values, norms, definitions of desired results, or other productivity-related factors. That clear conflict helps you understand how wide the gap is, and where you can begin to narrow it.

Understanding these realities can help teams become aware of conflict as a phenomenon and develop a sense of perspective about it. Learning to view conflict as a potential source of creative energy rather than as something destructive can change the paradigm of how it is viewed. And when teams establish their operating norms, attention needs to be paid to how team members will deal with their eventual differences. Just as the sun comes up in the morning, conflicts will most assuredly show themselves. But with the awareness of the conflict process itself, knowledge about people's personal styles or preferences in handling conflict, and a realization that our methods of managing conflict are in some ways a product of our cultural background, team members can gain insight, skills, and techniques that will help them manage this most natural of occurrences.

One of the most powerful and useful examples of dealing with diversity-related conflict was reported to us by a team member from an organization with whom we were working. This story is poignant because of its sensitivity, honesty, and complexity. Here's what happened. One competent associate, a native of India, felt very demeaned by a fellow employee. The statement the East Indian heard was, "If you're going to live here, why don't you learn to speak English?" This employee did speak English, and very well, we might add. Both her syntax and vocabulary were excellent. She has a slight accent, and herein lies the issue. Although she shared the episode with a colleague, she did not feel comfortable bringing it up in her group. However, her feelings of exclusion and diminishment did not go away. The obvious manifestation of it was that she became less engaged with others. It is hard to continue to do good work when you feel devalued.

Finally, the colleague she confided in, who happens to have exceptional communication, facilitation, and "human being" skills, decided to address the issue, through the back door. She convened a series of small-group meetings throughout her division. The sessions featured discussions about prejudice, stereotypes, assumptions about others, and the messages we give ourselves and others based on these assumptions. She used herself as the example, asking people what they saw or noticed about her. They started with physical characteristics, and she used that experience to tell her colleagues, in each of the five sessions, that she is a lesbian. They had fruitful discussions, with noticeable victories in the increased sensitivity department. The woman whose accented English inadvertently provoked the session finally spoke out about what happened to her and how she felt. These sessions were used to promote dialogue about how co-workers would agree to treat one another in ways that enhanced rather than diminished fellow employees. The team member who orchestrated this whole experience on her own helped people deal with the suppressed conflict that was eating away at performance and commitment. She did so in a way that left everyone more whole than when they started. That sort of elegant facilitation is possible on every work team. Since it is possible, that kind of outcome could be your vision.

In order to make good results happen, there are some things you need to know about how people manage conflict cross-culturally. Table 7–2 lists some mainstream American attitudes and viewpoints about conflict in one column, and views that are more dominant in 70 percent of the world in the other column. At the very least, it should raise your awareness and understanding about the reasons we might respond the way we do. And, needless to say, the cultural influence doesn't acknowledge individual preferences and habits in dealing with conflict. These are mighty factors as well.

TABLE 7–2

Dealing with Conflict as a Cultural Phenomenon

Mainstream American attitudes, behaviors, and belief systems regarding conflict on teams:	Other cultural attitudes, behaviors, and belief systems regarding conflict on teams:
• Communication is very direct: "Put your cards on the table." "Don't beat around the bush." "Tell it like it is."	• Communication is much more contextual and indirect.
• Airing of differences is seen as helpful to the team.	• Harmony is prized more highly than airing of differences.
• Emphasis is on being assertive and using "I" messages (I feel, I think, I need, I want).	• Being direct in resolving differences is viewed as offensive and crass; formal team structure is seen as a very inappropriate forum for negotiation.
• Conflict is negotiated within team structure as joint problem solving.	• Conflicts are solved informally after hours in social situations.
• In a legalistic culture, mediation and arbitration are viable options.	• Denial and suppression are tools of the trade.
• Frustration is felt from avoidance behavior or refusal to deal with conflict directly and openly.	• Third-party interveners are useful and can function as negotiators, but it is best done informally.
	• Confrontation is seen as potentially face-losing.

A purposeful way of using this chart with your team might be to distribute it in a meeting designed to focus on how the team can deal effectively with its differences. You can use this chart and the following questions as a good jumping off point:

- What is your reaction to these descriptions? What parts match the team's reality? What parts don't?
- Based on your experiences on our team, how accurate do these cultural manifestations of conflict seem to be?
- Which of these behaviors and beliefs do you see on the team?
- Which are your own preferences?
- What conditions, and what kinds of behaviors, need to exist on this team in order for you to willingly broach the discussion of differences?
- What behaviors and conditions would make you avoid or deny discussion of conflicts?

Discussing conflict while in a nonconflict situation can be one of your best investments of time. Your introductory comments should indicate that all groups have differences that need to be attended to, and that this team is no different. The conflicts don't need to be a problem, and they needn't cause fear. They are simply one aspect of life and human relationships. The message a team leader should convey is, "We will help ourselves a great deal as a team if we decide how we want to approach them ahead of time." Then you can distribute the table, "Dealing with Conflict as a Cultural Phenomenon" while pointing out that dealing with conflict is in part cultural. After the full discussion, the team leader or facilitator can capture any comments or suggestions made. Some behaviors may need to be added to the norms chart.

One way to begin the discussion of conflict and how to deal with it is to have team members share their feelings and views on the topic by using the following exercise.

WORKSHEET 7–13

Conflict: You and the Team

Directions: Pair up with another team member and discuss your responses to the following open-ended statements, each taking a turn with one statement, then continuing to trade off.

1. The hardest conflicts for me to deal with are . . .

2. I was raised to deal with conflict by . . .

3. The thing I most fear in conflict is . . .

4. When someone is in conflict with me, I wish they'd . . .

5. I don't confront in conflict because . . .

6. I feel most vulnerable during conflict when . . .

7. I usually hide my feelings when . . .

8. When someone confronts me in conflict, I . . .

9. My greatest strength in handling conflict is . . .

10. When we have conflict on the team, we should . . .

11. Conflict could help our team if . . .

12. What I would like to do better in dealing with conflict is . . .

Once the pairs have completed sharing responses, the whole team can talk about team issues such as:

1. What are our strengths in dealing with conflict?
2. What might prevent the team from dealing effectively with differences?
3. How can we handle conflict constructively?

"Conflict: You and the Team" is a safe tool for sharing individual views and perceptions of conflict that may impact a team. "Conflict Quiz" is another way to help team members focus on their own responses to conflict. This forced-choice questionnaire delves into attitudes toward conflict a little more specifically and deeply. It also presents avenues for individual or team exploration.

WORKSHEET 7–14

Conflict Quiz

Directions: Answer each of the following questions with a number from the scale that best represents your reaction.

Scale:
0 = No or Never   3 = Usually
1 = Not Usually   4 = Almost Always
2 = Sometimes

_____ 1. I confront as soon as I'm aware of a problem or tension in a relationship.
_____ 2. I'm happiest when I get my own way.
_____ 3. I try to determine the underlying issues in the conflict.
_____ 4. I take my conflicts to higher authorities for resolution.
_____ 5. I am clear about what I want and need from the other party.
_____ 6. Disagreements and arguments are upsetting to me.
_____ 7. I try to analyze how the other party perceives the situation.
_____ 8. I try to avoid confrontation at all costs.
_____ 9. I examine my own feelings regarding the situation.
_____ 10. I tend to ignore disruptive or difficult situations.
_____ 11. I approach conflict negotiation as joint problem solving.
_____ 12. I am upset when others disapprove of my actions.
_____ 13. I speak up when my needs are being ignored.
_____ 14. I am uncomfortable with aggressive or bossy people.
_____ 15. I show the other party what's in it for him or her to work with me to resolve the conflict.
_____ 16. I feel that I'm right and the other party is wrong.
_____ 17. It is easy for me to talk about my feelings (anger, fear, etc.).
_____ 18. Revenge is sweet to me.
_____ 19. I am willing to be flexible in order to achieve a resolution.
_____ 20. My anger gets me in trouble.

Conflict Quiz Scoring
1. Put a checkmark if you responded with 3 or 4 on any odd-numbered item.
2. Put a checkmark if you responded with 0 or 1 on any even-numbered item.
3. Count your checkmarks.

The higher the number of checkmarks, the more effectively you tend to deal with conflict. Items for which you did not have a checkmark indicate your weaker areas in dealing with conflict.

Share your score and perceptions with other team members, focusing on questions pertinent to the team:

1. How can my weaknesses become a hindrance to the team? For example, if my anger causes me to break off contact or pout, then it may keep me from engaging in working toward resolutions. Or perhaps if I feel I'm right and the other party is wrong, my mind might be closed to a third option that could work.

2. Which of these 20 items may be most difficult, based on cultural influences? What might the impact of these behaviors be on the team and what alternative behaviors might help teams get beyond cultural differences to effectively solve conflict? For example, trying to avoid confrontation at all costs is one behavior that might be culturally influenced. A good discussion might center on ways to bring differences to the surface that might feel less confrontational.

3. What can we do as a group to make dealing with conflict easier for everyone? Perhaps we need to have a small-group sessions at meetings where budding problems can be brought to the surface, and then bring them to the whole group. Or the team might need a mediator, who could serve as a facilitator to help two other team members work through a difference.

Suggestions for Resolving Conflicts

Ultimately, your team has numerous options for handling their differences. You might discuss each of the following options and ask team members when they might use it. This way, you are planting the idea that there isn't a best or an only way to handle differences. Rather, numerous vehicles are at their disposal. The challenge and the opportunity lie in determining under what circumstances each might be the most appropriate.

WORKSHEET 7–15

Options for Handling Conflict

Directions: The following options give you alternative methods for handling conflict on a diverse team. Check any methods you would use and think about the circumstances under which each would be appropriate.

___ *1. Approaching another person directly, one-on-one, to resolve the differences.* This approach is mainstream American in its directness. Theoretically, it involves only those who need to be involved. It intends to keep the conflict at its lowest, least-volatile point. Depending on the depth of the difference, it can provide the quickest resolution. *Hint*: Before approaching someone to solve this difference, be very clear about what you want, and be equally clear about what you're willing to pay or do to get what you want.

___ *2. Initiating an issue in the team environment and negotiating it on the spot in the group.* Resolving conflicts when they occur can be very productive for the team because it eliminates the performance blocks that exist when people are upset, frustrated, or angry. You do, however, need to be or have a skilled facilitator, particularly when different cross-cultural norms are part of the dynamics. There is strong conflict aversion in Pacific Rim and Latin American cultures, for example. And although team members may feel the conflict, that doesn't necessarily mean they are at all willing to deal with it openly. This reality brings to mind wisdom from a former boss of ours, who used to say, "Don't open a can of worms unless you have the recipe for worm soufflé." A few considerations will help you create the soufflé you want. First, avoid criticizing the person. Ground rules are helpful because they depersonalize the issue and focus instead on behaviors. Remember the group of advanced diversity trainers we previously mentioned? They were voracious learners and a dream class. But the noise level came up in several discussions as something that disrupted learning. By sticking to behaviors, the class kept the issue both concrete and fixable. Noise level, not personalities, was the issue.

    Those who are feeling the conflict need to be specific in stating the changes they want and be need to be open to seeing different points of view. All parties need to be flexible. The facilitator skill comes not only in keeping the group focused on specific behaviors, but also in seeing smoke screens—those conflicts that may be labeled "noise level," for example, but are in fact based on one person's dislike of another. This leads to the next option.

___ *3. Using a cultural interpreter.* Often, conflicts on teams feel explosive and intractable. It's at this moment of great volatility and misunderstanding that a cultural interpreter can be of assistance. The role of an interpreter is to help team members from different cultures understand each other better and come together less painfully. But an interpreter can also give quiet, one-on-one feedback to team members. In one situation, team members of two very different cultural backgrounds, one an immigrant from the Philippines and the other an African-American, nearly came to blows because of their differences in style regarding conflict. One wanted to deal directly and openly with the differences; the other wanted to continue to avoid the issue. As each retrenched further into her own style, the rift widened until both filed grievances. This escalation could have been avoided if a cultural interpreter had been able to work with them, helping each understand the cultural factors behind their reactions.

4. *Making use of a mediator.* Mediators are third-party negotiators who help facilitate resolution by getting the parties in conflict to talk to one another. One of us, Lee, used this technique with a group of secretaries at an accounting firm. Two of the seven could not get along and could barely stand to be in the same room together. Lee started by getting each person's perception of the problem separately, then fed back to them the information they gave her to check for accuracy; she then shared her own perceptions as well. Finally, she set up another meeting, to which each had to bring two lists: (1) specific behaviors they want and/or need from the other, and (2) what they are willing to do differently to eliminate the conflict. The two secretaries never grew to love one another, but they could once again work with each other, and that's all the client needed.

Using a mediator won't always fix personal conflicts, as Lee was reminded on one team she facilitated recently. An interpersonal conflict exploded between two team members who traveled to the monthly task-force meetings together. Their outburst was abrupt and startling. Lee wanted to facilitate it, but the person who was angry said the issues were personal, not team-related. Ultimately, one team member quit. Lee tried to function as a mediator, but each side saw the situation very differently. It reminded us of Roshoman, the Japanese parable in which there are many different versions describing truth. In this case, there was no way, and no desire, to come together. As a team leader or facilitator, your role is at least to give feedback and some coaching to the appropriate parties so that when team members are willing and able, they will grow into managing these conflicts on their own.

5. *Calling in an arbitrator.* This role is often used when an outcome must be reached and there seems to be no other way around the impasse. When there is a binding-arbitration mentality or when team members consent to reach some agreement with the help of an outsider, the outcome can be accomplished. You can raise the odds of success by making sure the arbitrator has credibility with all parties. Here's the caveat: Unless both sides feel that they won (best case), or

at least that they didn't lose ground, you will have a flimsy solution, and one that will be subtly, or not so subtly, sabotaged. Those "I will get even" voices we carry around in our heads show up at the damnedest times and have been known to wreak havoc.

___ *6. Denying or suppressing.* Although these responses are not your best option, they can offer some short-term benefit as a way to integrate a new reality. However, in the long run they are unattractive choices. We held a cross-cultural training seminar in Tokyo last July and discussed the issue of conflict. One Japanese man in the group stated that in his culture, people are taught to bury their feelings, and the result is negative. He felt that people reacted in ways that weren't constructive or helpful to the individual or the team. That conversation made Lee remember a seminar she had done in Los Angeles with a group that was extremely diverse ethnically. At lunch, she ate with two Korean nurses, one who had come to Los Angeles only 2 years before, and one who had been here 22 years. When Lee asked if they could remember their initial impressions of the United States and what subsequent views they held of Korea upon returning, the one who had been here longest responded that when she goes back, what she notices is how everyone buries their feelings. She said she never learned how to deal with her anger until she came to the United States, and for that reason alone, she could never "go home."

Resolving Conflict on the Team

Whether conflict on the team is between two members or among all in the group, following a step-by-step sequence can aid in creating a resolution that works. Utilize the following "Five-Step Guide to Resolving Conflict" by working through answers to the questions under each step to guide the team. Discuss them, step-by-step with those involved in the impasse.

FIGURE 7–2

Five-Step Guide to Resolving Conflict

Step 1:   *Establish a Supportive Climate*
- Are parties ready to talk and listen?
- Can they suspend judgment so they can hear each other's perceptions and feelings?
- Can each think in terms of "I" statements rather than "you" statements?
- Does each want to resolve rather than blame?

Step 2:   *Determine Each Party's Perceptions*
- What perceived loss or threat of loss has led each party to perceive a conflict?
- What does each think about the conflict?
- What does each think about the other?

Step 3:   *Isolate the Causes of the Conflict*
- Is the conflict substantive (about specific behaviors and conditions) or affective (about values and opinions)?
- What assumptions and cultural differences underlie each party's behavior?
- How does each party's behavior influence the other's?
- What is the nature of the differences—facts, goals, methods, values?

Step 4:   *Select the Appropriate Strategy*
- How is each party approaching the situation—collaborating, sharing, avoiding, competing, or accommodating?
- What does each party feel is an acceptable outcome? (More than two alternatives are a must.)
- What can both agree on?
- What is best for the team?

Step 5:   *Troubleshoot*
- What will prevent the resolution from jelling?
- Are there follow-up issues that need to be taken care of later?
- Do you need to set up a date for follow-up?

While there are no ideal or best ways to deal with conflict, the team does have a variety of options available. All that is required is an open mind and heart, a willingness to learn about others, a genuine desire to resolve differences, and the realization that each of us has a piece of the truth.

As a facilitator, keep in mind that you are the human engineer. By utilizing processes and strategies that reinforce the fulfilling of ego and affiliation needs, you give yourself the best chance to create an extraordinary team experience. You won't win every time, but you'll have more successes than disappointments and you'll learn a lot as you go. The diversity on a team, like a beautiful kaleidoscope, reflects light most brightly when all the pieces come together in a configuration that gives each piece of glass its place in the whole.

Chapter Eight

Where Do You Begin?

*"The greatest thing in this world is not so much where we are,
but in what direction we are moving."*

O W Holmes

When we work with teams to facilitate their task accomplishment, or when we teach classes several times a year at University of California, Los Angeles Extension to show people how to build high-performing, diverse teams, we always get the same feedback. It amounts to questions like these:

1. "The strategies you've shared are helpful, but do you have a planned sequence that can ensure our success?"
2. "The tools you suggest make good sense, but where do you start?"
3. "These techniques work in our class, but we elected to be here. How would they work on teams made up of people who don't want to participate?"

This chapter addresses all three of these questions. Let's begin with question 1. The answer to the first question is both yes and no. Yes, because there are some areas of team development that are sequential, and we will share the order with you later. For example, setting group norms collectively makes good sense and is most advantageous when done early in the process of working together. But the answer to that question is also No because each team is a unique, living organism. Just as there is no formula for raising kids because each is different, each group is its own entity. In this chapter we explain the stages of team development and suggest appropriate team-building strategies to use at each stage.

While the interventions you use to motivate members, get the team back on track, or help the group clarify thinking and redefine goals have the purpose of moving a team forward, when and how you use them always varies depending upon the group, its members, maturity and sophistication, its history, its team cohesion, and many other factors. This chapter, then, will help answer nuts-and-bolts questions that predictably show up at some stage of the team's existence.

OPTIONS IN SELECTING FUNCTIONAL TEAM MEMBERS

For starters, a team is helped considerably by having the right players. If you are looking at ongoing work teams, team-member selection involves hiring and recruiting the right people to begin with. A recruiter needs to keep several considerations in mind when scouting out talent for ongoing work teams:

1. What skills or competencies are "must haves" regarding your current employee base and the jobs you have to perform?
2. What skills or competencies add value but under certain circumstances are not a necessity?
3. What kinds of on-the-job experience would make this candidate a credible team member, one who gains respect just by walking in the door?
4. What are the human dynamics of the existing team? What kind of new team member would be an asset interpersonally? Is there any personality trait that you must avoid bringing on board?
5. When considering demographic diversity, what groups are underrepresented? How can we gain qualified potential employees from different backgrounds to round out our membership and ensure other viewpoints? What kind of climate will that person find when he or she arrives? How open and tolerant is the current team climate? If that person is hired, will the team environment be inclusive enough that the new employee will want to stay?

Options for Selecting
Short-Term Team Members

The previous questions are relevant for new hires entering functional teams, but considerations in selecting team members on task-force teams, or any variation of a time-specific or project-specific work team, are a little different. Here are a few options, complete with strengths and weaknesses.

Volunteer method. When putting together teams that are composed of volunteers, you theoretically get members who really want to participate, regardless of their reasons for doing so. The assumption is that the desire to participate makes for greater motivation of team members, which results in fewer necessary applications of the carrot or the stick. Those assumptions are all well and good; however, they may not always be valid. The volunteer selection method of team membership is a two-sided coin. Sometimes you end up with members who have axes to grind. While they may be passionate and motivated, their energy can be misguided. Bringing an objective viewpoint to the issue at hand is sometimes difficult.

Furthermore, if you take only volunteers, you are leaving to chance the skill composition of the team. Rarely do you start with a team that has the exact, perfect blend of skills. Competencies can be developed and cultivated, but the volunteer path can leave gaping knowledge and performance holes. You also may end up with functional parts of the organization unrepresented, or miss viewpoints you need to hear in order to deal effectively with a particular issue. When we work with diversity task-force teams, even those made up of volunteers, our contacts in these organizations are smart enough to know that the team itself must reflect the diversity of the company and the community. This is a good principle to keep in mind when you consider the volunteer path, no matter what your team's issue. Too much homogeneity inadvertently quashes options and creativity.

Recruitment method. When we work with teams and ask how participants were chosen, we sometimes get humorous references to the military and the concept of the draft. Whatever you choose to call it, people are frequently on project teams, for example, because someone asked them to do the job. They can be asked, recruited, drafted, appointed, or selected. The advantage to the organization is that if the selector chooses well, a magnificently blended team can exist in terms of skills and competencies, dynamics, parts of the organization represented, and any other consideration that is important. Furthermore, those selected may get an esteem boost from being invited. However, for a person agreeing to participate, the task may be demanding and make an already busy schedule more crowded. Even with that downside, though, there can be perks such as visibility, meeting and working with different people, accruing new experience, the prestige of being selected, and a chance to see and learn about the organization from a different vantage point.

The negative side of this selection method is that the person doing the picking may choose the wrong combination of people, may choose for the wrong reasons, or may end up with people who feel it would be career suicide to turn down the experience, when in truth they are short of interest, time, knowledge, or all of these.

Combination method. Many organizations use the volunteer method as a starting point, but the orchestrator of the team has clear membership needs. If voluntary selection doesn't produce all the necessary membership requirements, the invitation or draft method may become a necessity. The downside of that method is that when some people are selected to work with volunteers, others in the organization may wonder why they weren't asked. The potential exists for bruised egos, but then that potential exists under almost all circumstances. If you want to go with the volunteer method for reasons of motivation and interest, do so. But you may also want to do a little selecting behind the scenes to make sure that your team has a mix of skills, values, and viewpoints.

In considering the best method for building a short-term team, we would suggest that you first ask some pertinent questions. Before putting even one person on this team, make sure you have answers to the following queries:

1. For what performance objectives will this team be held accountable?
2. In order to meet these objectives, what skills, competencies, viewpoints, experiences, and diversities are needed on this team?
3. What's the best selection method for ensuring the right composition?
4. What are long- and short-term consequences of bruising the egos of people who won't be on the team?
5. What is the time commitment being asked, and is there a way to shuttle people in and out over time to give more employees a chance to participate?

While there are no perfect answers to the selection process, the considerations we mentioned and the questions we raised should at least help you have a rationale for how and why team members are determined. There is a postscript as we leave this issue. There isn't a right answer about how to get team membership. In looking to form a diversity task force, one organization was hoping to have 20 interested participants; it got 57 volunteers. Because there was so much energy and enthusiasm for the project, we asked the organizers how they'd feel about forming four task-force teams, each with different areas of responsibility. They agreed immediately because no one wanted to lose that kind of interest and passion. It was a good move, and options like that exist in your organization as well. There's not one best way, just a way that is well thought out and makes sense in terms of the objectives you're striving for and the resources you are willing to commit.

ASSESSING WHERE THE TEAM IS AND WHERE IT NEEDS TO GO

As we said earlier, teams are living organisms. There are many models for describing how teams grow and develop. One of the models most frequently referred to is Bruce Tuckman's four stages which begins with forming, moves to storming, evolves to norming, and then ends with performing. It's a wonderful model that articulates appropriate behaviors for both leaders and participants at each stage. We too see the growth of teams in stages, but our model is analogous to human growth and development. These stages are relevant in the context of task and maintenance behaviors. We suggest sharing this with your team and discussing not only the predictability of the stages, but the fact that not all progress is straightforward. As with humans, just because someone is mature in age doesn't mean he never regresses or acts like an adolescent. So too with teams. You can chart their growth, and you'll be less disappointed if you expect fits and starts rather than straightforward progress. Following this chart, we'll suggest techniques that will move your team from infancy to maturity.

WORKSHEET 8–1

Assessing Where the Team Is: A Checklist

Directions: Check any of the following statements that describe your team now.

Infancy
_____ 1. We keep asking what we're doing and why.
_____ 2. Team members don't know each other.
_____ 3. We're unclear about what we're supposed to do.

Adolescence
_____ 4. We're having trouble getting along.
_____ 5. Members are jockeying for power.
_____ 6. We disagree about how to proceed.

Middle Age
_____ 7. We're seeing the progress of our work.
_____ 8. Team members are open and honest in asking questions and giving feedback.
_____ 9. As we get to know each other better, we are working more smoothly together.

Maturity
_____ 10. We feel pride in our accomplishment.
_____ 11. We're really "cookin'."
_____ 12. We all do what it takes to get the job done.

Notice where your checkmarks fall. Based on your responses, look at Table 8–1, "The Phases of Team Growth and Development" model and see where you are.

As you look at the "Phases of Team Growth and Development" model, there are some important questions for the team to discuss:

1. What phase of development are you in? How much variety in perceptions exists in the answer to this question?
2. What problem behaviors seem to jump out?
3. What task and maintenance behaviors need to be addressed in order to move the team to the next phase?
4. What diversity issues might impact the team's ability to progress from one phase to another?

TABLE 8–1

The Phases of Team Growth and Development

Phase of Team Growth	Task Behavior	Maintenance Behavior
Infancy At this stage, the team is newly formed. Members jockey for position and work to create their own niche and demonstrated expertise. Often a tone of confusion or a "Why are we here?" mentality exists.	The team is trying to get started and needs some very basic and clear information in order to move forward. Fundamental questions asked in this stage: • Why are we here? • Are we really functionally interdependent? • What is our mission? • What are our goals? • What kind of resources and time lines exist?	The group decides how it will work together. It establishes ground rules that it believes will create a productive, supportive, harmonious environment in the service of accomplishing performance objectives. Team members need to get to know each other and share expectations.
Adolescence There is a beginning sense of connectedness and being a team, but also a challenging of the norms, a sense of rebellion against authority. Effort to exert one's will emerges in this stage. The struggle can be between team members or against the formal powers that be.	Disagreement exists about goals and how to accomplish them; members challenge the leader; intergroup conflict blocks clear definition of goals and objectives; some team members press for their own viewpoints without being open to others. This stage is short on negotiation, long on will power.	The norms that were agreed to at the beginning are sometimes violated. Not everyone participates, some people are closed-minded, and there's not necessarily much support for good ideas if they come from someone else. The leader continues to work on ego/affiliation needs and gives people room to disagree. Ample opportunity exists for rapport building and clarifying work content. Bridge-building interventions can be helpful.
Middle Age The group is more settled and humane in its interpersonal relationships. There is a sense of confidence in its ability to perform and accomplish its stated objectives. It can also change course without derailing. There is enough history together to breed a sense of confidence.	By this stage the group is seeing progress. Goals are being achieved and people are asking good, hard questions; gathering important information; and reality-testing solutions.	The group members know one another well enough to capitalize on strengths and weaknesses. They encourage and support the strengths and cover for each other when they need to. They can laugh and have fun together. There is general acceptance of team members as they are.
Maturity The team has a track record. It has proven itself. It functions well together, like a well-oiled machine, with each part making its contribution.	The team has been to the wars and back. They have midcourse corrected, implemented, followed up, evaluated, and revised. They continue to monitor and change as necessary.	Roles change, expertise is shared, and not much grandstanding is seen. A lot of joint pride in tasks accomplished and a willingness to do what it takes to keep doing the job is evident.

Discussing these issues with team members can be very enlightening, partially because of the variety of perceptions that exist, but also because of the awareness that team growth and development is a natural process influenced by team members' constructive (or destructive) behaviors. It will be an especially helpful discussion if team members reach a conclusion about where they are and agree to engage in some behaviors and a course of action that will move them forward. For example, if there is agreement that the team is in the adolescent stage and one of the problems is the violation of team norms, the group can go back one phase and rethink the norms they have set up. Which ones are key to working well? What is going on that causes participants to violate the rules? By omitting those rules that aren't useful, and by adapting or modifying ones that are, the "Phases of Team Growth Development" model can be an instructive tool. If you need help looking at task and maintenance behaviors, review that section in Chapter 7. Team growth and development is rarely straightforward. Your team will progress, and then it may regress. But specific, helpful task and maintenance behaviors will give you a good opportunity to move forward.

Regarding diversity as it relates to these stages of development, there is an exercise the group can engage in that will be a catalyst for exploration and insight on teams where diversity may be a major source of misunderstanding and conflict.

Use Worksheet 8–2 to explore how various dimensions of diversity may reveal themselves at different stages. Look at the examples presented on age and race in the Infancy stage, or the issue of cross-functional team members as it relates to brainstorming in the Middle Age phase. Use this grid to identify any diversity-related obstacles to performance during each of the four phases. Sharing perceptions can lead to a fruitful discussion about how your team is capitalizing on diversity or being stymied by it.

A SEQUENCE OF TEAM-BUILDING ACTIVITIES

To help you deal with the issues that you identified in Worksheet 8-2, we have categorized on the next page all the tools and team activities in the book and referenced them by chapter. They can be used at the appropriate stage. You will notice that some tools can be used in more than one stage.

WORKSHEET 8–2

Diversity as It Relates to Phases of Team Growth and Development

Directions: Identify any dimensions of diversity that may be at the root of some team growth and development obstacles.

Phases of Team Growth	Dimensions of Diversity	Task Issue	Maintenance Issue
Infancy	Example: *Age:* Young employee, new to the organization; youth and newness cause timidity Example: *Race:* African-American male	Example: Too timid to ask clarifying questions	Example: Unsure how to respond to those who tell jokes about other groups; they say there's no fun anymore since political correctness is a factor.
Infancy			
Adolescence			
Middle Age	Example: Work experience differences, cross-functional teams	Example: Varying degrees of experience impact brainstorming, not all equally.	
Maturity			

Infancy Stage

Need at this stage: Define mission, purpose, and goals; begin interpersonal relationship building; and establish norms for group behavior

- Ten Characteristics of an Effective Pluralistic Team (Chapter 1)

- Drawing Your Personality Profile (Chapter 2)
- Personality: What's Your Style? (Chapter 2)
- Analyzing Your Diversity Filter (Chapter 2)
- Dimensions of Diversity: Same and Different (Chapter 2)
- Assessing the Impact of Diversity on Our Team (Chapter 2)
- Keeping Your Filter Clean: Confronting Your Own Assumptions and Expectations (Chapter 2)
- Values: The Critical Underpinning (Chapter 4)
- Goals: Charting Our Course (Chapter 4)
- Defining Clear Goals and Objectives (Chapter 4)
- Measurement Criteria: Holding the Team's Feet to the Fire (Chapter 4)
- Creating a Mission: An Artful Process (Chapter 4)
- Trust Building on a Diverse Team (Chapter 5)
- Sharing Perspectives on the Team (Chapter 5)
- Trust on Our Team (Chapter 5)
- Being a Productive Team Member (Chapter 7)
- Who Am I? (Chapter 7)
- Establishing Norms on Our Team (Chapter 7)

Adolescence

Need at this stage: Clarify goals and directions; rethink norms that aren't working; utilize feedback mechanisms; assess team strengths, deal with conflict; and continue to build relationships

- Assessing the Team's Functioning: A Feedback Tool (Chapter 3)
- Team Busters (Chapter 3)
- Diversity Variables on the Team (Chapter 3)
- Trust Eroders on Your Team (Chapter 5)
- Interpersonal Problem-Solving Worksheet (Chapter 5)
- Identifying Behaviors Necessary for High Team Performance (Chapter 7)
- Improving Performance on the Team (Chapter 7)
- Diversity Assumptions Impacting Problem Solving on Your Team (Chapter 7)
- Dealing with Conflict as a Cultural Phenomenon (Chapter 7)
- Conflict: You and the Team (Chapter 7)

- Conflict Quiz (Chapter 7)
- Five-Step Guide to Resolving Conflict (Chapter 7)
- Diversity as It Relates to Phases of Team Growth and Development (Chapter 8)

Middle Age

Need at this stage: Use problem-solving and decision-making strategies; reality-test solutions; begin implementing strategies; continue strengthening interpersonal dynamics through shared work

- Developing Mutually Supportive Relationships on the Team (Chapter 5)
- Individual and Group: Maintaining the Balance (Chapter 5)
- Accountability for Team Tasks (Chapter 5)
- Group versus Individual: A Group Experience (Chapter 5)
- How Inclusive Is the Team Environment (Chapter 5)
- Structuring Work-Related Interactions for Task Accomplishment (Chapter 6)
- Defining a Problem on Your Team (Chapter 7)
- Diversity Assumptions Impacting Problem Solving on Your Team (Chapter 7)
- Blocks to Problem Solving (Chapter 7)
- Decision Making: What's Your Style? (Chapter 7)
- The Characteristics of an Effective Team Member on a Diverse Team (Chapter 7)
- Diagnosing Problem Spots (Chapter 8)

Maturity

Need at this stage: Finish implementation; get feedback, evaluate, monitor and follow up; continue to revise as needed; enjoy fellow team members

- Structuring Work-Related Interactions for Task Accomplishment (Chapter 6)
- Maximizing the Learning from Every Experience (Chapter 6)

- Cross-Training Self-Analysis (Chapter 6)
- New Team Member Integration (Chapter 8)
- Bringing New Members Up to Speed (Chapter 8)
- Team-Members, Celebration and Acknowledgment List (Chapter 8)
- Bringing Closure to a Work Team (Chapter 8)

DIAGNOSING PROBLEM SPOTS AND REDIRECTING THE TEAM

No matter how productive and cohesive your team is, at some point you'll face obstacles and, as marathoners say, "hit the wall." At times like these you need to retrench and redirect. We are frequently asked how we know we've hit problem spots, since so much teamwork involves problem solving. There are numerous indicators. Put a checkmark next to any that either currently do reflect or at some point have reflected your team.

WORKSHEET 8–3

Diagnosing Problem Spots

Directions: Check any problem spots that are visible on your team.

_____ The team is confused and has lost its way; it is unclear about what to do next.

_____ There is strong hostility between some members and an inability or unwillingness to move beyond it.

_____ The team's work seems repetitious and new ground is not being plowed.

_____ External circumstances have changed and many of the options that have been explored are no longer viable.

_____ The goal the team is working on is obsolete, or the team is fixing yesterday's problem.

_____ Attendance at problem-solving and decision-making sessions is dwindling and communication about attendance is spotty.

_____ The energy previously displayed in the group's work together is gone; in its place is apathy.

_____ People come late to meetings and leave early.

_____ Participation at meetings is uneven and unenthusiastic.

_____ Cliques and gossiping exist.

_____ People speak in languages other than English when they want
to leave people out.
_____ There's a caste system on the team in which some groups'
ideas carry more weight than others (e.g., men over women;
whites over people of color; managers over rank and file).
_____ People with accents no longer speak out because they feel
discounted.
_____ The team looks at high-impact organizational issues with a
narrow point of view.

There may be other indicators of roadblocks on your team. These
are just a few, but any of these could stall the team. When this happens,
there are several options for getting the team moving again. Going back
to the Infancy stage, for example, is one safe starting place if goal confusion is the issue. It will be very important to look at the team's goals
again. Consider the following task-related questions:

- Are the goals still meaningful?
- Do they need to be redefined?
- If they are still valid, what's the logjam?
- Is the problem about resource allocation?
- Is it a crunch time of year? Are you waiting for some
information that will impact your direction?
- Are people worn out? Have they been on this team
too long?
- On existing work teams, are downsizing realities or
rumors blocking concentration?

If the stall is more maintenance-related, pay attention to the human dynamics.

- Is there some interpersonal conflict that contami-
nates the whole team?
- Is there a general feeling of being overworked and
underappreciated?
- Does the team need some relationship building or
retreat away from the office?
- Are some team members upset about something having to do with the team, but unwilling to say what it is?
- Do norms and expectations need to be clarified?

Identifying whether the problem relates more to task or maintenance is the first item of business. Once you know that, your choices
become clearer. Look at Worksheet 8–2, match your team's obstacle to

the phase, and intervene appropriately. Whatever the stall at any stage, refer to the "Sequence of Team-building Activities" mentioned earlier in this chapter. This will provide a host of team interventions for you, any of which should propel the team forward. These will be particularly helpful on teams that have lost their steam, lost their way, or lost their clarity. Any intervention will break through the logjam.

INTEGRATING NEW TEAM MEMBERS; PHASING OUT LONGTIMERS

If you're on a functional work team, there will no doubt be turnover at some point, and if you're leading or serving as a member of a short-term project team or task force, there will also come a point in the life of that team where you phase out some members and bring in others. How you transition both old and new team members is very important, because any personnel change impacts the dynamics of the team. It will not be business as usual.

There are two essential points to consider when integrating and phasing out members:

1. Some formal process at a team meeting should acknowledge the changing of the guard and result in a recommitment to the norms.
2. Timing is critical.

Regarding point 1—that there needs to be a formal process—we have a recent example. Lee had been working with a team that was extremely cohesive and productive. This was a task-force team that was making recommendations about ways to make cultural changes. After 10 months, one person needed to leave and another was coming in her place. At the meeting before this change occurred, Lee brought the subject up and wanted to discuss what these changes would mean to team dynamics, particularly trust and openness.

It was easy to discuss the contributions of the person leaving. It was harder for the participants to discuss the new member because their perception was that any new person would meld into their environment, no matter who the person was. At the first meeting, they found it works a little differently. They were less comfortable and less open than they expected. They were also more tentative. When Lee challenged their consensus to see if all participants agreed with some of the new ideas suggested by the new member, who happened to be a top executive, some team members were forthcoming, while others were not. Their old ideas were hard-earned, but they said little. At the follow-up meeting, the group looked backward to understand its behavior and why members felt intimidated instead of engaging in their usual open process. Hindsight was helpful and served as a framework for moving forward. There's no magic tool, no one way to explore these issues. The important thing is that you do analyze and learn from your experience. Essentially, you are restating norms and expectations in a way that gives your new member input and also holds all members accountable.

Regarding the second point—that timing is critical—we like to equate team momentum and the energy of a rapidly moving train. There are stops made at appropriate, designated points, where people get on and off. However, when the train is going 125 miles an hour, that's not a good time to have someone try to jump on board. We have a pertinent example that clearly illustrates the second point. Anita was working with an ongoing task-force team in one organization when an employee indicated that she would like to participate. The team already had a rocky eight-month history. It had battled out issues together and was in the process of further exploring some alternatives and discarding others. But since it didn't want to hurt this person's feelings, curb her enthusiasm, or cut the team off from her viewpoints, the group agreed to bring her on board.

Anita had strong reservations about accepting a new member at this point. However, she knew that ultimately the team had to be given the opportunity to accept responsibility for its own choice, so she honored the team's decision.

What happened next was probably the most important lesson and insight about timing the team members ever received. Bringing on a new member was just short of disaster. Every time an issue was brought up, the new member inadvertently plowed up old ground. How was she to know that they'd "been there, done that"? The frustration came when her comments moved them backwards to old, already settled discussions. But the good news is that the members who thought they weren't a team, but only a loose-knit group that felt it had accomplished nothing, suddenly got a fresh picture of themselves. The new team member became a mirror for a group that now saw just how much progress it had made and how much of a team it had become.

There is a mostly happy ending to this story, and it involves the team being held accountable for its decision. The members believed that this new situation was totally unworkable. Anita told them that once they identified a spokesperson who would talk to the new team member, she would coach the spokesperson on how to explain, with grace and a considerable amount of face-saving, why the timing was wrong and how coming on board at this point would prevent the new person from having a real voice and influence while also keeping the team from moving forward. The issue was not the person they were trying to integrate, but how much old ground they'd have to cover again. And no matter how hard the team tried to bring this person up to speed by sharing an analysis of all options, she had missed numerous thoughtful and thorough discussions. There's no way to recapture that context, no matter how diligently someone tries to "tutor" a newcomer.

So what does this mean for you? It means that there are points in the process of team development, particularly on task-force or project teams, when it may be more harmful than helpful to integrate someone new. But there are also some natural closure points along the way when bringing someone on board can be very valuable. Newcomers bring a different perspective and fresh enthusiasm. They come to the team missing the bruises others may have accumulated in the process of doing the job. New blood and ideas are very worthwhile—just be cognizant of timing.

One tool, the "New and Existing Team Member Integration" form, Worksheet 8–4, will help new and existing members understand each other better and agree on new norms or recommit to already established ones. Have all team members, new and old, fill out the part of the form that applies to them first. Then a team leader or facilitator needs to go around the room, round-robin style, and, using an easel and a flip chart, replicate the worksheet and fill in each quadrant with the group's collective data. If items are said more than once, the best way to indicate repetitions is by making a checkmark with a different-colored marker. Once you have all the data on the flip chart for everyone to see, the content can be discussed. The discussion is best directed toward reinforcing those behaviors or norms that have already made the team effective and extinguishing or avoiding any that raise major concerns. The team leader can ask people to end with a public commitment to one thing they'll do to ensure effective teamwork.

There is no doubt that any team member who transitions into an ongoing team will have missed a lot in defining the issues, gathering information, proposing solutions, and working with fellow team members. The latter subject can be dealt with in Worksheet 8–4. But it will

WORKSHEET 8–4

New and Existing Team Member Integration

Directions: Depending on whether you are an existing or a new team member, fill out the appropriate boxes below with your most thoughtful and honest responses.

	Concerns about Changing Team Composition	Behaviors I Need for Effective Teamwork
Existing Team Member Concerns about Integrating a New Team Member	Example: Cover old ground; will waste time	Example: Get honest feedback
New Member Concerns about Becoming an Effective Team Member	Example: No shared history; new kid on the block; don't fit in	Example: Have my ideas count

also be helpful to new team members, less frustrating to existing members, and more productive for the organization if there is a vehicle for bringing new members up to speed quickly. Worksheet 8–5 can help in that process.

Although there is no way for new team members to ever fully capture the discussions they've missed, this worksheet and the discussion it elicits can encapsulate the team's major ideas and suggestions. Furthermore, meeting with one longtime team member provides an opportunity for relationship building and a more thorough and complex discussion of the issues than this limited worksheet can ever provide. The tool serves its constructive purpose as a catalyst for integrating a new team member.

WORKSHEET 8–5

Bringing New Members Up to Speed

Directions: Have an existing team member meet with the new team member to fill out this worksheet and to bring the new member up to speed.

1. The issues this team is working on are defined as:

   _____
   _____
   _____

2. Necessary information already gathered regarding each issue involves:

   _____
   _____
   _____

3. Solutions or actions being considered are:

   _____
   _____
   _____

4. The pros and cons regarding each of these solutions or actions are ...

Pros	Cons
_____	_____
_____	_____
_____	_____
_____	_____

APPROPRIATELY ACKNOWLEDGING COMPLETIONS AND MOVING ON

Ritual is important on teams. It kindles emotional ties and a sense that what the team does is important. It's also an opportunity for renewing commitment. Rituals on a team that has accomplished little will be empty, but ceremonies that celebrate real, genuine accomplishments touch people. Hans Selye, in his book *Stress without Distress*, and Douglas

McGregor, who discusses "Y" assumptions in his "X-Y Theory" in his book, *The Human Side of Enterprise,* take the position that humankind derives meaning from work. It can be a source of deep satisfaction and pride. Good team leaders build on this satisfaction.

On a team that has truly met its performance objectives, the individual and collective achievements will be worth acknowledging, and so will the process that people went through toward that end. Individual recognition is also important for people who leave the team early. The following suggestions are worth considering:

- A symbolic toast, where everyone on the team publicly recognizes this person for the unique skills and qualities he or she brought to the team
- A picture collage taken over time of team members engaged in various activities. This can be mounted on cardboard and used as a greeting card, with people writing nice tributes. It can also be framed.
- Personal gifts or mementos, such as a gift certificate at the local bookstore for avid readers or a CD of Beethoven's Fifth for the classical music lover. Money is not the intended measure; noticing unique interests is.
- A potluck dinner or visit to a local restaurant to celebrate and have time together away from work
- A skit, a poem, or a tribute, such as a calligraphied list entitled *Our Favorite Memories of . . .*

Individual endings are one thing, but there are whole teams that phase out after a specified amount of time. Depending on the satisfaction tied to the achievement of performance objectives and the enjoyment of the process itself, you will find varying passions about the endings and whatever constitutes completion.

It is important to have some time set aside to mark the work the team did together. If the team accomplished its goals, surely carving out a small piece of time to validate the learning and salute the job completed is an important way to close one experience and send people on to their next ones. At the very least, there is something in the experience itself that will apply to future team ventures, so marking the growth brings closure and enables you to move on feeling complete.

Some team experiences, however, are more than just getting the job done. They are peak moments for team members, and the attachments are deep and the results whale size. On teams like this, which are unique, there is a sadness and loss at reaching an ending. People on these teams don't need just to mark the experience, they need to grieve its ending and mourn the loss of something that was so meaningful. Once they do that, they too can move on. They won't necessarily duplicate that experience again, but they can have other satisfying jobs. We remember when Los Angeles hosted the Olympics in 1984. Most people associated with their respective teams and tasks still talk about that experience reverentially. We recall Peter Ueberroth saying he'd "been to the top of the mountain." He'd have other satisfying adventures in the future, not the least of which was serving as baseball commissioner, but directing the Olympics stood out for him as unequaled.

Moving on from special events like that is difficult. The important thing to recognize is that there must be a formal team closure so that you can fully feel the value and gifts gained, truly appreciate the empty spaces left in the ending, and thank one another, individually and collectively, for a job well done. We use the following process for that purpose. It has several parts and takes a couple of hours if you're going to fully milk the learning and give people a sense of completion.

For starters, the facilitator needs to set the tone and objectives. To so, offer comments to the effect of: "We've worked together for a year now, and as we end this experience, it's important to acknowledge how we've grown and what we've accomplished and learned, individually and collectively. It's also important to see how the organization benefits from our work and how we will use what we've learned here in future efforts." The facilitator then puts two open-ended statements on a flip chart and has everybody answer each:

1. One way I am clearly different as a result of this experience is . . .
2. One thing I'd change if we could redo our work together is . . .

You can have people give their responses publicly one at a time, or have each person complete both at once. Either way, it will be important to hear the different perspectives and talk about them. Once each team member completes each of these two statements, the facilitator distributes the handout, "Bringing Closure to a Work Team," Worksheet 8–6.

Each team member fills out this form individually. You will probably need 20 or 30 minutes for people to respond on their own work

WORKSHEET 8–6

Bringing Closure to a Work Team

Directions: Think about your experiences on this team, then respond to all of the open-ended statements.

Product

1. My original hopes and expectations were:

2. My realized hopes and expectations were:

3. The greatest gains (potential or actualized) for the organization are:

4. My biggest concerns that still exist are:

5. I'm proudest of:

Process

1. The clearest, most worthwhile part of the experience was:

2. The time of greatest confusion during our work together was:

3. I learned from the confusing times that:

4. My biggest frustration with the whole process was:

5. My biggest gain or lesson from the process, which will translate to other experiences at the organization, was:

Personal Growth

1. My greatest satisfaction is:

2. My most important lesson was:

3. My biggest contribution was:

4. The greatest gains for me personally were:

5. One thing I will never see the same is:

sheets. Once they have done so, break up the team into small groups that will rotate for three different discussions. The first discussion will focus on the statements under the Product heading. After the members discuss them in small groups, the facilitator picks a few of the statements to discuss as a whole group. When finished with that discussion, team members rotate so that the small-group compositions are different, and repeat the process for the second set of five statements. After that discussion, repeat the same process, with a newly rotated group, for the section labeled Personal Growth. In all three cases, you combine small-group discussion with whole-group discussion, working toward learning, insight, and awareness to be applied to future team experiences. For what it's worth, one team that just finished this process had a very memorable and, for some, life-changing experience accomplishing its task. After we finished discussing what a positive and fruitful process this was for the members, Lee asked if they could enumerate the reasons. The ones they gave are shown below. See if any of theirs match what happens on your team.

- Confidentiality was honored and maintained.
- Team members never attacked one another.
- All viewpoints and people were respected.
- People were comfortable sharing any idea.
- Team members had learned from previous team experiences.
- They stayed "in the moment" by discussing what they felt about any idea as soon as they understood their feelings and reactions.
- Team members recognized (and were honest enough to acknowledge having) their own agendas.
- All members were open-minded.
- They valued intuitive processes, not just analytical ones.
- They are *leaderful,* meaning they all have leadership capabilities.

When this process is finished, the final closure involves having each team member fill out Worksheet 8–7.

WORKSHEET 8–7

Team Members' Celebration and Acknowledgment List

Directions: Write the name of each team member in one column and a strength or characteristic you want to acknowledge in the other.

Team Member	Characteristic to Celebrate or Acknowledge
1. _____	_____
2. _____	_____
3. _____	_____
4. _____	_____
5. _____	_____
6. _____	_____

As leader, tell team members that they will be sharing these acknowledgments about everyone publicly when all participants are finished filling out their sheets. You might even suggest that people copy down the words that others say about them, since the qualities saluted will make people feel good. You may get some resistance initially from those who feel this process is awkward. Most people aren't used to telling others in a semipublic forum that they admire or appreciate them. But this exercise not only feels good, it works. It is one of our "never fails," and we have yet to hear people complain because they received too many compliments from fellow team members. It's a wonderful ending to a team experience.

While there is no foolproof way to build and develop teams, there are stages of team growth and specific strategies to utilize at each stage of development. If you pay attention to task and maintenance behaviors, if you acknowledge the realities of timing, and if you're open to accommodating and capitalizing on the diversity on your team, you will not only meet your performance objectives, you'll probably exceed them and have a satisfying experience as you do so. Leadership is a critical variable in this process, and that's the next item on our agenda.

Chapter Nine

The Critical Role of Leader

"People seldom improve when they have no other model but themselves to copy after."

Goldsmith

In the last few hundred pages, we have discussed ways to build, shape, refine, and create productive, high-performing teams. We have talked about the many variables that impact the growth, development, and productivity of effective work groups. Factors such as group size, knowledge about cross-cultural norms, attention to diversity issues, an emphasis on task and maintenance behaviors, a clear understanding of the group's values and a clear definition of mission and goals were among the subjects on which we focused. Woven through all discussions about building cohesive teams were comments about the role of the leader. Sometimes points about leader behavior were implicit. At other times, they were explicit, with leadership discussed in the context of a specific tool. This chapter, on the other hand, focuses specifically on leadership. It considers the critical role of leader on diverse teams, delineating leader behaviors that are helpful on any team but absolutely essential on pluralistic ones. And we will share a new model of leadership that we believe is appropriate for the times in which we live and for the teams that you are leading.

VARIABLES IMPACTING LEADERSHIP

The literature on what constitutes effective leadership is voluminous. For years writers and thinkers such as James MacGregor Burns, Douglas McGregor, and Kenneth Blanchard have provoked us with thoughts on the components of effective leadership. More recently, Marilyn Loden and Judy Rosener have factored in the diversity issue by looking at differences in the

214

leadership styles of men and women. Effective leadership models and definitions are as fluid as the world we live in and are significantly shaped by the following six variables:

1. *Degree of control.* No matter how broad the vision or how high the authority, there are always limits to the amount of control a person has. Whether you're the president of the United States answering to the American people and negotiating with Congress, a CEO who has to answer to shareholders and boards of directors, or a team leader who reports to managers and executives, no leader is a free agent. Part of the challenge of effective leadership comes in influencing others so that your control over situations is greater. However, even the most articulate and inspiring salesperson for a particular cause or position is often at the mercy of world events, the global economy, or even natural phenomena such as fires, floods, and earthquakes. Leadership is always exercised within boundaries, and it is the wise leader who pushes where she can and understands when she can't.

2. *Speed of change.* The speed of change at the end of this century is both lightening-fast and frightening. It strikes with swiftness and constancy. Obsolescence is built into everything. The newest high-tech accomplishments are continuously evolving, upgraded, and outdated. Furthermore, stable institutions no longer represent the security they used to, and the relationship between employer and employee has undergone radical change. It is in this mercurial environment that leaders must help employees come to terms with rapid change and adaptation as a lifestyle and survival skill. It is also a business competency. Role-modeling acceptance of and comfort with change is step one.

3. *Maturity and competence of staff.* The answer to how a leader should lead is, "It depends." Significant variables that impact leader behavior are the maturity level and competence of staff. Employees just learning a new task will be led very differently than one that has been doing the same thing for years. The evolutionary leadership model shared later in this chapter will show you the different leader behaviors required to match the maturity stage of the followers.

4. *Time.* This is the resource, universally, of which there is a chronic shortage. For leaders, it takes time to teach employees when they need new skills, it takes time to empathize when someone needs support, it takes time to coach when a team participant needs feedback—

and these are just a few of the essential leader behaviors needed to build effective personnel. There is a difference between micromanaging tasks and building people. The role of leaders on teams, as we view it, is to facilitate task accomplishment. The surest way to do so is to invest in people, but it is a labor-intensive, time-consuming responsibility. There is no shortcut, nor is there any substitute for investing in the development of your team members. It doesn't distract leaders from the job—it *is* the job.

5. *Resources.* It is certainly easier to be an effective leader when you have resources to allocate, whether you provide money for a new information system; training that the staff needs; or decent, spacious facilities so people can do their work. It is hard to be competitive and effective in any marketplace without the many resources needed to keep the organization or team moving forward. Like time, the amount of money will always be insufficient, but there are some bottom-line resources in any organization beneath which you cannot go if you have any intention of being effective. Determine what the "must haves" are and then remember the aphorism about being penny-wise and pound foolish.

6. *External environment.* We touched on this issue briefly when we mentioned the number one leadership variable, the degree of control. Some specific external environmental factors that can impact leadership are the following: global and domestic competition in your industry's marketplace; the strength or weakness of the dollar; and the economy. All of these can impact risk taking, decision making, and regulations (or lack thereof). The external environment can raise union issues, influence the stock market, or alter world events. These are variables that can influence the output, cost, and productivity of your goods and services, but they often leave the leader in a reactive rather then proactive position. There are always choices, however, and frequently it is in the minimal- or poor-choice environment that leadership is most severely tested and most brilliantly demonstrated.

Take some time to explore your perceptions about leadership by working through the following activity on Worksheet 9–1 with one of your leader colleagues.

WORKSHEET 9–1

Leadership and You

Directions: Think of yourself in situations when you are leading your team. Pair up with another leader whom you trust and with whom you can communicate easily. Take turns sharing your responses to these open-ended statements.

1. I lead best when . . .
2. When the followers don't follow, I . . .
3. I think a strong leader should . . .
4. I feel least confident as a leader when . . .
5. I'm most successful in getting others to follow when . . .
6. The most difficult aspect of leading a diverse team is . . .
7. I'd be more effective as a leader if . . .
8. I'd describe my leadership style as . . .
9. My followers would describe my leadership style as . . .
10. When my followers make a mistake or have problems, I . . .
11. As a leader I'd like to be more . . .
12. I get most frustrated when my followers . . .
13. My followers expect me to . . .
14. My leaders expect me to . . .
15. What I like best about leading others is . . .
16. I admire leaders who . . .
17. A nontraditional leader I respect is . . .
18. A famous leader I don't respect is . . .   because . . .
19. One area in which I'd like to grow as a leader is . . .
20. Two examples of feedback (one positive and one negative) that I have received about my leadership are. . .

Once you have shared your responses to these statements, discuss the following questions:

- What seem to be your greatest assets as a leader of diverse teams?
- What are your biggest stumbling blocks?
- What can you do to develop yourself to be even more effective?

Succeeding sections of this chapter will give you additional insight into these questions.

QUALITIES OF EFFECTIVE LEADERSHIP

Effective leadership, like beauty, may lie in the eye of the beholder or, in this case, the follower. However, there are some qualities that have withstood the test of time in a variety of circumstances, and it is those we offer as important in creating an effective pluralistic team. No one leader has all of these qualities, certainly not at the same time. And the best leaders are not static. They model the changes and growth they try to develop in their team members. In Worksheet 9–2 check any that you believe you demonstrate most of the time. They demonstrate the following ten behaviors.

1. *Effective leaders have self-esteem and confidence, which creates a nondefensive, open environment.* This sense of wholeness and confidence is important in any environment. But it is more so in a pluralistic one because perceptions of unequal treatment and conflict take on extra volatility when the racial, ethnic, and gender mix of the group is complex. Without a solid foundation of self-confidence, it is difficult for the leader to remain nondefensive and maintain an even tone of voice in dealing with hot spots. The self-esteem and confidence a leader feels is broadcast and extended to others. It creates a feeling of security and stability on which the team can build group confidence.

2. *Effective leaders have a vision that generates enthusiasm and commitment.* Former President George Bush talked about "that vision thing." Not having one was part of the bad rap he faced in the 1992 elections, and that phrase was proof positive to students of leadership that he didn't have any. On the other hand, his predecessor, Ronald Reagan, is almost always described as a master leader because he had a clear picture of where he wanted to take the country and he engendered enough support to accomplish most of his goals. Reagan's "vision thing" was crystal clear and was a key aspect of his leadership.

   Above all else, distinguished leaders earn their reputations because they have committed and passionate followers. Strong leader–followers relationships won't occur in the absence of a decisive vision. Painting a picture of where you want to lead a team and then sharing it with those who can help you achieve the goals imbue team members with a sense of purpose and clarity about why, beyond a paycheck, team members even bother to show up for work. The truth is that leaders with unarticulated visions unwittingly squander opportunities to make the difference they hope to and in fact can make—if they capitalize on their positions visually.

3. *Effective leaders expand their knowledge and awareness of culture and its influence, as well as other diversity-related issues.* Diversity, as we have been saying throughout this book, includes everyone. It's not a black thing, a gay thing, or a woman's thing. A leader who wants to maximize output and help *all* people grow and contribute understands that diversity includes white men too, discusses cultural norms with team members, and stops perpetuating the myth that you have to be a person of color to have a culture. An effective leader doesn't advocate any particular group's position, but understands or is willing to explore issues and customs of members from all group. "It's the modeling and openness, stupid" to paraphrase campaign manager James Carville from the 1992 presidential campaign.

4. *Effective leaders catalyze support for the collective common good, not just parochial self-interest.* Real leadership gets beyond enlightened (or even unenlightened) self-interest and helps followers minimize the myopia so common in organizational and national life these days. In the "what's in it for me" era we live in, it takes courage, integrity, and vision to stake out positions that go for the larger good, often at some sacrifice to self and others. Beyond courage, integrity, and vision, it takes leadership to advocate positions, often unpopular, that ask people to stretch and grow, be less selfish and more generous, be less narrow and more compassionate. It is risky behavior, but that is just the stuff of leadership legends. (May we discover more of them!)

5. *Effective leaders maintain a sense of humor and perspective.* This is sometimes very tough to do when it appears that it's "Chicken Little and the sky is falling" time. We have a very recent example. As we finish this book, the November 1994 elections have just ended. It's no secret that, however you interpret these election results, they were not an endorsement of President Bill Clinton's presidency to date. One of his areas of disagreement with Republicans pertains to term limits. Although the president believes term limits are built in because voters can retire any elected official, Republicans want a

formal policy limiting terms. The day after the election, White House reporters stated that the president, joking about having to work with an adversarial Republican Congress, said that term limits were starting to look more attractive. He may have lost a lot of things on November 8, but his sense of humor wasn't one of them. It can make difficult situations a little easier, and it also helps team members realize that what they do may be meaningful and important, but it doesn't have to be dour or earth shaking. Humor can be risky, but when not directed at others' expense, it has real value as a salve and a catharsis.

6. *Effective leaders are trustworthy and dependable.* Leadership is, ultimately, about trust. We have talked about trust before in this book. Part of what makes trust so complicated cross-culturally is that it is defined and demonstrated differently. With that in mind, since this book is written for domestic audiences and their work teams, we believe strongly that in mainstream American culture, your word is your bond. Being able to count on someone's performance, being able to predict that the leader is a straight shooter is invaluable. When conversations can be taken on faith, most team members can deal with, work around, or problem-solve most any issue. The other bonus regarding trustworthiness is that when the leader is perceived to be trustworthy, no one spends time on parking-lot and restroom agendas trying to get the real story, because the real story has already been told.

7. *Effective leaders have an internal standard of excellence.* This quality may be intangible, but it becomes noticeable over time when people work together in an organization. Part of why it's noteworthy is because in most organizations, people are afraid of rejection and risk, so they let others set the standards.

It can be invigorating and sometimes frustrating to have someone use his or her own standard of excellence if it becomes an obstruction to the team. It is possible that a perfectionist who imposes perfectionism on others, for example, would ultimately have the effect of dampening people's motivation, since many might feel that whatever they do isn't good enough. This scenario is possible and would not yield a positive outcome.

However, try this picture on for size. Imagine a leader who keeps challenging herself to do better and to exceed her own expectations. She isn't perfect and doesn't expect herself to be. But she won't take an honest day's pay for less than a full commitment to excellence or to continued growth and improvement. This leader not only role-models high standards, but also works to clear away obstacles that get in the way of those she leads. She rewards people for setting their own high standards within the context of the team objective. We like this picture and have seen it work well. We hope you have too.

8. *Effective leaders are responsive and empathetic toward others.* For those of you who read the word *empathetic* and worried that we're turning the work environment into a therapy session, relax. We aren't. What we are saying, though, is that we humans have both head and heart. We respond to the intellectual, idea part of the job, but we also respond with a strong emotional component to the things that happen to us and to others. Our emotional responses are based on the interpretations we make about events, and those interpretations aren't always valid. But valid or not, they are real. Good leaders are willing to invest a little time in listening to and empathizing with team members about these issues. Much good can come from this. Sometimes venting frustrations can be both helpful and cleansing. But a good leader isn't only a passive listener. There is also a chance, once people vent, to instruct, teach, and challenge. There is an opportunity to help people see the other side of the coin. After you've listened and empathized, you can legitimately ask, "What are you going to do about it?" Being responsive builds leader–team member relationships. It also builds more empowered people.

9. *Effective leaders match their words with their deeds.* Authenticity is not a word frequently used to describe effective leadership, but we think it could and should be. In the broader culture, this thought or behavior is commonly attributed to author and business consultant Tom Peters and his "walk the talk" mentality. Ralph Waldo Emerson, in the mid-1800s, said, "I can't hear what you're saying because what you are rings so loudly in my ears." Translation? If your words and deeds don't match, people will believe the deeds. A good leader has consistency between the two. It is worth noting that when we are asked to conduct focus groups around diversity issues, what comes up almost every time relates more to excellent management than diversity. It is the complaint that management has a double standard. We cannot even estimate in dollars the damage to companies when this is the perception. Leadership excellence presumes and necessitates no ambiguity between what you say and what you do.

This authenticity is more noticeable on sticky issues. We remember when John Sculley was CEO of Apple Computer. The Gay and Lesbian Coalition in his organization actively pushed for same-sex partner benefits. The issue had not yet been resolved, but it was being explored. In the meantime, Sculley's leadership was evident by his presence at the Gay and Lesbian March on Washington in 1993. He did not have the company of many other CEOs at this event, but he was there, walking his talk. For him it was a human rights issue and he didn't duck.

10. *Effective leaders are aware of their own feelings and reactions to interpersonal experiences and try to maintain objectivity.* Just because you're a leader at some level in the organization doesn't mean you're not human. You don't relinquish your right to feel things deeply, to be hurt, to feel joy and pride and/or a host of other responses on life's emotional palette.

But what it does mean is that effective leaders know their own issues, and are aware of buttons that can be pushed and predictable reactions that are their patterns. They are, to quote a member of one of Lee Gardenswartz's teams, "in the moment." By understanding themselves and their responses, they have a greater chance of maintaining objectivity. Doing so will be a real plus. It will lead to less defensiveness, a more open climate, a sense that one can suggest anything and it will be given a hearing, and a belief that the team has a leader whole enough and healthy enough to listen to others, value their views, and defer to their suggestions when appropriate. All of these benefits can't happen when you react out of your feelings but don't know that you're doing so, why you're doing so, and that it can have harmful effects.

These 10 overall leadership qualities are worth striving for. On your good days, you probably demonstrate them all. On those bad days we all have, you may violate your own standards of leadership excellence, being unable to respond in any way but impatient, irritable, and judgmental. The best of leaders occasionally have those days. But what you are striving for is to behave consistently in ways that bring out the best in you and others, so that on your bad days, team members will give you the high standard of trust, empathy, patience, and responsiveness you usually give them. Take a look at Worksheet 9–2 and make a commitment to three of the behaviors that, if improved, might make the most difference in your leadership effectiveness. Use that information to fill out Worksheet 9–3, then get feedback from someone whose judgment you value and trust. This person should have a sense of your strengths and weaknesses and a clear sense of you as a leader. Seek feedback on your responses. Are you on the right track in terms of how you see yourself? Have you missed some pictures of yourself that feedback from a trusted colleague or follower can fill in? One caveat here: Make sure you get feedback from those you respect, and make requests for feedback as concrete as possible. The more specific you are, the more helpful that feedback will be.

WORKSHEET 9–2

Essential Leader Behaviors for Effective Teams

Directions: Place a checkmark next to any of the behaviors on the list below which you believe you demonstrate most of the time.

_____	1.	I have esteem and confidence . . .
_____	2.	I have vision . . .
_____	3.	I expand my knowledge . . .
_____	4.	I catalyze support for . . .
_____	5.	I maintain a sense . . .
_____	6.	I am trustworthy . . .
_____	7.	I have an internal . . .
_____	8.	I am responsible and . . .
_____	9.	I match my words with . . .
_____	10.	I am aware of my own . . .

LEADERSHIP: AN EVOLUTION

"It ain't the way it used to be" is a cry heard in businesses across the country. As society has changed, so has organizational life, and the role of the leaders has had to keep pace. Once the captain of the ship who kept it on course, today's leader faces very different expectations and requirements.

Two fundamental shifts in the expectations of the workforce have transformed the job of leader during this century. The first is the movement away from top-down, command-and-control management to an emphasis on bottom-up, team-based, employee-driven control. More and more, decisions are made, problems solved, goals set, and responsibility

WORKSHEET 9–3

Improvement of Overall Leadership Characteristics

Directions: List in the boxes on the left three leadership characteristics that if improved would make the most difference in your effectiveness as a leader. Then list on the right actions you can take to improve and develop that characteristic.

Characteristics	Things I Can Do to Improve
Example: Words and deeds match	Example: Confront homophobic jokes

taken at lower levels within the organization. The inefficiency of a top-heavy management structure, a complex chain of command, and many layers in the hierarchy is giving way to more employee control and team empowerment.

Workers expect to have more autonomy, to have their input listened to, and to be more than just a means of production and the hands that get things done. Both employees and organizations know that workers themselves hold the key to increased productivity and innovation. It is this fundamental belief that propels this shift to greater and greater employee control.

The second powerfully impacting change is the move away from conformity and toward greater diversity. Demographics clearly drive this shift, but so do social attitudes. As the makeup of the workforce changes, with more women, people of color, and immigrants entering the workplace, diversity has a greater presence in organizations from coast to coast. However, it is not only a shift in numbers, but also one in attitude and expectations that propel this growing attention to diversity. Today's employees are not satisfied to blend into the melting pot, to assimilate by adopting the behaviors and methods of the old guard. Rather than make a blanket adaptation to the existing norms and policies, employees expect the adjustment to be a two-way street. Although anyone coming into a new situation clearly understands the need to learn the ropes in order to succeed, today's employee also expects the organization to respond with some flexibility as well. Newcomers bring new perspectives, different approaches, and more ideas that can spur creativity and reenergize the environment. However, these benefits of diversity only accrue if organizations capitalize on the variations employees bring. If "different" equates to only "less than" or "deficient," then the push will continue to be for sameness.

The increasing concern for diversity comes not only from employees, but also from the organization. Although workers want to be recognized for their uniqueness and see their differences as adding value to the organization, companies see that when diversity is capitalized on rather than suppressed, it is an asset. Increased creativity, greater commitment, and higher morale, as well as decreased turnover, absenteeism, and grievances are a few of the benefits. These two changes—increasing employee control and greater concern for diversity—have propelled an evolution in leadership.

The Four Roles of Leaders

Leaders aren't leaders without followers. Leadership rests on a relationship with followers that implies mutual benefit. As James MacGregor Burns, in his seminal book *Leadership*, says, "Leaders and those led have a relationship not only of power, but of mutual needs, aspirations, and values." Leaders continue to lead as long as followers get their needs met through the relationship. It is critical, then, to look at the connection between the needs of followers and the leader behaviors that fulfill those needs. Followers' needs are not static. They evolve over time and change due to both internal and external circumstances. Let's take a look at the role of the leader and how it responds to different follower needs.

FIGURE 9–1

Leaders and Followers
An Evolution

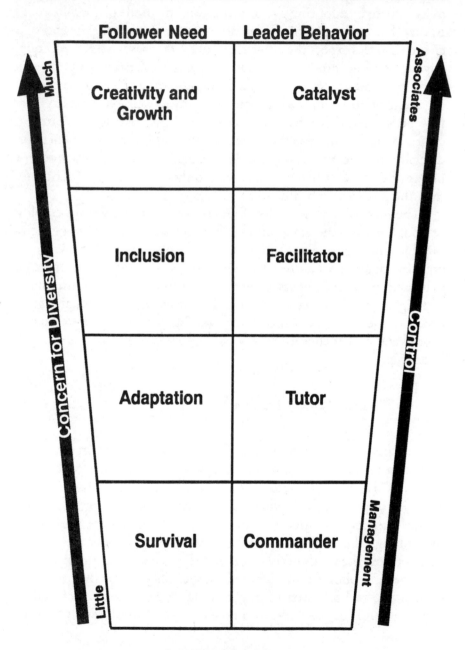

Leader as commander.   Command-and-control leadership works well when survival is at stake. Generals on the battlefield, surgeons in the operating room, and managers during a crisis are called on to use this kind of leadership. Followers during these times may have little concern for diversity and little desire to take control. Their focus is on getting through dangerous or particularly unsettling, confusing times. During the January 1994 earthquake in Southern California, many leaders were called on to take command of the situation in their organization, giving directives and making unilateral decisions that were both necessary and accepted because of the emergency status. These methods would have undoubtedly met with much resistance had they been used during normal or nonemergency times.

Leader as tutor.   Leaders are also teachers who show employees how to negotiate through the system. When followers need to adapt to the organization, the leader can be most effective when acting as tutor, guiding them through the land mines, explaining the informal organization, or giving them feedback about behaviors that may be holding them back. In this leadership mode, the follower's diversity is less an asset than a liability and the emphasis is on adaptation. During periods when the motto of assimilation "When in Rome, do as the Romans do" is the expectation, the leader can be the best guide to Rome.

Leader as facilitator.   When followers have a sense of the organization and the rules, they begin to express a growing need for inclusion in decision making and problem solving. They recognize that their views, while perhaps somewhat different from the prevailing "way we do it around here," are valuable, and they want a voice in changing those ways. It is at this point that the leader functions best as facilitator. In this role, the leader solicits input and encourages staff members to identify problems and solve them and to share in both decision making and accountability. As facilitator, the leader leads from behind rather than in front, encouraging employees to participate in the control.

Leader as catalyst.   Employees will eventually move beyond giving input about existing conditions and fixing problems. They will want to flex their own creativity and growth muscles, to see beyond "what is" to "what could be." This need calls for a fourth kind of leader—the catalyst. In this style the leader stimulates deeper thinking by staff members, allows them to push the boundaries, and helps them venture into uncharted territories. In this mode the leader has solid confidence in the thinking and decisions of staff members and trusts their ability and commitment; hence, this mode gives the most control to employees. In this mode, the staff is set free, and in fact is prodded to grow and create and to take the organization to the next level. This mode requires great trust between leader and follower and a high level of confidence both in self and other. Catalytic leaders have faith in the ability of the staff to take control and a belief in the value of the diversity they bring.

Each of these leadership modes can be effective in some situations and ineffective in others, depending on the followers' needs in particular situations. However, today's societal and organizational shifts point to a movement up the ladder, toward catalytic leadership.

The following questionnaire in Worksheet 9–4 will give you a chance to find out which is your preferred leadership style.

WORKSHEET 9–4

Leader: What's Your Type?

Directions: Circle the letter of the response most true for you.

1. As a leader, I'm at my best when I'm:
    a. giving directions.
    b. showing people how.
    c. helping the staff find their own solutions.
    d. creating opportunities for people to grow.

2. When the going gets rough, I:
    a. jump in and take charge.
    b. coach the staff through the rough times.
    c. support employees in working their way through it.
    d. trust the staff to find creative approaches to dealing with it.

3. When I'm challenged, I:
    a. explain my reasons or choices.
    b. spend time showing people why my ideas are valid.
    c. listen to the feedback from my challenger and work with him or her to find a mutually agreeable solution.
    d. stop, listen, and learn from my challengers.

4. When things are going well and productivity is high, I:
    a. keep tabs on things.
    b. watch for problems so I can help out.
    c. ask questions that keep the staff looking ahead to prevent problems.

d. challenge the staff to think bigger or try something new.
5. When staff is in the doldrums, I:
  a. try to energize them.
  b. find out what's wrong and work them through it.
  c. get the staff together to discuss what's going on.
  d. trust that the staff will work its own way through it.

6. When there's conflict on staff, I:
  a. jump in to resolve it.
  b. talk people through it.
  c. act as a third-party intervener, mediating the difficulty.
  d. use it as a growth experience for me and my staff.

7. If I don't like what's going on, I:
  a. tell people what I see is wrong.
  b. show people how to correct the problem.
  c. get the staff together to figure out what's wrong and how to fix it.
  d. allow the staff to learn from the consequences.

8. When people come to me with questions, I:
  a. give them answers.
  b. show them how to get the answers.
  c. get them to figure out how to get the answer.
  d. help them reframe the question or issue.

9. I see problems on the staff as something:
  a. I need to fix.
  b. I need to show the staff how to fix.
  c. I need to help the staff figure out how to fix.
  d. that needs more investigation and questioning.

10. My concept of the ideal leader is:
  a. one who takes responsibility and is clear and direct in laying out expectations.
  b. one who is a role model and teacher, showing the staff how to do things better.
  c. one who gets the staff to take part in setting goals, planning actions, making decisions, and solving problems.
  d. one who asks questions, pushes limits, and gets the staff to see things differently.

Scoring: Count up the number of *a, b, c,* and *d* responses —

_____	*a* responses = Commander
_____	*b* responses = Tutor
_____	*c* responses = Facilitator
_____	*d* responses = Catalyst

The greater the number of responses in any one category, the more you utilize that style of leadership.

What does your score tell you? Which is your favored, knee-jerk style? What other styles do you use? You might get interesting feedback by having some of your employees take this questionnaire about you. How do they see you? How close is their perception of your style to your own?

Now consider the effects of your style. When and where does it work to your advantage? How well does it suit your followers' needs? When does it work against you and become an inhibitor of productivity or teamwork? What can you do to develop your ability to expand your range of leadership styles?

The Qualities of a Catalytic Leader

Catalytic leadership is called for when there is high concern for diversity, a high degree of bottom-up rather than top-down control, and when employees desire opportunities for growth and creativity. These three conditions are becoming more and more apparent as organizations approach the next century. What qualities do leaders need in order to be able to deal effectively with a wide variety of employees and to give staff members the autonomy to take on responsibility and control? Seven qualities at the core of catalytic leadership emerge:

1. Tolerance for ambiguity
2. Valuing differences
3. Capitalizing on change
4. Belief in the wisdom of the team
5. Maintaining a balance between product and process
6. Building responsibility and accountability
7. Inviting, using, and giving feedback effectively

1. *Tolerance for ambiguity.*   Because leaders who act as catalysts operate in uncharted territory, the ability to live with the unknown is essential. Allowing employees to innovate and take charge requires a leap of faith. Diversity tests this ability further. Leading groups of staff made up of individuals from different backgrounds, with wide ranges in priorities, values, needs, and preferences, presents more questions than answers. Catalytic leaders are able to create new ways of responding to these exciting yet challenging situations because they have the inner strength to tolerate the anxiety of not having an immediate answer. They can live in limbo and confusion without pushing for premature solutions.

2. *Valuing differences.*   When the leader sees differences as an asset to the team, a diverse staff is well led. However, different is often viewed as substandard or, as one seminar participant called it, the "B team." The subtle, and sometimes not so subtle, assumption that differences equate to deficiencies forms a powerful stumbling block for anyone wanting to lead today's multifaceted staffs. Catalytic leaders are those who build on differences and see them as providing options, not presenting obstacles.

3. *Capitalizing on change.*   Change is both a stimulant and a stress inducer, both exciting and fear producing. Yet it is unlikely that the pace of change will decrease in the years ahead. Leaders that remain proactive will stay ahead of the game by looking forward, anticipating conditions and events, and preparing for the consequences. Not only do they prepare, but they also take the initiative to make these changes work for them and their organizations. Change is seen as presenting opportunities rather than problems, with each turn of the road offering a new chance.

4. *Belief in the wisdom of the team.*   Leaders who are able to stimulate their groups to produce at an accelerated level have a fundamental belief in the ability of the team to do so. There is ample evidence that the Pygmalion effect is a powerful one. What we believe about others' capabilities has a great effect on their actual behavior and performance. This belief keeps the leader from rescuing the group when it reaches a rough spot, or taking control to set things right. Catalytic leaders believe that the team ultimately can find its own answers and has the ability to push itself beyond its present limits.

5. *Maintaining a balance between product and process.*   Catalytic leaders know that both the ends and the means count. The two are

inextricably tied, and the success of the team depends on an appropriate balance between them. Attention to product gives the team focus and a sense of accomplishment that is central to its existence. Yet equally important is attention to process, which keeps the group from being hindered by human obstacles such as conflict and misunderstanding.

6. *Building responsibility and accountability.* Catalytic leaders also know that if staff members are to have the motivation and self-esteem to perform at high levels, they need to feel a sense of responsibility and accountability for their work. This means they are encouraged to take risks and deal with their outcomes, and they are expected to make their own decisions. The real test of both responsibility and accountability comes when things don't work out as planned. It is at these times that catalytic leaders demonstrate their ability to allow team members to grow and learn from the situation. By not riding in on a white horse to save the day, the leader helps team members develop this fundamental ownership of their own actions.

7. *Inviting, using, and giving feedback effectively.* For a catalytic leader to keep a finger on the pulse of diverse staff members, she must know their needs, understand their decisions, and have open and clear two-way communication. This requires a complete feedback loop, letting employees know what's expected and when they are on and off target as well as listening to the same in return. For the leader to be a real catalyst, a stimulator of growth and learning, a further step is required. It's what organization development theorist, Chris Argyris, calls "double-loop communication." It involves going beneath the initial feedback to the reasons and causes, as well as prompting deeper thinking and greater responsibility. If, for example, staff members report a problem, the leader does not respond with only a "let's fix it" discussion but with some probing questions as well. When did this problem become apparent to you? What is causing it? What prevented you from taking care of it or reporting it earlier? How can we remove these barriers? What other obstacles are there right now that we aren't talking about or working on removing? These discussions call for a nondefensive posture by all that requires a strong foundation of trust and openness between leaders and followers. Two-way feedback can both build and benefit from such mutual credibility and confidence.

The following questionnaire on Worksheet 9–5 will give you an opportunity to assess yourself to see the degree to which you have adapted these seven aspects in your leadership approach.

WORKSHEET 9–5

How Much of a Catalytic Leader Are You?

Directions: Think about yourself as a leader and respond to the following statements by putting a checkmark in the appropriate column.

		Almost Always	Some-times	Almost Never
1.	I am intrigued by uncharted territory.			
2.	I find value in a wide range of attitudes and views.			
3.	I can and do make midcourse corrections easily.			
4.	The team produces better ideas than I do alone.			
5.	It's worth the time it takes to have the team's involvement in solutions and decisions.			
6.	I let staff deal with the consequences of their own choices.			
7.	I depend on employees to give me clear, honest feedback.			
8.	I have the patience to live with the uncertainty and confusion of unsolved problems.			
9.	I am energized by different opinions and points of view.			
10.	I continually look to create new and better ways of doing things.			
11.	The collective judgment of the group is sound.			
12.	The airing of differences through discussion is as important as the decision that results from it.			
13.	I reward the staff for taking risks and dealing with the outcomes.			
14.	I find prime moments for giving feedback that helps people learn and grow.			

Scoring:

Tolerance for ambiguity (Items 1, 8)   _____

Valuing differences (Items, 2, 9)   _____

Capitalizing on change (Items 3, 10)   _____

Belief in the wisdom of the team (Items 4, 11)   _____

Maintaining a balance between product and process (Items 5, 12)   _____

Building responsibility and accountability (Items 6, 13)   _____

Inviting, using, and giving feedback effectively (Items 7, 14)   _____

Total: _____

Give yourself 3 points for every Almost Always response, 2 for each Sometimes response and 1 for each Almost Never response. Then add the points for each of the seven categories, as well as the overall total. The higher the score, the more you exhibit the qualities of a catalytic leader.

Take a look at the individual scores for each of the seven factors to see where your stronger and weaker areas are. Ask yourself a few questions. On dimensions where you have only 2 or 3 points, how does not doing this action hinder your effectiveness in leading your team? What could you do to develop yourself in this area?

Leadership is an art, not a science. There are few "always" and "never" rules and no formulas giving a template for success. Each leader negotiates his or her way through the maze with a unique style and pattern all his or her own. The proof is ultimately in the pudding. Effective leaders create environments in which teams can and do achieve success.

Chapter Ten

Making Team Building Pay Off
Considerations, Challenges, and Caveats

*"Unless you try to do something beyond what you
have already mastered, you will never grow."*

Ralph Waldo Emerson

When all is said (or in this case, read) and done, do these tools and ideas work? The answer is yes. We know they do because we have used them. Having claimed the value of the strategies and techniques offered, we also have to accept the fact that taking the time to use team-building processes as a means to a more productive end can sometimes fly in the face of real life. When it's the 24th hour and key deadlines loom large, you may not care about anyone's diversity issues. You just want the job done, and rightly so. The question then becomes, How do you balance the use of these team-building tools, which can increase productivity, with real organizational life, where people are continually asked to produce more in less time and with fewer resources?

Therein lies the dilemma and the opportunity of all we've presented in this book. The following considerations are critical in determining which tools to use, and when and how to apply them.

TEAM-BUILDING CONSIDERATIONS

1. *Balance long- and short-term goals.* It may be hard to keep your eye on both long-term and short-term outcomes at the same time, but successful team leaders accomplish that feat. Doing so means that you are building a human infrastructure of highly skilled, communicative, collaborative, and productive teammates who can grow together

as a work unit. Balancing long- and short-term goals means that you understand, and also help team members understand, the connection between the team-building strategies we've offered and a group's ability to be creative, to use individual team member's strengths, to be tenacious in problem solving, and to have a sense that their organization and team can be tops at what it does. In practical terms, it means when push comes to shove, team building doesn't get pushed out because of the most-urgent crunch.

2. *Always have a rationale for using any tool, and let everyone know why you're doing so.* Find opportunities to utilize the tools in this book, particularly at the beginning of a team's formation or when the team hits a plateau. Any diet of too much sweet food is unhealthy and the desserts themselves can lose their allure. Likewise, team-building tools done in excess and not anchored to real-life tasks and time lines will leave team members scratching their heads. When you do use these interventions, carefully select the appropriate ones, and then explain their purposes to the group. If people understand why you are investing time and what the team will gain, they'll cut you slack in using these tools, even when they're cynical. This leads to consideration number three.

3. *Trust the process.* There is no doubt that John Jones was our best teacher in the field of group dynamics. In a whole library full of valuable information, many of his gold nuggets stand out—none more so than this one about trusting the process. Learning exercises that are well designed, introduced, and presented are undeniably captivating because they focus on the interaction between an individual's core self, interpersonal dynamics, and the task at hand. As John used to say when describing his rationale for different processes, "Nothing is as interesting to me as me," meaning that learners can't help but get seduced by issues relevant to them. The processes offered in this book are designed to engage and instruct even the most initially resistant team members.

4. *Gauge your reality. Timing is everything.* There are times to use processes, and times when they are nowhere on the priority list because deadlines are so tight and crucial. These team-building strategies are an investment that, in Maslovian terminology, will help your team achieve self-actualization, or peak performance. That level of accomplishment is great, but when you're down at the bottom rung of the ladder trying to deal with survival issues, peak performance seems irrelevant. When teams can barely manage the basics, the top

priority is getting through the crunch. Then, in a less crisis-oriented time, process tools can serve as an investment in a smoother operation and the creation of a more proactive climate.

5. *Go beyond lip service and really accept the diversity on your team.* Team members will not react uniformly to the strategies you utilize on your team. Some will relish interpersonal processes as a life-enhancing learning opportunity; others will champion the task accomplishment to the exclusion of interactive tools because they see their job as just doing the work. Still others may see that both the task and relationship focuses have their place, while on some teams, there are members who value neither and contribute little. This wide range of human reactions is what we have been speaking about throughout the book. It is easier to accept rebuffs and not take them personally when you realize that it's just the way we humans are: unique and different. The objective of using these methods and strategies is to create a sense of value for contributions that come from differentness, which is especially difficult to do when demonstrating value causes frustration.

6. *Use feedback, both solicited and unsolicited.* The team will constantly and informally be giving you feedback, if you only pay attention to it. Are people confused about their tasks? If so, what needs to be cleared up? Do they seem discontented? What is the cause? Might they be energetic, committed, and creative? If so, what's fostering this positive environment? As a leader, you need to walk around and talk to people because that's how you'll build trust, develop relationships, and get the truth that unavailable leaders never hear.

   This is another of those time-consuming investments that pays dividends in the long term. Imagine yourself with an invisible satellite dish on your head. It picks up all these signals from your work team. Some are warning signs; others are an indication that productivity is humming. The point is that not all feedback has to be done in a formal process. Hone your radar, walk around, talk to people, find out what's going on, and learn how you can help make things better.

There are no easy answers to how you build high-performing teams. We have given you ways to balance task and relationship and ways to appreciate individual differences while building a common team culture. We've suggested strategies for individual and collective growth and learning, but we've also looked at ways to heighten team performance and accomplishment, the real objectives of all of the techniques in this book.

Regardless of which methods you use or how you implement these tools, ultimately team leadership and facilitation are the most critical variables in team performance. With that in mind, we end with a list of recommended leadership challenges and caveats.

How you treat team members not only influences productivity and commitment, but also impacts job satisfaction, loyalty to the organization, and enthusiasm for the job. Leading a diverse group can be challenging and rewarding. The following challenges and caveats for team leaders give suggested rules for building a collaborative and constructive group and for ensuring that your team experience is a positive one.

TEAM-BUILDING CHALLENGES

1. *Respecting and valuing the differences.* Variations in thinking styles; problem-solving approaches; technical expertise; and outlooks on priorities arising from varying diversities such as geographic location, ethnicity, gender, age, energy, and creativity are frequently sources of challenge and sometimes frustration. But they can also be the source of great energy. The challenge as a team leader/facilitator is to help team members find value rather than exasperation in their myriad diversities.

2. *Treating staff as they want to be treated.* There is a Golden Rule presumption that implies that you should treat people the way you want to be treated. It is certainly easy to make this assumption. The problem with that premise is that differing cultural norms make a single standard impossible. For example, in mainstream American culture, it is usually appropriate and appreciated when individuals are singled out for praise. But in Asian cultures that kind of attention would be embarrassing, not motivating. The challenge is to avoid assumptions and learn about your staff so you know their preferences and can honor them.

3. *Developing relationships as a source of trust.* Communicate openly and honestly. There's no substitute for trust on a work team, and in the United States, trust and integrity are shown by coming through on your commitments. Trust, which is based on repeated and successful experience with people, takes time to build and develop. You spend time on relationships, you invest in the future of the

team, and you enhance opportunities for trust and effective communication. The challenge will be to make sure that necessary relationship building isn't sacrificed when the alarm clock is about to go off.

4. *Sharing information.* In order for all team members to do their jobs, they need the most current information. But in some cases, individuals hold onto information as a way of maintaining power. Sharing it is the best way, not only to get the job done, but also to ensure that everyone has appropriate data to make good decisions. The challenge is to create an environment in which positive reinforcement is given for sharing rather than hoarding information and resources.

5. *Being a role model of the behaviors you want to see.* There is no substitute for practicing what you preach, walking the talk, or generally teaching excellence and high performance through your behavior. Role modeling is a powerful teacher. The challenge and the opportunity come from recognizing your impact on others and behaving consistently and ethically. Hopefully, your leader behavior will broadcast the message you want to send.

6. *Being flexible.* Working in a group or team structure when co-workers depend on and need one another to get the job done is a little like living in a family. You have to be sensitive to others, and you don't always get your own way. Teach members how to be more adaptive, and, more to the point, actually reward the flexibility. Doing so will advance harmony, tolerance, and results more than any fancy or costly idea you can think of. It will also help team members deal better with any challenges that continue to surface.

TEAM-BUILDING CAVEATS

1. *Making remarks against or belittling other employees.* Such comments spread divisiveness, pettiness, and cliquishness. If you have complaints about a team member, telling that person directly and then solving the problem is appropriate. Bad-mouthing isn't.

2. *Being all talk and no action.* Doers are the kind of people most employees want to be in the trenches with. There is nothing attractive about working with those who boast and brag but don't come through. While accountability may differ across cultures, nowhere in business do people appreciate talk that isn't backed up.

3. *Being defensive.* Good leadership means you're open to criticism and suggestions. On a good work team, you will have honest communication.

That means people may not like your ideas, or in some cases your behavior. If they don't, hopefully you'll hear about it from them in a nonconfrontational tone. Rather than feeling defensive, use the feedback as an important tool to help you and the group become better and more cohesive, and show team members that they too can learn from honest feedback.

4. *Giving feedback in an attacking, finger-pointing way.*   Part of helping fellow workers not be defensive is giving them feedback in sensitive, nonaccusatory ways. This can best be done by using "I" messages that focus on behaviors and situations and by using a passive rather than an active voice. "I appreciate deadlines that are met" is a far better way to give feedback than saying, "You never seem to come through."

5. *Showing favoritism.*   It may be hard not to have favorites since chemistry between people is personal and hard to define. But showing it can be very divisive. The opportunity for "spreading the wealth," so to speak, comes in finding something positive about every team member and in ways suitable to each person. It is helpful to acknowledge the contributions of each employee.

6. *Being a rescuer.*   It is not uncommon for leaders to attempt to fix things, to intervene as the buffer in conflict-ridden relationships, or to be the safety net that rescues people from their mistakes. Doing so is costly in the long term, however. In order to build whole, healthy, and fully responsible and accountable team members, you have to be there to help them when they fall, but not to prevent their falling. Reward the effort, the learning, and the results from each experience rather than trying to save people from their mistakes.

Finally, creating a high-performing team involves equal amounts of both the magic and the mundane. On the best teams, there is an intangible kind of spark and chemistry that puts individual egos aside and relishes the collective effort toward meaningful accomplishment. But even on those rare, magical teams, the hard work and notable outcomes derive from mundane efforts that occur from plugging away, working hard, making commitments, and following through, one day at a time.

Developing a high-performing, diverse team is not the sexy stuff of Madison Avenue. But it can be thrilling, and in the case of the diverse teams we've seen, it is life changing. Perhaps the best case for diverse teams comes from a seminar participant of ours who talked about the joys of diversity. He said, "It's amazing. I get my own way more often now that I have more than one way."

Resources for Building Diverse Teams

The following resources may be helpful in developing diverse teams as well as training team leaders and members.

Diverse Teams at Work is also available as a video from corVISION MEDIA, Inc. The video dramatically portrays a diverse task force, actually charged with exploring the ways to build tolerance within an organization. Prime aspects of the four layers of diversity within individual team members are profiled, and the subsequent effects these layers have on the way the team interacts and operates is shown.

Comments from team members contrast their initial fears with subsequent experience in the team, emphasizing the positive aspects of diversity. This video is available from corVISION MEDIA, Inc., 1359 Barclay Boulevard, Buffalo Grove, Illinois 60089. For further information, please contact corVISION at 1-800-537-3130.

GENERAL BOOKS ABOUT DIVERSITY

Gardenswartz, Lee, and Anita Rowe. *Managing Diversity: A Complete Desk Reference and Planning Guide.* Homewood, IL: Business One Irwin, 1993. This comprehensive guide gives both conceptual information as well as practical techniques, strategies, and activities for managing diversity. Over 80 worksheets, checklists, and charts are provided for use by managers and trainers.

Gudykunst, William B. *Bridging Differences: Effective Intergroup Communication.* Newbury Park, CA: Sage, 1991. This book explains the process underlying communication between people of different groups and presents principles for building community with people from diverse backgrounds.

Hall, Edward T. *Beyond Culture.* New York: Anchor Books/Doubleday, 1989. This fundamental work on culture gives an in-depth analysis of the culturally determined yet unconscious attitudes that mold our thoughts, feelings, communication, and behavior. This continues from Hall's *The Silent Language* and *The Hidden Dimension* to discuss the covert cultural influences that impact cross-cultural encounters.

Hall, Edward T. *The Hidden Dimension*. New York: Anchor Books/Doubleday, 1969. Written by a leading anthropologist, this book discusses proxemics, the ways humans use space in public and private. It provides insights about how this aspect of culture affects personal and business relations and cross-cultural interactions as well as architecture and urban planning.

Hall, Edward T. *The Silent Language*. New York: Anchor Books/Doubleday, 1973. Insights into the cultural aspects of communication are given in this fundamental work by a foremost anthropologist. The author explains how dimensions such as time and space communicate beyond words.

Loden, Marilyn, and Judy B Rosener, PhD. *Workforce America! Managing Employee Diversity as a Vital Resource*. Homewood, IL: Business One Irwin, 1991. This foundation piece in the literature about diversity makes a case for creating an organization that capitalizes on the richness in differences. It offers an insightful look at the issues as well as the managerial and organizational strategies to deal with them.

Simons, George F, Carmen Vasquez, and Philip R Harris. *Transcultural Leadership: Empowering the Diverse Workforce*. Houston, TX: Gulf Publishing, 1993. This latest addition to the literature on diversity offers new insights into managing and leading diverse employees.

Thiederman, Sondra, PhD. *Bridging Cultural Barriers for Corporate Success: How to Manage the Multicultural Work Force*. Lexington, MA: Lexington Books, 1990. This handbook for cross-cultural communication gives managers and human-resource professionals practical information about motivating, attracting, interviewing, retaining, and training the multicultural workforce. This reader-friendly book is full of applicable examples, how-tos, and exercises for overcoming obstacles to intercultural communication.

Thiederman, Sondra, PhD. *Profiting in America's Multicultural Marketplace: How to Do Business Across Cultural Lines*. Lexington, MA: Lexington Books, 1991. In practical, readable terms, the author explains cultural effects on person-to-person behavior and how to communicate effectively with people of different backgrounds. This book gives anecdotes and tests that involve and teach.

Thomas, R Roosevelt. *Beyond Race and Gender: Unleashing the Power of Your Total Work Force by Managing Diversity*. New York: Amacom, 1991. This book puts forth a plan for managing diversity, coupled with practical examples of how organizations capitalize on their diverse staffs. It includes a strategy for a cultural audit as well as an action plan for change.

BOOKS ABOUT SPECIFIC GROUPS

Astrachan, Anthony. *How Men Feel.* New York: Anchor, 1988. How men feel about women is the topic of this book, which contains a number of chapters focusing on work relationships.

Blumfeld, Warren J, and Deane Raymond. *Looking at Gay and Lesbian Life.* Boston: Beacon Press, 1988. Lesbian and gay lifestyles in the United States are examined and discussed in this book.

Condon, John C. *With Respect to the Japanese: A Guide for Americans.* Yarmouth, ME: Intercultural Press, 1984. In this handbook, the author discusses aspects of Japanese values and behavior that affect communication, business relations, and the management styles. He goes on to make recommendations on how to deal with the Japanese during face-to-face encounters.

Condon, John C. *Good Neighbors: Communication with the Mexicans.* Yarmouth, ME: Intercultural Press, 1985. In this concise book, the author describes how the culture of the United States and Mexico differ, how Mexicans and their northern neighbors misunderstand each other, and what can be done to bridge the gap. Vital information for those working with Mexicans is provided in a readable, interesting way.

Davis, George, and Gregg Watson. *Black Life in Corporate America.* Garden City, NY: Anchor Press/Doubleday, 1982. This book sheds light on the impact of American organizational culture on black employees.

Fernandez, John. *Racism and Sexism in Corporate Life.* Lexington, MA: Lexington Books, 1981. This book discusses the findings of a major study of black and white men and women in the workplace, focusing on how racism and sexism affect their work life.

Fieg, John Paul, and Elizabeth Mortlock. *A Common Core: Thais and Americans.* Yarmouth, ME: Intercultural Press, 1989. Both commonalties and differences between Thai and American cultures are explained in this book. The authors go on to discuss the implications of the differences for those engaged in cross-cultural encounters on and off the job.

Gochenour, Theodore. *Considering Filipinos.* Yarmouth, ME: Intercultural Press, 1990. This intercultural handbook contrasts the values and perspectives of Filipinos and Americans and offers guidelines for successful interaction between these two groups. It gives suggestions for bridging cultural differences in social and workplace settings, as well as case studies showing cross-cultural dynamics in action.

Gray, John. *Men Are From Mars, Women Are From Venus: A Practical Guide for Improving Communication and Getting What You Want in Your Relationships.* New York: HarperCollins, 1992. This look at male-female differences argues that communication problems between the sexes are rooted in gender-related value differences.

Grier, William H, and Price M Cobbs. *Black Rage*. New York: HarperCollins, 1991. This classic in the diversity field offers the views of two black psychiatrists on the inner conflicts and desperation of black life in the United States.

Gutek, Barbara A. *Sex and the Work Place*. San Francisco, CA: Jossey-Bass, 1985. This book examines a critical aspect of male-female interaction on the job—the impact of sexual behavior and harassment on women, men, and organizations. The issue is looked at from managerial, legal, psychological, and social perspectives.

Heim, Pat, and Susan Galant. *Hardball for Women: Winning at the Game of Business*. Los Angeles, CA: Lowell House, 1992. Differences in male and female leadership skills are the subject of this book. Tracing gender differences to the play of boys and girls, the authors apply these preferences to adult behaviors in the workplace.

Knouse, Stephen B, Paul Rosenfeld, and Amy Culbertson, eds. *Hispanics in the Workplace*. Newbury Park, CA: Sage, 1992. A comprehensive exploration of Hispanic employment factors, problems at work, support systems, and Hispanic women and work. Contributors deal with specific topics such as recruiting, training, and language barriers.

Kochman, Thomas. *Black and White Styles in Conflict*. Chicago, IL: University of Chicago Press, 1981. This classic study of black culture helps illuminate racial misunderstandings and explain the values and style differences that may be at the heart of problems in interethnic communication. This book serves as a practical guide for crossing racial barriers in business and education.

Kras, Eva S. *Management in Two Cultures: Bridging the Gap Between U.S. and Mexican Managers*. Yarmouth, ME: Intercultural Press, 1989. This book pinpoints the principal differences between Mexican and U.S. cultures and management styles that cause misunderstandings and conflict. Concrete recommendations to both U.S. and Mexican managers for dealing more effectively with each other are given.

Lipman-Blumen, Jean. *Gender Roles and Power*. Englewood Cliffs, NJ: Prentice-Hall, 1984. This book explains the way in which the gender system is a foundation for all other power relationships.

Loden, Marilyn. *Feminine Leadership: Or How to Succeed in Business without Being One of the Boys*. New York: Times Books, 1985. This book delineates differences in male and female leadership styles, with implications for enhancing the workplace.

Nydell, Margaret K. *Understanding Arabs: A Guide for Westerners*. Yarmouth, ME: Intercultural Press, 1987. This readable cross-cultural handbook gives a concise and insightful look at Arab culture. It dispels common Western misconceptions regarding Arab behavior and it explains the values, beliefs, and practices of Arabs, particularly in terms of their impact on interactions with Europeans and Americans.

Pearson, Judy C. *Gender and Communication.* Dubuque, IA: Wm. C Brown, 1985. This book focuses on the gender gap in interactions and discusses the difficulties and differences in communication between men and women.

Renwick, G, P Pedersen, and K Smith. *Communicating With Malaysians.* Yarmouth, ME: Intercultural Press (in press). This new addition to the Inter-Acts series offers insights and practical help in interacting with Malaysians.

Richmond, Yale. *From Nyet to Da: Understanding the Russians.* Yarmouth, ME: Intercultural Press, 1992. This succinctly written book is a cross-cultural guide for dealing with Russians. The author outlines ways of responding most effectively to Russians on a personal level as well as in business.

Rodgers-Rose, LaFrances. *Black Women.* Newbury Park, CA: Sage, 1983. Issues and conditions confronting black women are discussed in this book.

Rosener, Judy. *America's Competitive Secret: How Organizations Can Gain the Advantage by Promoting Women to Top Management.* New York: Oxford University Press, 1995. This new book discusses the cost of and reasons for the underutilization of women in organizations and explains how companies can benefit from capitalizing on this underused resource. It includes chapters on sexual static and how men and women feel.

Sagarin, Edward, ed. *The Other Minorities.* Waltham, MA: Xerox College, 1971. Nonethnic minorities, such as the differently abled, are the subjects in this collection of articles.

Simons, George F, and G Deborah Weissman. *Men and Women: Partners at Work.* Los Altos, CA: Crisp Publications, 1990. The objective of this book is to help men and women approach each other openly, creatively, and with effective communication tools. Exercises and worksheets help readers identify and resolve gender issues that inhibit productivity and understanding.

Stewart, Edward C. *American Cultural Patterns: A Cross-Cultural Perspective.* Yarmouth, Me: Intercultural Press, 1972. Using the value-orientation framework of Kluckholn and Strodtbeck, the author examines American patterns of thinking and behaving. He goes on to analyze the assumptions about human nature and the physical world that underlie these values, and to compare and contrast them with those of other cultures.

Tannen, Deborah. *You Just Don't Understand: Women and Men in Conversation.* New York: William Morrow, 1991. In a down-to-earth, reader-friendly style, the author explains gender differences in communication that produce obstacles. Recognizing and understanding these differences can help avoid barriers to clear communication between men and women.

Tingley, Judith. *Genderflex: Men and Women Speaking Each Others' Language at Work.* New York: Amacom, 1994. This book gives suggestions about overcoming the gender gap in work communication.

Wenzhong, Hu, and Cornelius L Grove. *Encountering the Chinese: A Guide for Americans.* Yarmouth, ME: Intercultural Press, 1991. This useful book goes beyond description to explain Chinese behavior. It provides a cross-cultural analysis that can guide Westerners toward more effective relationships with the Chinese.

BOOKS ABOUT TEAMS

Chang, Richard Y. *Building a Dynamic Team*. Costa Mesa, CA: Richard Chang Associates, Inc., 1994. This book offers a practical model for understanding the phases of team development and how to plan for the next step.

Chang, Richard Y. *Success Through Teamwork*. Costa Mesa, CA: Richard Chang Associates, Inc., 1994. This book provides a guide to improving team effectiveness through interpersonal skills in areas such as communication, conflict, and diversity.

Chang, Richard Y, Audrey E Bloom, and Gloria E Bader. *Measuring Team Performance*. Costa Mesa, CA: Richard Chang Associates, Inc., 1994. This reference offers tools and techniques to set team objectives, and to track and evaluate performance of the team and individuals.

Elledge, Robin L, and Steven Phillips. *Team-building for the Future*. San Diego, CA: Pfeiffer and Co., 1993. This comprehensive team-building resource provides training designs to intervene effectively to overcome difficulties such as trustless teams and teams in chaos.

Fetteroll, Jr, Eugene, Glen Hoffherr, and John Marian. *Growing Teams: A Down-to-Earth Approach*. Methuen, MA: Goal/QPC, 1993. This practical handbook gives practical steps and 29 exercises for beginning, developing, and growing successful teams.

Francis, Dave, and Don Young. *Improving Work Groups: A Practical Manual for Team Building*. San Diego, CA: Pfeiffer and Co., 1992. Aimed at those responsible for developing effective teams, this resource gives a step-by-step system for evaluating and improving team performance.

Katzenbach, Jon R, and Douglas K Smith. *The Wisdom of Teams: Creating a High-Performance Organization*. Boston, MA: Harvard Business School Press, 1993. Based on research with over 50 high-performing teams, the authors share both commonsense and uncommonsense findings about what makes teams work.

Kayser, Thomas A. *Building Team Power: How to Unleash the Collaborative Genius of Work Teams*. Burr Ridge, IL: Irwin Professional Publishing, 1994. This practical guide to building team power gives how-tos for facilitating teamwork and collaborative techniques for work groups.

Kayser, Thomas A. *Mining Group Gold: How to Cash In on the Collaborative Brainpower of a Group*. El Segundo, CA: Serif Publishing, 1990. This rich resource presents how-tos for facilitating collaboration in groups in order to forge consensus, work through differences, and solve problems.

Kelly, P Keith. *Team Decision Making Techniques.* Costa Mesa, CA: Richard Chang Associates, Inc., 1994. This guide explains potential pitfalls of team decision making and offers six decision-making techniques for groups.

Kossoff, Leslie L. *Closing the Gap: The Handbook for Total Quality Implementation.* 2nd Edition. Knoxville, TN: SPC Press, 1994. This book gives the management structure to support quality-improvement teams through the implementation process.

Mears, Peter. *Healthcare Teams: Building Continuous Quality Improvement.* Methuen, MA: Goal/QPC, 1994. This book provides a thorough understanding of team building in a healthcare environment, including healthcare related exercises.

Mears, Peter. *Organization Teams: Building Continuous Quality Improvement.* Methuen, MA: Goal/QPC, 1994. This book for both public- and private-sector organizations provides exercises that help team members learn about cohesiveness, empowerment, and handling difficult members.

Phillips, Steven L, and Robin L Elledge. *The Team Building Source Book.* San Diego, CA: Pfeiffer and Co., 1993. This basic guide to team building provides activities, assessment tools, and reproducible handouts to lead a group through the process.

Scholtes, Peter R, Ed. *The Team Handbook: How to Use Teams to Improve Quality.* Methuen, MA: Goal/QPC, 1988. This guide for leaders and team members gives databased methods to form and maintain groups, plan and manage projects, and design and conduct meetings.

STRUCTURED EXPERIENCES, GAMES, AND TRAINING RESOURCES

Bafa Bafa: Cross-Cultural Orientation. Gary R Shirts, PO Box 910, Del Mar, CA 92014; (619) 755-0272. This experiential activity simulates the contact between two very different cultures, Alpha and Beta. The activity is structured so that participants learn through direct simulated experience and then apply that learning to real-life situations.

Barnga: A Simulation Game on Cultural Clashes. Sivasailam Thiagarajan, Intercultural Press, Inc., PO Box 700, Yarmouth, ME 04096; (207) 846-5168. Through playing a simple card game in small groups, participants experience the effect of simulated cultural differences on human interaction. This activity is easy to complete in a relatively short time.

The Diversity Game. Quality Educational Development, Inc., 41 Central Park West, New York, NY 10023; (212) 724-3335. This multiplayer board game provides insights, raises awareness, and stimulates discussion about diversity issues in the workplace. Questions focus on real workplace issues such as communication, motivation, reward, recognition, respect, and trust in the context of gender, race, and cultural diversity.

The Diversity Tool Kit. Lee Gardenswartz and Anita Rowe. Irwin Professional Publishing, 1333 Burr Ridge Parkway, Burr Ridge, IL 60521; (800) 634-3966. This resource contains over 100 diversity training activities in reproducible format. Exercises designed to build awareness, knowledge, and skills are categorized by topic such as stereotypes and prejudice, culture, communication, and team building.

Diversophy. Multus, Inc., 46 Treetop Lane, Suite 200, San Mateo, CA 94402-3234; (415) 342-2040. This board game is designed to be played by line managers, supervisors, administrative personnel, salespeople, customer-service representatives, and senior executives. Easy to play, the game delivers thought-provoking information, deals with critical attitudes, and teaches useful skills for meeting the challenges of diversity.

Earthquake Survival. Arlette C Ballew and Marian K Prokop. Pfeiffer and Co., 8517 Production Avenue, San Diego, CA 92121; (800) 274-4434. This fun, experiential activity shows the benefits of using all the resources of the team, group member styles, and how to improve communication skills.

Ecotonos. Nipporica Associates and Dianne Hofner-Saphiere. Intercultural Press, Inc., PO Box 700, Yarmouth, ME; (207) 846-5168. This simulation deals with problem solving and decision making in multicultural groups.

The Encyclopedia of Team Activities Set. Edited by J William Pfeiffer. Pfeiffer and Co., 8517 Production Avenue, San Diego, CA 92121; (800) 274-4434. This collection of 99 team activities is designed to boost team and individual performance through the learn-by-doing approach.

Jumpstarting Your New Team: Establishing Norms. Ken S Keleman. Pfeiffer and Co., 8517 Production Avenue, San Diego, CA 92121; (800) 274-4434. This experiential activity focuses the team on developing group norms that contribute to the team's success.

The Managing Diversity Survival Guide. Lee Gardenswartz and Anita Rowe. Irwin Professional Publishing, 1333 Burr Ridge Parkway, Burr Ridge, IL 60521; (800) 634-3966. This resource provides over 80 reproducible checklists, questionnaires, and worksheets for raising awareness and building knowledge about diversity in the workplace.

Team Learning System: A Team Self-Assessment and Action Planning Tool (For Windows). John E Jones, PhD and Wm. L Bearley, EdD. Organizational Universe Systems, PO Box 38, Valley Center, CA 92082; (619) 749-0811. This software provides a series of assessment tools that make it easy to take the pulse of the work group in two dimensions. This system gives clear data reports that enable the team to make clear action plans for improvement.

DIVERSITY VIDEOS AND FILMS

Age & Attitudes. corVISION MEDIA, 1359 Barclay Blvd., Buffalo Grove, IL 60089; 1-800-537-3130. Produced by ABC News for "Prime Time Live," this video explores discrimination among older workers.

Bill Cosby on Prejudice. Budget Films, 4590 Santa Monica Blvd., Los Angeles, CA 90029; (213) 660-0187. This film presents a monologue by Bill Cosby on prejudice.

Bridges: Skills for Managing a Diverse Workforce. BNA Communications, Inc., 9439 Key West Avenue, Rockville, MD 20850; (800) 253-6067. This eight-module, video-based program is designed to train managers and supervisors in managing diverse workers. Both awareness about cultural/racial/gender differences and the skills to deal with them are presented. The series includes manuals for trainees and participants.

Bridging Cultural Barriers: Managing Ethnic Diversity in the Workplace. Barr Films, 12801 Schabarum Avenue, PO Box 7878, Irwindale, CA 91706-7878; (800) 234-7878. This half-hour film featuring Sondra Thiederman, PhD, teaches the effective management of diverse workers through simulated examples of a manager resolving situations with two culturally different staff members. Vignettes are interspersed with lecturettes by Thiederman.

The Fairer Sex? corVISION MEDIA, 1359 Barclay Blvd., Buffalo Grove, IL 60089; 1-800-537-3130. Produced by ABC News for "Prime Time Live," this video explores what happens when a man and a woman are put in identical situations including reserving a tee time at a public golf course and applying for the same job.

Gay Issues in the Workplace. United Training Media, 6633 West Howard Street, Niles, IL 60714; (800) 424-0364. This video features gay, lesbian, and bisexual employees speaking about workplace issues that concern them.

Managing Diversity. CRM Films, 2233 Faraday Avenue, Carlsbad, CA 92008; (800) 421-0833. This film combines dramatizations and information from experts in the field to focus on diversity issues such as stereotyping and communication as well as differences in perception regarding teamwork, power, and authority. It ends with a useful list of things people can do to improve communication in a diverse environment. A guide is included.

Managing a Multicultural Workforce: The Mosaic Workplace. Films for the Humanities and Sciences, PO Box 2053, Princeton, NJ 08543-2053; (800) 257-5126. This video training program consists of 10 videos addressing the issues of the diverse workplace. It covers topics such as understanding different cultural values and styles, men and women working together, and success strategies for minorities.

Sandcastle: A Film about Teamwork and Diversity. Salinger Films, 1635-12 Street, Santa Monica, CA 90404; (310) 450-1300. Teamwork and the unique contribution of each diverse team member is illustrated in this Academy Award–winning, non-narrated 13-minute video. In a unique story about the building of a sand castle, the film demonstrates the value of diversity.

Valuing Diversity. Copeland Griggs Productions, 302-23 Avenue, San Francisco, CA 94121; (415) 668-4200. This seven-part film/video series for managers and other employees focuses on the advantages inherent in diversity. Segments deal with issues such as managing/supervising differences, upward mobility in a multicultural organization, and communicating across cultures. The series includes users' guides.

A Winning Balance. BNA Communications, Inc., 9439 Key West Avenue, Rockville, MD 20850; (800) 233-6067. This 34-minute video-based training program introduces the topic of diversity and its importance to all employees. It goes on to deal with attitudes toward differences, the impact of biases, becoming a diversity change agent, and making a personal commitment. Trainer's participant manuals are included.

The Workforce Kaleidoscope: A Systems Approach to Diversity. United Training Media, 6633 West Howard St., Niles, IL 60714; (800) 424-0364. This video raises awareness about diversity and gives suggestions about how diverse employees can work together productively.

Working Together: Managing Cultural Diversity. Crisp Publications, 95 First Street, Los Altos, CA 94022-9803; (800) 442-7477. This video-book program teaches how to work productively in a multicultural environment. Users learn how to manage their attitudes and communication in interactions with people from other cultures. The kit includes a leader's guide.

Bibliography

Adams, James L. *Conceptual Blockbusting.* New York: W W Norton and Co., 1974.

Argyris, Chris. "Good Communication That Blocks Learning." *Harvard Business Review,* July/August 1994: 77–85.

Arnold, John. *Make Up Your Mind: The Seven Building Blocks to Better Decisions.* New York: Amacom, 1978.

Burns, James MacGregor. *Leadership.* New York: Harper & Row, 1978.

Josefowitz, Natasha. *Is This Where I Was Going?* New York: Warner Books, 1980 (pp 6–7).

———. *Paths to Power: A Woman's Guide from First Job to Top Executive.* Reading, MA: Addison-Wesley, 1980 (p 99).

Katzenbach, John R and Douglas K Smith. *The Wisdom of Teams: Creating the High-Performance Organization.* Boston: Harvard Business School Press, 1993 (p 12).

Loden, Marilyn, and Judy Rosener. *Workforce America! Managing Employee Diversity as a Vital Resource.* Homewood, IL: Business One Irwin, 1991 (pp 17–21).

Maier, Norman R F. *Problem Solving and Creativity in Individuals and Groups.* Belmont, CA: Brooks/Cole, 1970.

McGregor, Douglas. *The Human Side of Enterprise.* New York: McGraw-Hill, 1961.

Rosener, Judy. *America's Competitive Secret: How Organizations Can Gain the Advantage by Promoting Women to Top Management.* New York: Oxford University Press, 1995.

———. "Ways Women Lead." *Harvard Business Review.* November/December 1990 (pp 119–25).

Selye, Hans. *Stress without Distress.* New York: New American Library, 1975.

Tannen, Deborah. *You Just Don't Understand: Women and Men in Conversation.* New York: William Morrow, 1991.

Tuckman, Bruce. "Developmental Sequence In Small Groups." *Psychological Bulletin,* 1965. Referenced on pg. 181, *Paths To Power* (see N. Josefowitz).

Index

Other books of interest to you

The Diversity Tool Kit
Lee Gardenswartz and Anita Rowe
A complete "training program in a box." Inside are 100 activity cards, including sample agendas, skill-building exercises, questionnaires and many other structured tools covering virtually every area of diversity training.
    0-7863-0266-6   100 training tools

Mining Group Gold
How to Cash In on the Collaborative Brain Power of
a Group, Revised Edition
Thomas A. Kayser
Reveals the philosophy and techniques of management and teamwork that were the fruits of a handful of Xerox employees' labor, who devoted their time exclusively to working on a new approach to doing business.
    0-7863-0429-4   178 pages

Why Teams Can Fail and What to Do About It
Essential Tools for Anyone Implementing Self-Directed Work Teams
Darcy Hitchcock and Marsha Willard
Co-published with Association for Quality and Participation
Identifies the most common problems faced by teams, offering specific suggestions for spotting and solving the problems and creating teams that really work.
    0-7863-0423-5   225 pages